71623

W9-ASC-046

GERMAN FOREIGN POLICIES, WEST & EAST

Studies in Comparative Politics

Peter H. Merkl, *editor*

Studies in Comparative Politics is designed to make available to students and teachers comparative studies of substantive interest and innovative approach. Written for classroom use, they range over a broad spectrum of topical subjects and lend themselves in particular to supplementing course content in a comparative direction.

RIGHTS & LIBERTIES IN THE WORLD TODAY
Constitutional Promise & Reality
    Ivo D. Duchacek

POWER MAPS
Comparative Politics of Constitutions
    Ivo D. Duchacek

GERMAN FOREIGN POLICIES, WEST & EAST

On the Threshold of a New European Era

Peter H. Merkl

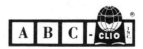

SANTA BARBARA, CALIFORNIA
OXFORD, ENGLAND

Library of Congress Catalog Card Number 73-92506
ISBN Clothbound Edition 0-87436-133-8
Paperbound Edition 0-87436-134-6

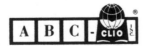

American Bibliographical Center—Clio Press, Inc.
2040 Alameda Padre Serra
Santa Barbara, California

European Bibliographical Center—Clio Press
30 Cornmarket Street
Oxford OX1 3EY, England

Designed by Barbara Monahan
Composed by Graham Mackintosh
Printed and bound by Publishers Press, Inc.
in the United States of America

TO

Lisa, Jacqueline & John Peter

Contents

Muna Lein two

Contents

Acknowledgments

The writing of this book involved the assistance and cooperation of many persons and agencies. For the statistical parts in
particular, credit is due the Institut für Demoskopie, DIVO (Frankfurt), EMNID (Bielefeld), and the helpful staff of the Zentralarchiv für empirische Sozialforschung at Cologne. The writer
would like to thank Profs. Rudolf Wildenmann of Mannheim and
Stonybrook, Klaus Montag of Babelsberg, and Lawrence Schein-
man of Cornell University for their generous encouragement and
assistance. "Politico-Cultural Restraints on West German Foreign
Policy: Sense of Trust, Identity, and Agency," by Peter H. Merkl
is reprinted in revised form as chapter 1 from Comparative Political Studies, vol. 3, No. 4 (January 1971), pp. 443-57 by permission
of the Publisher, Sage Publications, Inc. Finally, a debt of gratitude
is owed Mrs. Nancy Davidson and Ms. Barbara Monahan of
Clio Press in whose competent hands the final product took shape.

GERMAN FOREIGN POLICIES, WEST & EAST

The Two Germanies & the International System

Few countries of the world present to the student of international affairs such problems of definition and analysis as does Germany. If the international system is thought to be made up of known basic units, nation-states subject to relatively little change, then Germany becomes an ever-changing, Protean enigma. Within the last 100 years alone it changed from a loose confederation of sovereign princedoms to one extremely centralized nation-state and back to two fiercely antagonistic states, the Federal Republic and the East German Republic.

If a certain territorial basis is taken for granted, such a foundation is equally uncertain here. The old German Confederation (1815-67) still included the vast lands of the Austro-Hungarian Empire which were excluded at the formation of the Bismarckian Reich (1871-1918). The Weimar Republic (1919-33) had to accept a substantial loss of the imperial territory under the Peace Treaty of Versailles (1919). The Nazi era (1933-45) witnessed the *Anschluss* of German Austria and, for a brief spell, German wartime control over immense territories of which the German government intended to keep large parts ranging at least from eastern France to the Ukraine. The two postwar Germanies (1949-) again are smaller in their combined territory than pre-Nazi Germany as a result of the possession of the large areas beyond the Oder-Neisse line by Poland and the Soviet Union. Thus the territorial character of Germany as a basic unit of the international system never seems to stand still. It is further complicated by the persistence of unresolved border questions, the precarious status of postwar West Berlin, still an occupied area, and such loaded questions of interpretation as whether the Federal Republic represents all of Germany or only itself, a question laid to rest only in 1972 in the Basic Treaty (Grundvertrag) between East and West Germany.

If these changes baffle the student of German foreign policy, the changes in the foreign policy-making institutions and in the policies themselves will do so even more. A hundred years of drastically changing internal political forces and forms of government leaping from semifeudal autocracy to parliamentary democracy with a detour to totalitarian dictatorship appear to lack even the most elementary continuities. Foreign policies, changing from a static policy of self-preservation to the dynamic imperialism of the Third Reich and from there to a desire to merge either with other Western countries or with the Soviet bloc, hardly relieve the stark contrasts.

Behind these drastic changes of recent German history lie the vast social and economic transformations of German society, which within a few generations burst the crust of a semi-traditional society, released vast productive energies as capable of good as of evil, and ushered in an era of painful identity crisis for Germany in the midst of almost a whole world in equally uncertain transition.

The difficulties of systematically analyzing the perplexities of constant change suggest an approach which seeks internal consistency in something other than the discontinuous lines of German political development. Short of a historical account that attempts to order facts and relationships chronologically, the only way of doing justice to the problem would seem to be a *political culture* approach which stresses the subjective elements, the changing attitudes, visions, and role conceptions of German groups and individuals, including successive teams of foreign policy leadership, during the period in question. Such an approach, it is hoped, will be capable of identifying the elements of continuity in German foreign policy thinking and at the same time also explain the changing directions in the situation and in the groups that hold the various views discussed.

THE POLITICAL CULTURE APPROACH
TO FOREIGN AFFAIRS

The uses of a political culture approach in the comparative study of political systems hardly require extensive discussion.[1] In brief outline, political culture is the sum total of a people's political attitudes and beliefs acquired by the processes of political socialization. The study of a country's political culture usually begins with an assessment of the popular levels of political knowledge and participation, which may well result in the isolation and identification of well-informed "attentive publics" and of the politically more involved "active publics" from among the general population. Furthermore, students of political culture focus on the popular feelings toward the political system and toward other political actors, feelings which may range from love of country to disaffection and from social trust to distrust. The political culture also includes a sense of individual and collective identity and specific notions of the roles that citizens, leaders, parties and institutions ought to play as parts of the system.

Political culture of the system further involves the feelings of individual or group actors of the system toward the other role players. The political culture of any given country is likely to be divided into a variety of political subcultures distinguished by social class, ethnicity, and different ideologies. The feelings of hostility or cooperation among these subcultures are as crucial to the operation of a political system as the trust, or lack of it, among its citizens. The operation of the channels of political communication also contribute to the nature of a given political culture. The nature and circulation of a country's press and other media and the newspaper readers or other receptive publics are crucial to the operation and change of the political culture.

The policy-making institutions and elites of a given political system are embedded into the web of the political culture and its subcultures. In fact, they may make up a distinctive subculture whose values and style of political evaluation are derived from those of relevant parts of the larger political culture. The recruitment patterns of foreign policy makers, for example, may indicate what subculture their thinking comes from. There are also the style and the procedures of formal decision-making processes to consider, which again reflect community values of how public policy should be made.

Applying the political culture approach to the international system entails some additional points of emphasis because there is no central government as a natural focus for affection or alienation. Now it is the entire "anarchic" international system which some citizens, groups or entire nations may consider a legitimate order while others regard it as threatening or badly in need of drastic revision. The legitimacy of the international system is usually viewed also in terms of whether the citizens of a given country accept the place accorded their country in the world or whether they feel discriminated against. The great powers and their conflict or cooperation are today a chief object of trust or distrust. International organizations such as the United Nations or the International Court of Justice or instrumentalities such as international law may also be the recipients of a subliminal sense of trust or of manifest ridicule or hatred. A citizen may also view the role of his own government in the larger system with misgivings. Many Americans today, for example, question whether their government should play the role of the policeman of the world, while others would like to see it do more policing. Some would prefer that the United States discontinue bankrolling a significant part of the operations of the United Nations or of the economic development of former colonial nations. Others see in American foreign policy the only reliable instrument toward world peace.

An important dimension of the political culture of any given country relative to international politics is the degree of awareness among the population of the complexities of the international system. Even within highly advanced democracies the level of information about the domestic system is rather low. In developing countries large pockets of parochial political culture often are hardly aware of the existence of their central government. The level of accurate information about the international system and its special requirements is likely to be far lower yet. The flow of political communications about foreign affairs is a mere trickle and often subject to government control. To make matters worse, it is difficult even for the rare individual who is well informed to check on the veracity of his information in time to influence decisions. Crucial foreign policy decisions are sometimes sparked or impeded by popular sentiments that may be as erroneous as they are explosive. This difficulty of obtaining information also means that international political culture may often be comprised of the attitudes and opinions of organized groups, such as political parties, communications media, or the staffs of governmental and military institutions, more than of mass sentiments.

While governments of sovereign states and international or regional organizations may appear to be natural role players of the international system, there are others that are sometimes considered. Is an international partisan or ideological movement such as the Communist International of the 1920s a legitimate player? What about the international activities of the CIA or, for that matter, of the Vatican? Should foreign policy be made by governments alone or, presumably by democratic procedure, by the peoples of the countries? What about so-called people-to-people relationships and attempts to appeal directly to the good will of another nation? Not infrequently, individual Americans have attempted to crash through the iron curtains and State Department prohibitions keeping them out of Cuba or North Vietnam. Unauthorized West German officials have often tried to establish contacts with the East German government in the hope of initiating negotiations for German reunification. What instrumentalities are a proper way of dealing with international crises? Is a summit conference likely to accomplish what bilateral diplomacy cannot? Are international conferences or multilateral diplomacy the right means, or a better means, than bilateral negotiations? There are many ways in which the role conceptions and notions of legitimacy or trust of domestic political culture can be applied to the international system.

The attitudes of hostility or cooperation among domestic groups can be transferred to the feelings of hostility or friendliness among nations or alliances of states. This is all the more significant since hostile nations, unlike hostile domestic groups, can conduct war as a widely accepted way of dealing with each other. One can even speak meaningfully of international or regional subcultures such as pacifistic attiudes that rest on binational or regional patterns of consensus, as do the degrees of belligerence among parties and groups in domestic politics. The impact of war, defeat, and conquest or occupation often perpetuates the hostility that originally led to war.

A PREVIEW OF THE CHAPTERS TO COME

Following this introduction to the problems and perplexities of German foreign relations and appropriate methods of approach, this book will proceed directly *in medias res*. In chapter 1, some of the basic dimensions of contemporary German political culture are explored with particular emphasis on how the culture restrains the use of West and East German economic and military capabilities in the exercise of international power. For the political culture of the Federal Republic, this exploration is based on recent public opinion polls, while East German notions of identity and other indicators have to be surmised from official pronouncements and the literature. Chapter 2 probes more deeply into the historical patterns of consciousness and tradition surrounding the development and disintegration of German national identity. Chapter 3 considers the specific foreign policy goals of the two Germanies and earlier German governments which have attempted to mold the fluid German realities according to their desires.

Chapter 4 will discuss the changes in West German foreign policy after Adenauer's departure, and the rocky beginnings of *Ostpolitik*. Chapter 5 will deal with the policies of the Brandt regime vis-à-vis East Germany and the Soviet Union, and the problems raised for the two Germanies by negotiations on German reunification, the status of Berlin, and the recognition of Germany's eastern borders. Chapter 6 finally blends the domestic politics of *Ostpolitik* with a discussion of the continuing importance of *Westpolitik*.

Chapter 7 will deal with the West and East German economic and military capabilities in relation to the international environment and analyze the institutions and procedures of the process of foreign policy making in East and West. It will also come to grips with the group forces of West and East German society that influence the course of foreign policy making, such as political parties, interest groups, and social groups.

West and East Germany cannot conduct their foreign policies in a vacuum. Their location in the midst of Europe, along both sides of a twenty-five-year-old Cold War boundary that cuts the German nation in two, has placed the two states in the middle of continual East-West confrontations in the past. But since recent

German and European policies have increasingly defused the explosiveness of the Berlin situation and of confrontations between Bonn and East Berlin, the two states also happen to be at the hub of the unfolding new era of conciliation and cooperation in Europe. Willy Brandt's *Ostpolitik* and the various agreements between East and West Germany in the last few years are at the center of the evolving future of international relations in Europe, an era which was initiated by the 1967 Report of the NATO Council on the Future Tasks of the Alliance (Harmel Report) at Reykjavik. The "signal of Reykjavik" has been the guiding light of most concrete German foreign policy measures since 1967 to remove the knotty political obstacles in the way of a stable order of peace in Europe. As this book goes to press the *Ostpolitik* has succeeded in clearing out the most thorny of the obstacles, and the impending European Security Conference and another round of summit meetings among European heads of states promise to complete the great task of establishing a livable, tension-free *modus vivendi* in Europe. Yet the *Ostpolitik* was made possible only by the successful *Westpolitik* of an earlier German era. Looking back from this secular goal is the way to survey how the Germans and their leaders ever found their way from the hopeless beginnings of 1949.

Notes

[1]   For definition and details, see Gabriel A. Almond and Sidney Verba, *The Civic Culture* (Princeton: Princeton University Press, 1963), chap. 1, and Lucian W. Pye and Sidney Verba, *Political Culture and Political Development* (Princeton: Princeton University Press, 1965). See also this writer's *Modern Comparative Politics* (New York: Holt, Rinehart & Winston, 1970), chap. 3.

Germany and Neighboring States: Territorial Changes from
1918-Present

CHAPTER 1

Some Basic Dimensions of Current German Foreign Policy Orientations

German foreign policy today," Willy Brandt wrote in 1968, "bears not only the burden of the second lost war and not only the burden of the Hitler regime. It bears still another burden: the mistrust of many people in countries abroad as to the authenticity of our desire for reconciliation and as to whether the democrats in Germany are strong enough to assert themselves and implement their desire for reconciliation."[1] The plain meaning of these words is understandable enough. Nevertheless, a careful student of comparative foreign policy must wonder just what exactly such a "burden on a foreign policy" could be. Chancellor Brandt is obviously referring to a mental burden both on German minds and on the minds of other people regarding what trust they might place, for example, in a German policy of reconciliation with Eastern European countries such as Poland or Czechoslovakia.

Trust and distrust, and the West or East German sense of identity are among the basic dimensions of German political culture which this chapter will examine more closely. Reliable conclusions from public opinion polls, of course, will have to be limited to the West German population, although on many subjects the mass of East Germans may not differ drastically in their views. The attitudes of East German elites, on the other hand, are likely to be at variance with East German mass opinion due to the dictatorial nature of their regime, in contrast to West German elites who depend heavily on public support. The following text will indicate from time to time how East German opinion is likely to differ from the West German data.

ELITES & ATTENTIVE PUBLICS

Before specific West German attitudes toward foreign affairs can be examined, this politico-cultural information must be placed into the proper perspective. Analysts rely chiefly on mass opinions ascertained from representative samples of the entire population, but the actual making of foreign policy has always been far too oligarchic to bear any simple explanation relating its course to mass opinions. Even in the political give-and-take of democracy, it must be assumed there are at least two intermediary levels at work between the formal policy makers and the people at large. One is composed of the informal elites and opinion makers in influential positions who have been the object of several elite studies. The other far more inclusive level of intermediaries is the so-called "attentive public" of knowledgeable and interested citizens who probably constitute opinion leaders on foreign policy problems in the small groups of mass society. It is they who follow governmental policies closely and who have to be persuaded of their merits. Nevertheless, mass opinions have their effect on policy making via elections and on the deeper levels of consciousness for masses and elites alike, as shall be discussed.

Two recent West German elite studies illustrate the interpretation of the term *elite in* political science. A 1964 interviewing project of Karl W. Deutsch, Lewis J. Edinger, Roy C. Macridis, and Richard L. Merritt,[2] which concerned itself particularly with foreign policy attitudes, defined the West German political elite as follows:

(1) political (partisan) elites
(2) military leaders
(3) communication (media) elites
(4) civil servants
(5) business and business association leaders
(6) other professions (including the churches, labor and professional associations)

In five of these six groups, the researchers intended to interview a like number (thirty) of respondents and half that number among the military. Generally speaking, the bulk of this elite sample was about forty-five years of age and occupied highly influential positions in society and government. If there was a choice, ascending, younger elite persons were preferred to those near retirement. Only a small fraction of them actually were in formal policy-making roles, but it can be assumed that most of the basic foreign policy attitudes of the larger political elite are shared by policy makers and influential persons alike.[3]

The second elite study was conducted by Rudolf Wildenmann at the University of Mannheim in 1968 and aimed at a similar group distinguished by its formal rank. This project had singled out about 800 respondents as follows:

191 party leaders, mayors, land ministers, chairmen and vice-
chairmen of federal and land legislative committees
89 high federal or land civil servants
129 economic and managerial elites
150 communications media elites
88 functionaries of business associations
78 trade union leaders
90 university, church and other associational elites

Wildenmann decided to omit members of the federal government for fear of a high rate of refusal and to avoid the bias introduced into a measurement of opinion by loyalty to government policies. His definition of elites is "persons or groups who are capable of imposing their own views and guidance within recognizable social formations."[4] Like the Deutsch-Edinger sample, the Wildenmann sample is mostly over forty-five years of age and highly educated, which deviates markedly from the "attentive public" for foreign affairs, not to mention the West German public at large. Any study of the East German political elite by definition will have to concentrate its attention on the Communist leadership of the party, the mass organizations, and the state apparatus.

By common consensus, West Germany's "attentive public" for foreign affairs is rather large. A recent cross-national study by Daniel H. Willick found 27.1 percent of West Germans "very interested in international affairs," as compared to 16.9 percent Englishmen, 11.9 percent Frenchmen, 8.7 percent Japanese, and 4.4 percent Italians.[5] Richard Merritt and Ellen Pirro have supplied comparably high indicators of media attention and media exposure to foreign affairs for West Germany in contrast to other

European countries. Indeed, the newspaper-reading public is very large, with nine out of ten reading a paper at least once a week and more than half reading the paper daily.[6]

However, the levels of salience and cognition of the West German public are closely related to special circumstances and conditions of the country's international situation. And they have tended to fluctuate considerably in interaction with domestic issues and priorities. After the 1961 elections, for example, Viggo Graf Bluecher wrote persuasively that "the most salient issue among the electorate is the *grosse Politik* (foreign and world politics)" which is also far more stable and lasting than domestic issues tend to be. Only the small number of people highly involved and interested in politics, he claimed, tended to pay equal attention to domestic issues.[7] Nevertheless, he had to admit, such issues as access to Berlin and the desire for peace rose to high levels of saliency only after the alarming events of that year, beginning with the Kennedy-Khrushchev meeting in Vienna. Reunification, however, was the issue of highest salience every year from 1955 to 1963,[8] an issue of abiding if "cold enthusiasm." In October 1960, four-fifths of the respondents expressed their strong support for reunification, yet only a third was prepared to "do anything to attain it." Nearly all respondents regarded reunification as a matter of family or personal deprivation, a "nondiscussable fundamental value" in their lives.

But how long will people keep on longing for the unattainable? In 1964 the saliency of the reunification issue began a sharp downturn after having reached a high of 41 percent regarding it as "the most important question facing Germany today." The DIVO survey of late 1964 already rated inflation higher,[9] although the surveys of the Institut für Demoskopie continued to give reunification a generous edge over economic issues for another year. In 1966 and in January 1967, however, the economic recession in the Bonn republic had eclipsed the importance of reunification, with 62 percent naming economic issues over 18 percent for reunification.[10] Other foreign policy issues rarely rated a higher saliency than domestic issues either, except when accident or Soviet heavy-handedness happened to stir up East-West crises at nearly every federal election. The 1949 elections were overshadowed by the Berlin blockade and those of 1953 by the crushing of the East German revolt of June 17, 1953. The elections of 1957 were in the wake of the abortive Hungarian and Polish revolutions and the demise of John F. Dulles' doctrine of rolling back the Iron Curtain. The 1961 elections were preceded by the construction of the Berlin Wall and those of 1969 may well turn out to have been influenced by the invasion of Czechoslovakia by the Warsaw Pact nations, or the collapse of the Bonn policy toward Eastern Europe. Only the 1965 and the 1972 elections were undisturbed by foreign policy crises.[11] Since measurements of voter interest in foreign policy are most likely to occur at the time of elections, the claim of high West German attentiveness to foreign affairs may well have been exaggerated.[12]

What would be the East German equivalent of the "attentive public"? The answer to this question is contingent upon a comparative interpretation of circumstantial factors in East and West Germany. A member of the "attentive public" of a Western democracy plays a fairly well-defined role within the democratic interplay among a free press, government policies, and the policy alternatives of the opposition party or parties. His attentiveness is a critical stance toward his government and has to lean heavily on information and ideas contributed by the independent press and the opposition. The absence of a free press and legitimate opposition in a Communist people's republic deprives the equivalent role there of essential supports. Receiving foreign radio stations or newspapers is outlawed. Traveling abroad is very restricted, and impossible in the West. Life in social organizations and at work is politically supervised so that the individual of critical inclination can only withdraw into the privacy of his own mind and perhaps the company of trusted friends and members of his family. Thus there is no public opinion in the Western democratic sense, only official and private opinions. Attentiveness at best is directed only toward the official opinions and limited by what information people are permitted to have. This is particularly true of foreign affairs, a subject about which most people under any system and especially in East Germany have to accept on faith what they learn from the media.

Popular attitudes toward foreign policy in East Germany are also likely to be colored by the scale of the basic attitudes toward the dictatorial regime. People who have made up their minds to distrust the Communist regime are likely to believe very little of the official line without necessarily knowing what else to believe.

The regime's supporters, on the other hand, accept its propaganda without the mental reservations any prudent person would have. And there are many degrees in between the alienated and the supporters. Hans Apel, who has carried out informal public opinion polls since 1962, gives a telling description of the way stations of the mind between belief and disbelief. He distinguishes believers, supporters who have socially arrived in the system, the reconciled, the satiated, persons vacillating in their support because of strong conflicting motivations,[13] the discontented, and those who feel oppressed and alienated. Only the first and the last categories are truly interested in politics and their numbers are rather small. Most of the others are motivated primarily by economic and environmental considerations, a posture which seems rather consistent with the dominant ideology of the system. It would appear, then, that the East German equivalent of an "attentive public" is rather small and poorly informed, while the general East German public has relegated concern with international issues to a very low level of saliency.

A LACK OF TRUST IN
THE INTERNATIONAL SYSTEM

One of the basic dimensions of political attitudes toward foreign affairs, as in studies of domestic political culture, is the basic sense of trust or distrust in the international political system. This sense of trust or distrust is implicit in the expectations of individuals toward friendly, hostile or disturbing activities of the international system. Unlike domestically oriented political culture, which focuses its sense of trust or alienation mostly on the public order, the government and secondary groups, orientations toward the international system tend to focus on the absence of an international public order and on the anarchic forces that dominate it. The fear of war and other disturbing activities of the anarchic environment may well be greater with smaller and weaker nations than with superpowers who can take care of themselves. Smaller nations, therefore, understandably cling more to security arrangements, alliances and agreements, fearing any upset of the status quo.

East Germany, for many reasons including its size and dependence on the Soviet Union, presents in this sense the small-country syndrome of attitudes. At the elite level in East Germany, there is an intense and somewhat paranoid preoccupation with the alleged capitalist encirclement of the DDR. Since by terminating the rule of the capitalist class over the workers the DDR earned the unrelenting hostility of the capitalists all over the world, the capitalistic and "imperialistic" powers of the West through NATO are forever plotting the exclusion and discrimination of the DDR from the world's markets and organizations. The "revanchist," "imperialistic clique" of the Bonn government, moreover, is trying to isolate the DDR by means of denying it diplomatic recognition under the Hallstein Doctrine. More ominous yet to the East German elites, the friendly West German overtures to the East European neighbors of the DDR are seen as an attempt to isolate the latter within the Communist bloc. As Peter Florin, the East German ambassador to Czechoslovakia, wrote, evidently projecting his own anxieties upon the West:

> The unity and solidarity of the socialist states and their cooperation is a nightmare for world imperialism which tries again and again to destroy our unity. All the more reason for the socialist states to stand together against any supposedly new or more flexible Eastern policy of our imperialistic antagonist whose goals have not changed in the least.[14]

The best course for East German foreign policy, consequently, is "close friendly collaboration with the state of the great Socialist October Revolution, the Soviet Union, as well as with the other brotherly-linked members of the socialist family of states, especially of the Warsaw Pact."[15] Such collaboration, among other things, also led the DDR to participate in the Warsaw bloc military intervention in Czechoslovakia in 1968.

The tortured Marxist-Leninist reasoning of the elite is sharply confirmed at least in part at the popular level. Until recently East Germans knew that they were not free to cross the Polish or Czech frontiers at will, and they are still distrusted and disliked in most parts of Eastern Europe. Their feelings toward the Soviet Union are rather mixed in spite of official German-Russian friendship societies and observances, for many people remember the first decade of ruthless economic exploitation of the country by the Soviet Military Administration and its stratagems. There is also some awareness of continuing economic bondage in the form of highly unfavorable trade treaties. Older East Germans remember the violent entry of the Red Army into German cities on the heels of retreating German armies in 1944-45 when mass rape, killings, and depredations by the enraged victors were a common occurrence.[16] Today, the Soviet divisions stationed in East Germany are generally kept away from the civilian population to minimize potential friction.

As for the capitalistic West, East Germans on the whole are not taken in by the ideological propaganda of their leaders with the possible exception of personal diatribes against particular Western public figures ("Johnson, the murderer") or the stereotypes of Wall Street, the Pentagon, and the "revanchists in Bonn." There still seems to be a hidden reservoir of warm fraternal feelings slumbering under the decades of official East German vilification of West German governments and politicians. When West German Chancellor Willy Brandt met East German Premier Willi Stoph in the city of Erfurt (March 1970), the first such state visit ever, the People's Police could hardly hold back the friendly crowds. Somewhat to the embarrassment of Premier Stoph, the East Germans held up signs with the letter Y to signify which Willy they were cheering. Evidently, they have few neighboring governments to welcome.

West Germans, by way of contrast, do not feel as isolated or encircled by hostile forces as do the East Germans. Nevertheless, there seems to have been an underlying lack of trust in the international system in the Federal Republic as well which has come out every so often in public opinion polls. The dramatic impact of the construction of the Berlin Wall in 1961, for instance, and perhaps also the confused Western reaction to it, caught the West German population quite unprepared, giving them a sudden sense of insecurity and helplessness, and of their lives being directly threatened. It produced a regression to residual, older attitudes of dependence on leaders and powerful protectors, even old-fashioned German nationalism. In the polls then in progress, a solid two-thirds expressed their trust in the Allied guarantees for Berlin, the symbol of long-repressed German nationalism. A like number maintained their support for the Western alliance, evidently on the theory that "if we are loyal to them, they will come through for us." An acute fear of war and desire for peace rose sharply in reaction to the upset of the status quo.[17]

The fear of war is a ready barometer of distrust in the international system, especially for a country divided by or perched on the edge of the Iron Curtain. To be sure, the public awareness of threatening circumstances and rational evaluation of the likelihood of war should not be disregarded, even though we can now say with the benefit of hindsight that the East-West system was capable of avoiding outright conflict throughout the period in question. But there remains an irrational element in the fear of war after everything else is accounted for (Table 1a).[18] If we consider, for example, the great turning point of the 1950s, the Soviet

TABLE 1a   "Do you think there'll be another world war in the next three (3) or four (4) years?"   (*DIVO* 1959, p. 17)

	1953	1954	1955	1956	Jan. 1957	Dec. 1957	1958
Yes	10%	17	9	8	15	18	12
No	66%	60	69	71	56	52	69
Don't know or undecided	24%	23	22	21	29	30	19

intervention in Hungary, the Allied failure to counteract it and the growing European realization in 1957 that American military superiority in Europe had been replaced with something approaching a standoff, the rising fear in 1957 of "another world war in the next three to four years" seems plausible. The greatly reduced number of "nos" and the rising number of "don't knows" or "undecideds" could also be explained as a switch from trust to a reluctance to think the unthinkable. But why the basic level of 8-12 percent expecting a world war at all times and why the high level in 1954, the year of the post-Stalin thaw?[19]

In the 1960s, the Institut für Demoskopie in Allensbach asked a somewhat different question on a similar subject: "Do you think we have to expect another world war, or do you think no one would risk another great war anymore?" Table 1b shows the high level of fear as contrasted to the patterned reply "no one would risk it." The question probably exercised a kind of semantic compulsion upon the respondent to concentrate on whether it is reasonable to assert that no one would again risk war rather than to express the fear of the international environment. The figures also mirror the effect of the construction of the Berlin Wall (the first

TABLE 1b "Do you expect another world war, or would no one risk another great war anymore?" (*JOM* 1967, p. 419)

	1961	1963	1964	1965	1965 by age: under 30 yrs.	45-59	1965 by occupation: civil servants	independents, professions
No one would risk a war	45%	49	56	48	52	43	57	43
Expect another world war	46%	42	35	41	39	46	36	47
Other responses	—	—	1	2	—	—	—	—
Impossible to say	9%	9	8	9	9	11	7	10

survey was a month after this event) and reveal surprising differences between the young generation and that of their parents who entered politics between 1920 and 1940. The confidence of youth aside, still more surprising is that of civil servants as compared to the anxiety level of independent businessmen and professional people. In a second question (Table 1c), the institute linked the

TABLE 1c "Can young marrieds calmly face the future, or need they fear another war?" (*JOM* 1967, p. 420)

They . . .	1963	1964	1965	1965 by age: under 30 yrs.	30-44	45-59	over 60
can calmly face future	21%	32	27	33	28	26	21
need fear war	46%	35	38	33	40	37	41
Undecided and don't know	33%	33	35	34	32	37	38

fear of war to the domestic providence of young couples: "When somebody gets married and wants to start a family these days, do you think he can calmly face the future or need he fear the coming of another war?" Again the confidence of youth over old age is prominent despite the fact that it is the young and their new families, and not the old, who are most likely to have to face the risks of future wars.

The most likely sources of war and international insecurity are, according to popular perceptions in West Germany, certain powers, most of all the Soviet Union, in critical situations. Asked flatly whether they "felt that Russia threatens or does not threaten us?," West German adults exhibited the slow decline of the cold war feelings, but only to a midway point (Table 2a). Breakdowns

TABLE 2a   "Does Russia threaten or does it not threaten us?"   (*JOM* 1967, p. 456)

Respondents feel . . .	1952	1954	1956	1958	1964	1965	1966
Threatened	66%	64	45	51	39	50	38
Not threatened	15%	21	27	27	37	27	37
Undecided, don't know	19%	15	28	22	24	23	25

by age show those under thirty feeling 42 percent to 30 percent that they are not threatened while those over sixty hold 26 percent to 45 percent the opposite view. Respondents identifying with the CDU/CSU similarly feel threatened by 45 percent (versus 32 percent not threatened) while only 30 percent of SPD adherents feel that way (versus 46 percent). There are also many other polls which suggest that the popular impression of the Soviet Union is one of unrelieved hostility toward West Germany, but also of Soviet incapacity to take action against the Federal Republic as long as the latter is in league with the West. These findings receive further depth when they are contrasted with a poll in which undiminished numbers insisted in 1966 (59 percent yes, 16 percent no) and 1965 (61 percent yes, 14 percent no), as in June and September 1955 (54 percent yes, 17 percent no, and 56 percent yes, 14 percent no, respectively), that the most important goal of the Soviets would always be "to make the whole world Communist." There was also a poll in November 1960 in which respondents were asked whether "they believed the Russians by themselves would or would not start a war in Europe." Fifty percent responded in the negative and 12 percent in the affirmative, although 57 percent of the sample (as against 17 percent) denied that the "Soviets today have the basic good will to come to an understanding with the West." Red China, oddly enough, has become the coming menace to world peace and West Germany, according to 35 percent and 43 percent, respectively, of West German adults asked in 1963 and 1964. Forty-seven percent considered China "the greater menace to the West" as compared to 23 percent who expressed this opinion about Russia.[20]

West German elites, it should be noted, seem to feel little fear of an imminent war today, although they may well have shared the fears of the masses back in the 1950s. As Wolfram F. Hanrieder has emphasized, the need of the new-born Federal Republic for a permanent security arrangement against the Soviet and East German military threat coincided with the American and British desire to incorporate West Germany into the NATO alliance in the early 1950s. West Germany was rearmed and by 1955 became a full-fledged, though not equal, NATO member.[21] The rearmament policy of the Adenauer government had to be carried out in the face of strong opposition from rival elites and the public. Once West German rearmament was an accomplished fact and the opposition became reconciled to it, however, the level of anxiety among the political elites fell considerably. At the time of the Deutsch-Edinger interviews in 1964, West German elites (65 percent) professed their reliance on NATO more emphatically than the French elites whose overriding concern with an equal role in NATO for France was strong. Communist forces and communism as such were seen by most (70 percent) elite persons as the greatest threat to West German security. They took a dim view of any plans to withdraw troops (65 percent) or nuclear weapons (72 percent) from Central Europe while at the same time rejecting any national German nuclear role, a view widely shared among the masses of West German society.[22]

The other side of the coin from expectations of hostility is a trust in friendly powers and agreements. For purposes of analysis, it is advisable to separate the instrumental use of alliances, the sense of agency, from expressions of friendship, trust and distrust. A crude comparison of the two could contrast, for example, the liking expressed by West German adults for Americans, Frenchmen, Englishmen, or Italians to the percentages who propose "close collaboration" between these countries and the Bonn republic. A glance at Table 2b clearly shows that the inclination toward instrumental collaboration with a country far outruns the liking for its nationals as people (see also Table 2c). Traditional

TABLE 2b Liking foreign nationals versus proposing close collaboration with their countries. (*The Germans*, pp. 543-44, 565 and *JOM* 1964, p. 533)

	U.S.			Great Britain		France		Italy
	1957-59	1961-62	1963-65	1962	1963-65	1962	1963-65	1963-64
Liking the nationals of . . .	39%	54	58	32	46	44	39	19
Proposing collaboration with government of . . .	81%	81	90	54	65	61	71	31

TABLE 2c "Should Americans go Home?" (*JOM* 1964, p. 553 and *DIVO* 1960, p. 31)

	1951	1953	1954	1956	1957 (Jan.-Feb.)	1957 (Dec.)	1958
No	(58%)	57(67)	(71)	40(43)	48(52)	40(66)	55
Yes	(22%)	24(19)	(15)	33(41)	28(23)	32(23)	21
Undecided	(20%)	19(14)	(14)	27(16)	24(25)	28(11)	24

national stereotypes and ideological rigidity aside, the two are probably quite independent of one another although the data available were not adequate to demonstrate their independence.[23]

A more succinct measure of trust in the West German partnership with the United States emerges from the various degrees of American withdrawal explored by public opinion polls. In the 1964 elite study of Deutsch and Edinger, the question most upsetting to the German respondents was "How likely is it that the U.S. would abandon its commitment to defend Western Europe?" It was the year of the Goldwater-Johnson race and an American return to isolation was not implausible, although the respondents frequently insisted that the American presence in Europe was at least as much in the American interest as the German. De Gaulle, moreover, had argued persuasively that in spite of current American commitments future American leaders might wish to withdraw from Europe, or at least Americans might not wish to risk their cities in a showdown over Berlin. The contingency of an American withdrawal evidently produced a sharp sense of insecurity, if not rage, and threats of teaming up with De Gaulle or of making a "deal" with the Soviets.[24] In the years from 1953 to 1958, including the acquisition of sovereignty and NATO membership and during the crisis of 1956, the Allensbach Institute repeatedly asked representative samples of the adult population "Would you prefer that the Americans withdraw and concern themselves only with America?" Beginning in July 1956, the institute further asked respondents whether they would welcome it or regret it if they read in the newspapers that the United States troops were being withdrawn (Table 2d).

TABLE 2d   "Would you welcome or regret reading news of a withdrawal of U.S. troops?"   (*JOM* 1964, pp. 553-54)

	1956	1957 (Jan.)	1957 (Dec.)	1962
Welcome it	51%	33	34	12
Regret it	22%	34	34	59
Undecided	27%	33	32	29

Withdrawal means alienation of affection or abandonment, so to speak, a separation very likely followed by divorce. Frequently, however, such an ending is preceded by liaisons with third parties. And so the institute asked in 1957 "Suppose we would negotiate all of a sudden with the Russians, regardless of our American ties, do you think the Americans might turn away from us or not?" Forty-four percent of the respondents regarded such conduct as insufficient grounds for an American withdrawal, especially males, the age group from thirty to forty-four, the better-educated, the West Berliners, and adherents of the Social Democratic Party (SPD). Relatively more fearful of losing the American partner over such dalliance were women, older people and adherents of the Free Democratic Party (FDP).[25] On the other hand, respondents were also asked repeatedly whether they believed that "someday the United States would recognize the division of Germany in order to come to an understanding with the Soviets." (Table 2e).

TABLE 2e "Do you think the U.S. will someday recognize the German division in order to come to an agreement with the Soviet Union?" *(The Germans,* p. 549)

	1959	1961	1962
No	41%	39	44
Yes	27%	23	23
Undecided	20%	21	20
No opinion	12%	17	13

The amount of faith in American commitments was even higher (49 percent) among Christian Democratic Union (CDU) adherents in 1962 while the skeptics were more heavily represented among SPD- and FDP-oriented voters.

The choice between French and American partnership, by contrast, is not a genuine alternative for West German minds who regard the United States as irreplaceable for their national security at the same time that they may show a yearning for French friendship. In the 1964 elite study, four out of ten West German elite respondents insisted that the Bonn republic simply could not rely on France as an ally, and another three-tenths considered France "reliable only to a limited extent."[26] Regarding the Franco-German friendship treaty, on the other hand, 51 percent in 1963 considered

TABLE 2f "Is lasting friendship with France possible, or are there too many differences between the countries?" *(The Germans,* p. 535)

	1955	1962(July)	1962(Sept.)
Lasting friendship is possible	40%	52	59
Too many differences	32%	16	15
Undecided	28%	32	26

it "a good thing" as compared to 17 percent who thought it was "a bad thing." (See also Table 2f). The percentage of enthusiastic Francophiles was particularly great among white collar and independent groups and among CDU and FDP adherents. But De Gaulle was not preaching to deaf ears in West Germany when he counseled against placing too much confidence in the Americans and warned that Europe would lose its influence in world politics unless it developed atomic armaments. This lengthy De Gaulle quote (of which the confidence aspect is hard to separate from the German reaction to atomic armaments) was used in a poll and found agreement among 27 percent of the respondents.[27]

A SENSE OF FLAWED IDENTITY

The civic culture survey of 1959 turned up a curious aspect of the national self-image among West Germans. Unlike most of the other national groups, West Germans showed very little pride in their political institutions. When asked what aspect of their nation they were proud of, they stressed instead their economic system or retreated into the stereotypes of national character (Table 3a). This

TABLE 3a Aspects of nation in which respondents report pride (Almond and Verba, *The Civic Culture* [Princeton: Princeton University Press, 1963], p. 102).

	Political Institutions	Social Legislation	International Position	Economic System	People's Character
Great Britain	46%	18	11	10	18
West Germany	7%	6	5	33	36

complex of questions can be explored further from polls which reflect on the collective self-image and were taken both before and after the civic culture survey. Since surveys of self-ascribed German virtues always turn up two-thirds and more responses of "industriousness, ambition, achievement-mindedness, etc.,"[28] the Institut für Demoskopie asked respondents repeatedly "Do you believe we Germans are more able and gifted than other peoples?" (Table 3b). The responses have become progressively more self-deprecating over the years, and in 1965 the negative replies were

TABLE 3b   "Are we Germans more able (*tüchtig*) and gifted than other peoples?"   (*JOM* 1967, p. 1954)

	1955	1956	1959	1960(Jan.)	1960(July)	1965
No	38%	42	50	55	55	50
Yes, more or less	39%	33	30	29	27	28
Definitely yes	21%	23	18	13	15	17

even higher among those under thirty (56 percent), SPD adherents (55 percent) and respondents with secondary education (*mittlere Reife*). Less humble were respondents over sixty and adherents of the FDP. There was also an EEC study in 1963 which constructed a scale of relative self-ratings among European nations on the basis of surveys of self-ascribed national virtues. The French rated 284 points on the scale, the Italians 203, and the Belgians 135. The British and the Dutch came in at 122, but the West Germans only at 105.[29]

"Will Germany ever again be one of the great powers of the world?" was the second question asked over the same period of time. (Table 3c). The responses were rather evenly distributed over

TABLE 3c   "Will Germany ever again be a great power?" (*JOM* 1967, p. 155)

	1954	1955	1962	1965
No	41%	48	53	52
Yes	38%	25	19	17
Impossible to say	21%	27	28	31

the various groups of the population except for three groups: respondents from industrial North Rhine Westphalia and the best-educated respondents (with *Abitur*), both of whom took a slightly more sanguine view of the German future, and the adherents of the FDP, who answered 69 percent positively to 6 percent in the negative. Another question in 1966 quoted Franz Josef Strauss as having said he did not expect to see a revival of a German *Reich*, not even of one consisting only of West and East Germany (i.e., without the Oder-Neisse area). Thirty-five percent expressed agreement with Strauss, including nearly half of the FDP adherents, while 34 percent considered his statement too pessimistic.[30] At the heart of the self-deprecatory attitude underlying West German political culture, it is submitted, there lies a sense of *identité manquée*, of flawed or wounded identity. The question to be raised, then, is whether the flaw or wound is the territorial one of a divided nation, or the historical one of the "undigested past" of the Nazi era, or a combination of both.

TABLE 3d "Who is to blame for World War II?" (*JOM* 1967, p. 146) (Percentages have been rounded.)

	1951	1955	1956	1959	1962	1964	1967
Germany	32%	43	47	50	53	51	62
The "others"	24%	14	12	11	9	9	8
Both	18%	15	11	10	10	7	8
Other replies	11%	9	10	11	9	6	6
Don't know	15%	19	20	19	20	28	16

Regarding the division of Germany, the wound is deep and painful. Asked in 1963 whether they considered it "an intolerable situation" or had "gotten gradually used to it," 53 percent of a national sample called it intolerable (versus 32 percent "used to it"), a response practically identical to that of 1956 (52 percent "intolerable" versus 33 percent "used to it"). Similarly unchanged was the response to the question "Is there any point in demanding again and again that Germany be reunified, or should one just leave it to the passing of time?" In 1956, 65 percent answered "Yes, there is a point, etc.", while 25 percent wanted to leave reunification "to the passage of time." The positive response was 64 percent in 1958, 65 percent in 1959, and 69 percent in 1964, against 24 percent in 1958 and 21 percent in 1959 (there was no corresponding measurement in 1964).

It is not even clear whether "German reunification" in the popular mind refers only to the union of the Federal Republic and the East German Republic. In 1964, 51 percent of the respondents said they understood the phrase to include only East and West Germany while another 34 percent specified Germany within the borders of 1937.[31] In 1962 only 30 percent agreed (versus 54 percent who did not) that "one should not give up the hope for reunification." Asked how important *Deutschlandpolitik* (reunification) was to the respondent himself, 66 percent answered "very much," 13 percent "much," 10 percent "rather," 3 percent "a little" and 4 percent "not at all." Residents of the areas bordering on East Germany and refugees from there gave 6-12 percent higher salience responses. In 1962, 45 percent also said that the Oder-Neisse areas were hopelessly lost for Germany (versus 29 percent who did not), and 50 percent (versus 26 percent) said that Germans should resign themselves to the Oder-Neisse Line.[32]

The painful choices before West Germans were also explored by polls, one asking what was more important to the respondents, reunification or security from the Russians (Table 3e). The re-

TABLE 3e   "Is reunification more important than (1) security (1959); (2) general disarmament and peace (1962); (3) East German liberalization plus recognition (1960); (3a) almost identical question (1962); (4) refusal to recognize Oder-Neisse line (1966)?"   (*JOM* 1964, p. 484, 486-87 and *JOM* 1967, pp. 408-12)

	1	2	3	3a	4
Reunification	30%	45	48	51	51
Alternative priority	55%	25	18	28	25

sponses in favor of reunification varied only slightly from 33 percent in 1952 (versus 51 percent for security) to 35 percent (versus 55 percent) in 1959. Protection against the East, however, seems to be the only thing more important to the West Germans than reunification. A second question, "Should we renounce reunification in order to obtain general disarmament and peace for another decade," thus meeting Soviet desires, received only 15 percent affirmative and 61 percent negative replies in 1956. In 1962, this response had softened to 25 percent ayes and 45 percent nos. The same year, 42 percent (versus 27 percent who did not) indicated their readiness to renounce atomic arms for the German army if this would facilitate reunification.[33] A third question, in 1960, was whether Germans in East and West should solemnly renounce reunification if this would gain East Germans "freedom from Com-munist rule so that they could live just as in the West." The poll almost amounted to a measurement of suspicion of Russian (or Communist) motives. The highly-educated and refugees were the most skeptical. Another version of the same question in 1962 juxtaposed two opinions. One suggested renouncing reunification if East Germans could live in dignity and personal freedom, electing their own government and enjoying political freedoms. The other one insisted that reunification had first priority and the rest would follow. This time the alternative did somewhat better, but was still no match for reunification.[34] The fourth question, in 1966, asked respondents whether they were prepared to recognize the Oder-Neisse line in a peace treaty in exchange for reunification with East Germany. Fifty-one percent answered in the affirmative while 25 percent chose the alternative, holding out for the chance of eventually regaining the areas beyond the Oder and Neisse.[35] The uncertain territorial state of Germany, and especially the wound of the division between Communist-ruled and democratic Germany, is obviously a main feature of the West German sense of identity.

Some aspects of this preoccupation have come out also in the controversies about who represents *all* Germans and what East Germany should be called. The official claim of Bonn to speak for all of Germany had the support of 61 percent of West German respondents in 1967, and was gainsaid only by 14 percent, although 45 percent could not even cite any reason for such a claim to *Alleinvertretung*. The official line had also insisted until rather recently on referring to the German Democratic Republic (DDR) as the "East Zone" as if it were still occupied by the Soviets. As recently as 1966, 64 percent of West German respondents still called it the East or Soviet Zone when shown a map. Sixteen percent called it East or Central Germany, the latter name hinting that there is also an East Germany beyond the Oder-Neisse line. Five percent called it "over there" and only 11 percent were willing to refer to it as the DDR. During the same survey 44 percent also said they did not expect to see reunification in their lifetime (versus 28 percent who did). There is also a sharp and bitter sense of identification with the victims of the misdeeds of the East German regime. For example, 95 percent of West German respondents were aware of the hour-long agony of Peter Fechter, an escaping worker who was brutally slain at the Berlin Wall. In 1966, 55 percent supported the idea (as against 19 percent who did not) of trying and punishing upon capture the East German politicians responsible for the orders to shoot refugees.[36]

West German elites have undergone a telltale change of mind about reunification over the years. In the 1950s, reunification was proclaimed by the Adenauer government as a major goal ahead of European integration and second only to German security against the threat from the East. The opposition parties at every election accused the government of not doing enough for reunification. By the early sixties, the issue had become such a sacred cow that the Deutsch-Edinger study was afraid to ask elite respondents directly about it. Instead, they were asked whether or not they expected reunification to occur within the next twenty-five years, a question allowing rather ambiguous responses.[37] The salient point also seemed to have shifted more to the question of whether the DDR should be recognized or just what the relations between the two German states should be, a tacit abandonment of the doctrine that only nonrecognition could lead to reunification. The elite respondents of the Wildenmann study of 1968, asked about "the most important West German foreign policy problems of the 1970s," ranked (1) better relations with Eastern Europe, (2) with the USSR, (4) with the U.S., and (3,5-7) four different versions of European political integration all ahead of a "reformulation of the relationship between the Federal Republic and the DDR." Reunification itself ranked 11th on this list of priorities, still after (9) better relations with France and (10) "normalization of relations with the DDR," but before such security issues as (12) securing the peace and (13) reorganizing NATO.[38] This was only a year before Brandt's *Ostpolitik* was launched.

The East German political elites have undergone a change of their own on the reunification issue. Up until the time of the construction of the Berlin Wall, there was a great deal of official concern for German reunification, provided that an all-German government be chosen, not by free elections (the West German *sine qua non*), but in a manner safeguarding the continued existence and power of the unpopular Communist government in East Berlin. In 1957, Walter Ulbricht even proposed before the Central Committee of the East German Communist Party (SED) the establishment of an all-German confederation which was to be chosen by a permanent committee of which one-half would be East German appointees.[39] By 1961, however, the emphasis had shifted toward the assertion of a new "fatherland DDR," a separate state and nation whose consolidation had higher priority than the reunification of the German nation as such. In place of the West German complaint that East Germans were not allowed national self-determination and therefore had to be represented by "free Germany," East Berlin now stressed that it was West Germany that needed to be "liberated" from American and capitalistic-imperialistic control. In 1966, Ulbricht added further conditions for the Federal Republic in case the latter wished to take up his plan for a confederation, including reforming the West German parliament along East German lines, controls on the press, and the purge of "militaristic, revanchist and ultra-reactionary elements" in the army and civil service. He placed the onus of perpetuating the German division squarely upon Bonn.[40] The seventh SED convention of 1967, finally, adopted a manifesto which put off reunification until such time as West Germany became "anti-imperialistic" and "progressive," a thought echoed in the preamble and articles of the new DDR constitution of 1968.

How the mass public in East Germany feels about all this is difficult to gauge. There is a consensus among observers that the erection of the Berlin Wall, rather than inducing an explosive situation, has helped to consolidate the society and to achieve more popular acceptance of the Communist regime than anyone believed possible at the time. Rather than accepting uncritically some of the reports of a budding popular enthusiasm for the Communist regime,[41] it should be noted that there has been, along with the advance of East German prosperity, a substantial retreat from politics not unlike the "depoliticization" observable earlier in many western countries. Hans Apel may well be right when he reports that there has been less popular discontent in East Germany in the 1960s and that the de facto power of the DDR government is now less questioned than before. But it would be premature indeed to deduce from this the genesis of a new East German national consciousness in the place of the broader, all-German identity of the German nation.

The latent sense of German national identity, in fact, has often appeared to be more solidly embedded in the East German consciousness than in the Federal Republic's. For an outside observer conscious of German history, it is difficult to overlook the goose step of East German soldiers on parade or not to be reminded of Prussian militarism by the militarized education and indoctrination in the schools. It is no easier to escape the overwhelming parallels between the propaganda and police state of National Socialism and its Communist successors. An Israeli journalist, Amos Elon, wrote in his *Journey Through A Haunted Land:*[42] "Some aspects of the DDR exhibit a dismaying resemblance to the Third Reich," and he pointed especially to the thousands of political prisoners, killings by police and border guards, and the language of Communistic propaganda.

As Elon also pointed out, the East German reckoning with the German past suffers from curious doctrinaire distortions according to which "the Gestapo is the creation of 'powerful financial circles': Auschwitz and Treblinka are instruments of the Ruhr industry. An innocent reader would have to conclude [from school textbooks] that the bankers had converted Hitler and his cronies to racism in order to corner the stock exchange."[43] In spite of candid presentations of Nazi atrocities, East Germans seem to have managed to externalize and project their guilt feelings onto a scapegoat, chiefly the West German government and the capitalists, rather than come to grips with it in themselves. Unlike the Federal Republic, consequently, East Germany has paid no restitution to Israel or to victims of the Nazi regime, and it invariably takes the Arab side in the Middle East dispute. No attempt is made to purge the numerous ex-Nazis in the East German government and army either, although the DDR always likes to embarrass the Federal Republic with disclosures of the hidden Nazi past of some Bonn officials. Finally, the East German republic, after decades of concentrating on the future, has in recent years striven to incorporate German history in its self-image and insists that the DDR, not the Federal Republic, is the "true Germany."

If East Germany thus can hardly be said to feel a "sense of flawed identity," with the possible exception of the disoriented older generation of East Germans, such a sense certainly prevails in West Germany. Germany's "undigested past" is an inexhaustible subject of which only a few themes will be discussed here, such as the popular appraisal of Hitler and the Nazi state. As recently as 1955, 48 percent of West Germans still insisted to the dismay of Allied and German reeducators (versus 36 percent who did not) that Hitler would have been remembered as one of the greatest German statesmen had he not lost World War II. By 1959, however, Hitler's detractors began to outnumber his defenders 42 percent to 41 percent, and by 1967 the former had grown to a clear majority of 52 percent as compared to 32 percent who still defended him.[44] The change is probably generational in nature and may also be motivated by years of prosperity and well-being when economic necessities have receded into the background and moral reflections have moved into the public mind. In November 1960, for example, 41 percent of the respondents believed that the public schools taught children "too little about the events under Hitler and after the war," as compared to 21 percent who thought they taught "enough" and only 2 percent who felt they taught "too much" on this subject. There is indeed abundant evidence that German youth is not adequately informed on this subject.

This sense of a flawed past showed other results as well. The blame for starting World War II is now being accepted without subterfuge (Table 3d), even though some prominent foreign historians like A. J. P. Taylor have repudiated such a clear-cut assignment of guilt to Germany. In 1964, the Institut für Demoskopie also reported that as many as 53 percent (versus 31 percent who did not) regarded the Nazi state as a "criminal state,"-including as many as 58 percent in conservative Bavaria. And regarding the attempted assassination of Adolf Hitler on July 20, 1944, by army officers, 52 percent of the same sample supported the statement the conspirators were really "serving the fatherland," while 16 percent insisted they had been "traitors," a percentage somewhat higher among respondents over forty-five.[45]

While it may be difficult always to see in the sense of trust (or lack of it) in the international system a politico-cultural restraint on the making of foreign policy, this is not so in the case of the sense of flawed identity. West Germans evidently have been, like Hamlet, "sicklied over with the pale cast of thought" about their present predicament and horrid past. The call of the fatherland no longer moves them to great exertions. In a special study of *Bundeswehr* reservists by the Institut für Demoskopie, the respondents were asked whether the word patriotism (*Vaterlandsliebe*) had "a good sound" in their ears, or whether it no longer seemed to "fit into our time." Fifty percent said it was outdated, compared to 45 percent who still liked its sound. Army recruits were even more negative. Of the ranks, the officers were the most patriotic (53 to 43 percent) while sergeants (*Obergefreite, Hauptgefreite*) were at the opposite end (39 to 55 percent). In spite of their considerable economic and military capabilities, West Germans are evidently rather reluctant to use their capacity fully in the game of power politics.[46]

INSTRUMENTAL IDENTIFICATION:
THE SENSE OF AGENCY

The missing link between underlying attitudes, such as a sense of trust or of identity, and popular demands and supports for specific foreign policies are the evaluative processes which attentive publics use to arrive at specific judgments and conclusions. There are several approaches to understanding evaluative processes such as the study of political style, a culture-bound way of looking at political situations and of devising ways of coping with them. We are only concerned with the sense of agency, the instrumental identification with such tools of action in the international scene as one's own government, political groups and leaders, allied governments and leaders, national or common armed forces, and regional or international organizations. As was pointed out earlier, concerned citizens generally cannot resort to action in international politics as they can in domestic politics, and hence must find tools to do their work in the world.

The first level of analysis in exploring the sense of agency deals with the identification of individuals with the national government or with larger instrumental entities. Thus it also raises boundary problems, since we cannot take for granted the identification of a person with his own nation. In 1952, young West Germans surveyed by the Institut für Demoskopie were presented with a choice between "doing something which would be only in their own interest" and "something which would make Germany better off, but not themselves." To the surprise of interested observers, 37 percent of the respondents chose "something which would make only themselves better off" over 33 percent who preferred the interest of the country. Such a measurement may be crude, but it does draw a line between merely self-regarding orientations and identification with the national unit, without which it is hardly possible to speak of an instrumental relationship with a governmental entity in international affairs.[47]

While no public opinion material on East Germany is available, there is sufficient evidence to suggest that the nearly two million East Germans who fled to the West before 1961, and probably millions more like them, also have placed a higher priority upon their own private interests than on the public interest of their state. On the other hand, the schools and mass organizations, not to mention the Communist establishment, concentrate much of their socializing efforts on the inculcation of voluntary participation and on placing community-mindedness above individual interests. It would hardly come as a surprise to learn that there is an underlying popular pattern of community-mindedness which had been encouraged by the Nazi regime. The large numbers who feel alienated, persecuted, or indifferent today, however, are obviously not in the habit of regarding the DDR as their favorite instrument in world affairs.

In the West German case, on a more involved level, one can draw the boundaries between foreign policy orientations which stress (1) the national focus, (2) instrumental identification with the NATO alliance and the United States, or (3) with "Little Europe" (EEC) and France, as was done by the *Zentralarchiv* in

TABLE 4a   National versus western integrative orientation in 1968-69[a]

	Jan.	Mar.	1968 June	Sept.	Oct.	Dec.	Jan.	1969 Feb.	Apr.
National	29%	32	29	23	24	23	24	25	23
NATO-U.S.	16%	17	19	26	26	29	} 52	34 } 54	
EEC-France	29%	26	23	27	25	24		20	
Indifferent	26%	25	29	24	25	24	24	21	23

[a]From *Zentralarchiv* files, partisan differences in the shifting orientations can also be observed. Respondents of national orientation in January 1968, for example, were especially preponderant among those identifying with the NPD (61 percent), FDP (48 percent), and SPD (35 percent) while those identifying with NATO and the U.S. were more frequent among the CDU/CSU (23 percent) and SPD (19 percent) than on the average. By December 1968 the shift away from the national orientation was largest with the new voters (21 percent), the CDU/CSU (10 percent), the FDP (9 percent), and the SPD and NPD (7 percent each), while the increase for the NATO-U.S. level was largest with the CDU/CSU (14 percent), FDP (13 percent), SPD (12 percent), and the new voters (10 percent).

Cologne. The pre-election surveys in Table 4a show the distribution of these orientations in the West German public. They also enabled the *Zentralarchiv* to gauge the immediate impact of the Warsaw Pact invasion of Czechoslovakia in August 1968 as a considerable shift from the national to the Western regional and, in particular, the NATO-U.S. level. The armed threat from the East, in other words, made the U.S.-led NATO alliance the preferred instrument of the West German public in foreign affairs, more than their own government or even Little Europe. Whether East Germans aside from the political elites identified likewise with the Warsaw Pact on this occasion is extremely doubtful. There were, in fact, acts of sabotage and signs scribbled on the walls in many East German towns to signify popular displeasure with the Czechoslovak action.

The *Zentralarchiv* measurement recommends itself over earlier formulations which tended to emotionalize and thus cloud the issue. Frequently the pollsters had asked questions such as "Do you *personally* stand on the side of the West or the East, or on neither one, in the current world-wide conflict?" Given the cast of mind of the West German public, the responses for the East were usually negligible and the contest became, in a backhanded way, a test of neutralism with a generous admixture of low salience. Questions asking something like "Should Germany stay with the United States or go neutral?," on the other hand, produced a dramatically different and clearly instrumental response (Table 4b). It is evidently not the same matter whether an individual

TABLE 4b   Personal versus instrumental identification (*JOM 1967*, p. 435 and *The Germans*, p. 523)

	Stay with U.S. (West)	Go Neutral
Personal Formulation 1965	75%	16
Instrumental Form 1965	46%	37

"sides with the West" or whether he wants his government to do so. In all fairness, one has to concede that in the DDR, too, individual reservations may not keep the unsupportive public from approving of governmental foreign policies as rational or understandable under the circumstances, e.g., the building of the Berlin Wall.

Hardly more enlightening were the West German polls pitting "United States guarantees" against "closer cooperation with France" during the years of the Gaullist challenge to the Western alliance. Given the ambivalence of different situations, a general judgment about the relative attractiveness of the French and

TABLE 4c Functional differentiation of American and French helpfulness: "In [policy area], should the Federal Republic seek closer collaboration with France or the U.S.?" (*JOM 1967*, p. 445 and *The Germans*, pp. 537-38)

	General Foreign Policy	Defense	Culture	Reuni- fication	Economic
United States	60%	63	26	64	58
France	15%	11	37	8	20

May 1965

American allies to the West German public tended to blur the vital functional distinctions which appear in such differentiated questions as "which ally could do more for us in *defense questions*" as compared to *"economic questions"* (Table 4c). The sense of agency is quite sophisticated in sizing up the instrumental capabilities of a particular ally or alliance.[48]

In a rather different category again are questions having to do with the creation of a new instrument or instrumental level. A national sample in West Germany, for example, indicated in 1961 by 81 percent against 4 percent (1955: 68 percent to 7 percent) its willingness to vote for a united Europe. Seventy-two percent (versus 10 percent) were prepared to establish a European parliament. In 1960, 42 percent (versus 50 percent who preferred a national government) said they would rather have a European government than their own.[49] In the same category are responses indicating a desired level of agency, or one different from that which prevails. In 1963, after the Cuban missile crisis, 56 percent felt "Europe should have a say about the American use of nuclear weapons" as compared to 21 percent who were willing to leave this decision to the American president.

Once the level of agency is determined, we can also take a closer look at the popular evaluation of specific policies or instrumentalities. At this point, questions such as whether respondents approve or disapprove of their government's policy on any aspect of foreign affairs need to be differentiated as in Table 4c on France and the United States. West German popular identification with the government's foreign policy has been quite high[50] (see also Table 4d).

TABLE 4d Support for governmental policies in 1961 (Blücher, *Der Prozess der Meinungsbildung*, pp. 21-24)

	Western Alliance	NATO Membership	European Integration	Anti-Communism	Reunification
Favorable	67%	61	67	64	32
Negative or Critical	27%	25	22	30	60

The popular evaluation of particular leaders and their procedures in foreign policy can also be an appropriate subject of study here. There are some pathetic statistics, for example, about the popular belief in the efficacy of Adenauer's goodwill visits to various countries, most of them in response to the question "Do you think Adenauer's visit to [XX] did Germany any good?" Behind the popular approval stood a great faith in policies such as "Adenauer's effort to establish good relations with France" (65 percent for, 10 percent against) or in his ability to succeed against great odds by personal appearances. Adenauer himself was to West German minds a major foreign policy instrument, as can easily be demonstrated from public opinion surveys (Table 4e). The latest

TABLE 4e Perceived efficacy of Adenauer's visits (Institut für Demoskopie, *Umfragen über Adenauer* [Allensbach, 1961], pp. 117-20)

	United States	Greece-Turkey	France	England
	(1953)	(1954)	(1959)	(1959)
yes	47%	42	30	37
no	12%	16	13	14

of these polls was a question in 1967 asking respondents to single out his greatest achievements. They turned out to be nearly all in foreign policy: he "brought back the prisoners of war" from the Soviet Union (75 percent), "achieved reconciliation with France" (70 percent) and "international status and recognition for Germany" (65 percent), and "started European unification" (48 percent). These responses were the frontrunners, which were followed at some distance by a few domestic issues and by German reconciliation with Israel, German rearmament with NATO, the EEC, and the return of the Saar.

Also very revealing of the evaluative process are questions posing hypothetical situations, since they tie down the rather volatile attitudes to realistic, simple settings. A good example (and one having to do less with neutralism than with the fear of war) was "Suppose the Russians attacked the United States without at the same time attacking Europe, what should Germany do?" Fifty-two percent of the respondents in December 1958 replied "stay neutral," while 13 percent were prepared to come through with non-military assistance and 17 percent with military help. The same question had already been asked in October 1957, still under the impact of the Soviet invasion of Hungary but prior to Sputnik. At that time, 63 percent were for staying out of the conflict while 25 percent were willing to take sides, all on the American side, that is. But only 26 percent believed that it would be possible for West Germany to stay out of such a conflict (versus 31 percent who did not). What is particularly interesting about the West German response is that the same question in Holland produced 70 percent side-takers (versus 22 percent), in England 41 percent (versus 54 percent), and in France 28 percent (versus 66 percent). Only Sweden, Austria, Norway, Belgium and Italy had more situational neutralists than Germany.[51] Whether it is a deeply-rooted fear of war on German soil or memories of allied bombings in World War II that cause West Germans to think this way, evidently here again are potent restraints on foreign policy behavior.

The last example will bear out the discrepancy between tough talk and actual behavior in the West German foreign policy culture. According to Allensbach and DIVO polls in the late fifties, 72 percent of West Germans in 1957 (versus 13 percent) were opposed to arming the *Bundeswehr* with nuclear weapons, a percentage which changed only gradually to 62 percent versus 18 percent in 1960, with as many as a third favoring it among CDU/CSU adherents. Seventy-seven percent (versus 11 percent) were against stationing such weapons in Germany and 66 percent (versus 18 percent) against setting up launching pads there. The fear of atomic death was already evident in 1957 polls in which only 20 percent called atomic energy a blessing while 65 percent thought it a curse. A DIVO study of members of various parliaments early in 1958 also brought out the West German wariness of the unthinkable with a strength mirrored only by the Japanese legislators. The question had been whether the respondents agreed or disagreed with the statement "Considering the new weapons, some people think there will never be any more world wars." Evidently both the Japanese and the West Germans still remembered all too well the horrors of bombing and clung to the thought that it simply could not happen again (Table 4f).[52] But in spite of

TABLE 4f "Do the new weapons make war unlikely?" (*DIVO* 1957, pp. 18-19 and *DIVO* 1958, pp. 18, 70-74)

	Great Britain	France	West Germany	Italy	India	Japan	United States
True	36%	23	48	32	38	53	36
More or less	8%	—	9	4	—	—	—
False	36%	64	40	45	49	41	43

all this fear and actual reluctance, a West German sample in 1957 presented the usual tough front to the Soviet threat "to turn Germany into a veritable cemetery" if the *Bundeswehr* were to accept atomic weapons. Thirty-four percent replied the Soviet threat merely showed the deterrence value of atomic armaments, as compared to 42 percent who said West Germans should heed the Soviet warning. At least as many as two out of three of the tough talkers, in other words, were actually opposed to arming the *Bundeswehr* with these weapons.[53] There can be little doubt but that the DDR may have a similar gap between tough talk and popular readiness to act tough, although there it is mostly a contrast between a belligerent elite and indifferent masses.

Thus the politico-cultural restraints on either country's foreign policy are evidently present below the surface of much of the verbal give-and-take. Only the evaluative processes bring them out into the open and to bear upon what a country will actually stand for. The actual interaction between a conflicting elite and mass opinion will vary, of course, from case to case and, most of all, between democratic West Germany and the dictatorial DDR. The East German reaction to official participation in the Czechoslovak adventure demonstrates that popular disapproval cannot stop governmental action in the short run, no matter how many dissenters are arrested and punished. But even a Communist dictatorship cannot persist for long in foreign policies deeply repugnant to the people without jeopardizing their cooperation in other vital matters and endangering its own survival.

Notes

1 Willy Brandt, *A Peace Policy for Europe*, trans. Joel Carmichael (New York: Holt, Rinehart & Winston, 1968), p. 11. Brandt at the time of this writing was West German vice chancellor and foreign minister.

2 Karl W. Deutsch et al., *France, Germany and Western Alliance* (New York: Scribners, 1967), p. 14. See also the elite literature cited there, p. 5, footnote 1.

3 See also the approach used by Deutsch and Edinger in their earlier book, Karl W. Deutsch and Lewis J. Edinger, *Germany Rejoins the Powers* (Stanford: Stanford University Press, 1959), chaps. 5-9.

4 Rudolf Wildenmann, *Eliten in der Bundesrepublik*, unpublished draft manuscript, August 1968.

5 Daniel H. Willick, "Public Interest in International Affairs," *Social Science Quarterly* 50 (September 1969), p. 274.

6 See also W. Phillips Davison in Hans Speier and Davison, *West German Leadership and Foreign Policy* (Evanston: Row & Peterson, 1957), pp. 242-81. Deutsch and Edinger, *Germany Rejoins the Powers*, p. 112, cite a 1955 figure of 39 percent attentive to foreign affairs.

7 Viggo Graf Bluecher, *Der Prozess der Meinungsbildung* (Bielefeld: Emnid, 1962), pp. 14-15.

8 Institut für Demoskopie, *Jahrbuch der oeffentlichen Meinung, 1958-1964* (Allensbach, 1965), (hereafter cited as *JOM* with the last year polls were taken).

9 The respondents ranked the issues as follows: inflation, reunification, social security, crime, honest government, protection against the East, lower taxes, good relations with the United States, better housing, European integration, and better relations with the Soviets. By way of contrast, Wildenmann's elite sample ranked the "most urgent priorities of the

government" of 1968 as follows: sound public finances, educational re-form, economic growth, better East-West relations, economic reforms, better U.S.-German relations, diplomatic relations with Eastern Europe, including England in the EEC, better transportation, better relations with East Germany, better Franco-German relations, plurality voting, etc.

10 *JOM* 1967, p. 387.

11 Werner Kaltefleiter, "Konsens ohne Macht," Verfassung und Verfassungs-*wirklichkeit* (1969), pp. 18-20.

12 Using reunification as an indicator of attentiveness to foreign affairs raises an additional conceptual problem. As late as 1964, a DIVO study unearthed the fact that half of the respondents of a national sample considered reunification a "domestic" rather than a foreign affairs issue. DIVO, *Der Wähler vor der Bundestagwahl* (November 1964) (Stuttgart: Deutsche Verlagsanstalt, 1965), p. 57 (hereafter cited as *DIVO* with the last year of the polls taken).

13 For example, persons of liberal bourgeois background or strong religious convictions who have made their peace with the regime. See Hans Apel, *DDR 1962, 1964, 1966* (Berlin: Voltaire Verlag, 1967) pp. 22-96.

14 See Peter Florin, *Zur Aussenpolitik der souveränen sozialistischen DDR* (East Berlin: Dietz Verlag, 1967), pp. 55-56, 82-84. The Hallstein Doctrine threatened a withdrawal of West German recognition from any state that recognized the DDR.

15 Walter Ulbricht, *Die gesellschaftliche Entwicklung in der DDR bis zur Vollendung des Sozialismus* (Berlin: Dietz Verlag 1967), p. 26.

16 See the account of Zoltan M. Szaz, *Germany's Eastern Frontiers* (Chicago: Regnery, 1960), pp. 91-94 and the sources cited there.

17 However traumatic the crisis may have been, five years later only 55 per-cent could remember "what important event had occurred August 13, 1961." *JOM* 1967, p. 415. See also Bluecher, *Der Prozess der Meinungs-bildung*, pp. 16-18.

18 The data of Table 1a are from *DIVO* 1958, p. 17.

19 As a sobering thought on using war and peace as an indicator of trust in the international system, an expressed "foremost desire for peace" was correlated with levels of information and education. According to the *DIVO* survey before the 1965 elections, 29 percent of a national sample named peace as "the most important foreign policy problem after reuni-fication." Broken down by the degree of political information, however, this "desire for peace" varied from 20 percent among the well-informed to 58 percent among the least-informed, who may well not have been able to name anything else when asked. The well-informed named Euro-pean integration with 29 percent (versus 8 percent of the least-informed) and better relations with Eastern European countries with 21 percent (versus 7 percent of the least-informed) before peace. With the level of education, likewise, the highly educated gave the nod to European inte-gration with 32 percent (20 percent for the least-educated) and only 23 percent to peace (39 percent for the least-educated). (*JOM* 1967, pp. 52-56).

20   See *JOM* 1967, p. 456; *JOM* 1964, p. 559; and Institut für Demoskopie, *The Germans* (Allensbach, 1966), p. 584. The image of Soviet incapacity for aggression, however, does not extend to the most immediate points of friction, such as threats to Berlin. West Germans quickly anticipate a major crisis with every build-up of tension over Berlin, but they also return quickly to a feeling that the crisis is over and not worthy of further excitement.

21   Wolfram F. Hanrieder, *West German Foreign Policy 1949-1963* (Stanford: Stanford University Press, 1967), pp. 36-49.

22   Deutsch et al., *France, Germany and the Western Alliance*, pp. 142-47, 278-87. In 1959 public confidence in the protection afforded West Germany by NATO still stood at a low level (18 percent) but then increased rapidly to a two-thirds majority (*JOM* 1964, pp. 539, 542).

23   To illustrate the various kinds of intervening variables, there are the surprising 35 percent (in Hamburg 54 percent, in Bremen 44 percent and in Baden-Württemberg 41 percent) of the West German population who claim to have had in their family at least one emigrant to the United States and the 82 percent who are aware of Germans making up a part of the American melting pot. (*JOM* 1964, p. 550).

24   Deutsch et al., *France, Germany and the Western Alliance*, pp. 149-55.

25   *JOM* 1964, p. 555. German elite persons identify even more strongly with the United States and a German-American alliance, on the theory, among other things, that the two countries share common interests. See Deutsch et al., *France, Germany and the Western Alliance*, pp. 154-55 for an account of the depth of this feeling of dependency.

26   Deutsch et al., *France, Germany and the Western Alliance*, p. 156.

27   *JOM* 1967, pp. 566-67.

28   In 1965, 67 percent of a national sample gave this response (72 percent in 1952 and 71 percent in 1962) ahead of 19 percent naming "orderliness, reliability, cleanliness, etc." (21 percent in 1952 and 12 percent in 1962). (*JOM* 1967, p. 156). Nevertheless 73 percent (versus 11 percent) said in a 1967 survey that "they were proud to be German," again with more dissent (15 percent) among the young.

29   Institut für Demoskopie, Pressedienst (June 1965).

30   *JOM* 1967, p. 155.

31   *JOM* 1967, pp. 388-89.

32   *JOM* 1964, pp. 483, 504-5, and *DIVO* 1964, pp. 69-70.

33   *JOM* 1964, p. 486.

34   Nevertheless 36 percent agreed (38 percent did not) that one should extend recognition to the DDR if and when it would "turn into another Yugoslavia." One important reason West Germans are reluctant to trade East German recognition for assurances of guaranteed liberties for the East Germans as an alternative to reunification is the extreme credibility gap of the Soviet Union and the Communists in general in West German minds. Asked in 1958 whether American actions in the world dovetailed

with American statements, for example, 36 percent answered with a flat "yes" while 34 percent said "often not." The Soviets rated on the same question only 3 percent "yes" and 76 percent "often not" (*DIVO* 1958, p. 14). In 1965, 66 percent (versus 17 percent who did not) denied there was any less reason to distrust Communism today than before. Regarding the renunciation of nuclear weapons as a *quid pro quo*, it should be noted that majorities between 72 percent and 62 percent of the West German public were against nuclear arms for the *Bundeswehr* in polls taken between 1957 and 1960 (*DIVO* 1958, pp. 70-71).

35   In polls taken between 1951 and 1966, the percentage willing to accept the Oder-Neisse line has gradually grown from 8 percent in 1951 to 27 percent in 1966, while those unwilling to do so have declined from 80 percent in 1951 to 54 percent in 1966. By now there is solid public support for a government move in this direction.

36   *JOM* 1967, pp. 389, 395-96, 399 and 414. Needless to stress, the West German claim to *Alleinvertretung* is received by the East German elites with something close to apoplexy. See Florin, *Zur Aussenpolitik*, pp. 109-17.

37   See Deutsch and Edinger, *Germany Rejoins the Powers*, pp. 217-18. In January of 1965, reunification was still mentioned by 47 percent as "the most important issue" (Deutsch et al., *France, Germany and the Western Alliance*, pp. 174-77, 245-47, 288-89). Four out of ten respondents were willing to recognize at least the Oder-Neisse line as a step toward a relaxation of tensions.

38   Wildenmann, *Eliten in der Bundesrepublik*, pp. 154-55.

39   See *Neues Deutschland*, February 5 and 7, 1957.

40   See especially Fritz Kopp, *Kurs auf ganz Deutschland?* (Stuttgart: Seewald, 1965) and the articles by the same author in *Deutsche Fragen*, (June 1966, July 1967, June 1968), and the sources cited there.

41   See, for example, Apel, *DDR*, pp. 373-98, or Jean Edward Smith's presentation to the American Political Science Association in 1966.

42   Amos Elon, *Journey Through a Haunted Land* (New York: Holt, Rinehart & Winston), p. 113. See also his chaps. 7 and 8. Elon and other visitors have remarked that traveling from West to East Germany has struck them like a journey into the Germany of thirty years ago.

43   Ibid., p. 123. Simon Wiesenthal of the Vienna Documentation Center also recently spoke up to remind the East Germans that they have not yet begun to acknowledge their share of the responsibility for the holocaust. Neither has Austria.

44   *JOM* 1967, p. 144.

45   See *JOM* 1964, p. 354; DIVO, *Basic Orientation and Political Thinking of West German Youths*, 2 vols. (Stuttgart, 1956), I, pp. 44-48.

46   *JOM* 1967, p. 314.

47   *The Germans*, p. 171.

48   The West German elite responses of 1964 and 1968 bear out this differentiated evaluation by giving emphasis to German doubts about the French

capacity to defend the West side by side with the strong German interest in economic and cultural cooperation. Even the East German elite exhibits a desire to encourage Franco-German friendship, at least on a proletarian basis. Florin, *Zur Aussenpolitik*, pp. 88-89.

49   *The Germans*, pp. 525-26, and *DIVO* 1960, p. 18.

50   As many as two-thirds of the West German elite respondents of the 1964 study expressed general approval of their government's foreign policies (Deutsch et al., *France, Germany and the Western Alliance*, p. 141).

51   See *DIVO* 1957, pp. 26-27 and *DIVO* 1958, p. 23.

52   *DIVO* 1957, pp. 18-19 and *DIVO* 1958, pp. 18, 70-74.

53   *DIVO* 1957, p. 19.

CHAPTER 2

A German Nation?
Origins of German Political
Culture & Identity

The very uncertainty in the German sense of identity and the cataclysmic course of German development makes it advisable to probe German public opinion more deeply for the roots, structures, and images which fashion the foreign policy awareness of attentive publics in East and West Germany today. A subject such as foreign policy, in the German tradition and perhaps in that of other European states as well, is not to be compared to the study of passing fads in foods or motion picture idols. It has always been considered a *Wissenschaft* par excellence, a subject fit for historical and philosophical study by the best minds of the country, whether they were active participants in foreign policy making, publicists molding opinions on the subject, or just attentive publics following the course of government policies in the light of their understanding of their country's historical development and situation. The basic elements of their understanding are well distributed among the minds of the attentive publics in East and West Germany today, even though they may sometimes be in irreconcilable opposition to one another or serve only inadequately to define current issues. In any event, the evaluative processes of German political culture in foreign policy can be understood only if these elementary contents in the minds of policy makers and interested citizens are understood. These foreign policy postures

and archetypal situational images consist basically of three histor-
ically conditioned dimensions: one relating to the geographic
position of the Germanies, one to the historical discontinuities of
German development, and one to the social discontinuities of German society during the last hundred years of German history.

PARTICULARISM, NATIONALISM & EUROPEAN UNITY

The elements relating to the geographical position of the
Germanies in the heart of Europe call to mind how recently the
bulk of the German states of modern history were united into a
single nation-state. It was a mere 100 years ago, in 1871, that a
German national state was formed after a series of bloody wars,
including one between north German and south German states.
National unification had been deeply desired, and yet there was
also a stirring controversy about the merits and disadvantages
of this particular kind of national union, namely a narrow national state under the leadership of Prussia. The various sides of the
controversy were not new then nor have they completely disappeared now in the thinking habits of attentive foreign policy
publics in Germany. Advocacy of the particular interests of a state
or an even smaller part of Germany in the face of common interests, the promotion of national unity or reunification in various
forms, and the concern for integration into the European family of
nations are as prevalent today as they ever were.

Particularism in this context is the propensity to prefer one's
local or regional interests to those of the larger community. German particularism can look upon an ancient and deeply ingrained,
if not always honorable, past. Throughout the centuries of the
Holy Roman Empire of the German nation under the Hapsburg
crown particularism meant *Kleinstaaterei*, i.e., a prevalence of
small and tiny states. German princes and states followed the path
indicated exclusively by the pursuit of their own glory and petty
dynastic aggrandizement. On occasion, they even allied themselves with non-German powers such as France or Tsarist Russia
against other German princes and states. Later the bane of particularistic egotism, most notably that of Prussia and Austria,
prevented the German Confederation (1815-66) from growing into
a closer union and frustrated the attempt of the German revolutionaries of 1848 to create a German nation-state. Even after
national unification, particularism has been on occasion an im-

pediment to greater national unity whenever questions of federalism or relations between the federal government and the states are at stake. Particularism also plays a prominent role both in Bonn and in East Berlin today when it comes to questions of German reunification or of relations between East and West. As in past centuries, the establishments of both states think of their own positions first. As a habit of mind among German citizens and office-holders, particularism has always denoted an ambiguity of identification with the whole nation, its common interests and/or its government. Due to their past, Germans are evidently less likely to identify with their country than Frenchmen or Englishmen and somewhat more likely to take up the interests of smaller established units within the Germanies.[1]

German nationalism has long been the bugbear of neighboring states and especially of Germany's antagonists in World Wars I and II. An assessment of its current prevalence in German minds, however, requires first of all semantic clarification of a thicket of meanings and connotations of the word. In the sense of increasing identification with the existing German nation-state versus particularistic identification with locality, region or smaller component state, nationalism is a universal phenomenon of modernizing societies everywhere. In Germany, this shift of political identification began in the early nineteenth century and progressed especially in the years from the 1880s to 1945. In the last twenty-five years, however, the division of Germany into the Federal Republic, the East German Republic (DDR), West Berlin and such permanently separated parts as the areas beyond the Oder and Neisse rivers or Austria (which was a part of Germany only before 1866 and between 1938 and 1945) places the original question in the state of limbo indicated earlier. It is of course possible to ask whether the Federal Republic, the DDR, or Austria have become more unified as "nations," as indeed they have, or less unified. But the progress of a loss of identification with a larger, more inclusive Germany is under the circumstances not amenable to empirical inquiry. With the passage of twenty-five years and the ascendancy of new generations in all the separate parts, it seems reasonable to assume that there is less such identification today than in 1945.

In the sense of the political assertion of a nation, again, the understanding of German nationalism is complicated by the varying territorial claims of competing schools of nationalists. Just as today some Germans mean reunification to connote only the union of East and West Germany while others speak of including the Oder-Neisse areas or even the Sudetenland, there have always been widely divergent notions of how far the German nation extends.

The issue was posed clearly, for example, at the revolutionary Frankfort Assembly of 1848, where some of the delegates preferred a *grossdeutsch* nation-state, that is with the inclusion of at least German Austria, while the majority favored a *kleindeutsch* solution without Austria and under the leadership of Prussia. The latter was finally realized by Bismarck after a military victory over Austria at Königgrätz in 1866 and led to the dominance of Prussian traditions in the new (Second) *Reich* until the defeat and the fall of the monarchy in 1918. After World War I was fought by the German *Reich* and the Hapsburg Empire in fraternal alliance, the subsequent disintegration of the latter would have freed the German part of Austria for union with the *Reich* had not the victorious allies vetoed such a step. In 1938, however, an Austrian corporal named Adolf Hitler who had meanwhile come to power in the German *Reich* revived the *grossdeutsch* idea as a stepping-stone toward even vaster plans of German expansion which soon engulfed the whole world in another global war. As some Germans put it, he was Austria's revenge for Königgrätz.

The *kleindeutsch* nationalism of Prussia-Germany was generically different from the *grossdeutsch* nationalism of most Austrians and south and west Germans. The difference between the two was chiefly cultural and received special color from the historical religious division of the Germanies between Catholicism and Protestantism in the age of Reformation and Counter Reformation. To this day, Protestant areas tend to incline more toward the traditions of the self-contained Bismarckian *Reich*. The broader European traditions of the Catholic Church, as well as domestic reasons, prompted Catholic leaders like Adenauer to seek Catholic allies from Austria to France and Italy.

Hitler's brand of nationalism, by contrast, went far beyond the *grossdeutsch* idea in the direction of a racially conceived Pan-German nationalism. He actually rejected the word *nationalism*, which to his mind was bound up with what he considered an outmoded "liberal nationalism" of nineteenth-century vintage. He took a generous loan of ideas from the Pan-German League, which since the 1890s had advocated a greater German *Reich* including even the German minorities in Eastern Europe and overseas. In this he enjoyed also the anguished support of east Germans and Austrians fearful of losing all control over the Slavic populations of both empires. Thus he developed his idea of a German master race ruling over subject non-German peoples. In the attempted execution of his plans in World War II, national socialism lost even the last elements of German nationalism and became more and more a philosophy of fascist elitism over both German and non-German subjects. Germany's defeat and division and the expulsion of the German minorities from Eastern Europe were the final outcome of this endeavor.

An assessment of German nationalism also has to come to grips with the degree of assertiveness, or the intensity or aggressiveness of nationalism. Throughout this age of nationalism, in the individual citizen as well as in all political groups save the pacifistic extreme left wing, a basic level of assertiveness must be taken for granted, for example, enough to react belligerently to purported threats of invasion or imagined slights upon the national honor. This basic level of nationalism, however, would not be sufficient to warrant aggressive war or the annexation of foreign territory, unless inflamed by the machinations of propaganda and popular provocation, of which the Nazis were acknowledged masters. In this context, then, the question must be asked whether it is a sign of German nationalism for Germans in East and West to want the reunification of the Federal Republic and the DDR. Furthermore, is it not even more nationalistic for some West Germans to demand the Oder-Neisse areas, long-time German territories which have been settled, since the expulsion and flight of the Germans, by Polish families for about a generation now? And what about the handful of German refugees who still want the Sudetenland back, that German minority area of Czechoslovakia which gave Hitler the first excuse for major aggression toward the East?[2] It would appear that the dividing line between the basic level of nationalism and aggressive nationalism lies somewhat beyond the demand for reunification of the Federal Republic and the DDR, but definitely short of the demand for the Sudetenland, if not for the Oder-Neisse areas. The decision where to draw the line is, of course, a matter of subjective judgment in which the danger of causing another world war and a kind of historical justice must figure prominently.

A third basic theme of German political culture toward the world today is that of supranational integration. In East Germany, in spite of membership in the Communist Economic Community

(COMECON) and the Warsaw Pact, popular identification with the "socialist brother states" appears to be low. While the official propaganda on this point is loud and insistent, there is a pervasive popular feeling of German isolation among the bloc nations. Not infrequently, even the Ulbricht government had reason to feel isolated or neglected and there was considerable popular awareness of the quasi-colonial bondage of the East German economy to the Soviet Union. West Germany, by contrast, went enthusiastically pro-European in the first years after World War II and has remained so with minor fluctuations ever since. A DIVO poll in April 1960, for example, asked a West German sample whether the respondents preferred a common European or a national government. Only 50 percent preferred a national government, while 42 percent hoped for a common European government, including even higher percentages among the partisans of the CDU and residents of the *Laender* bordering on France.[3]

The identification with supranational communities in the West has precedents in the centuries prior to the age of nationalism and especially prior to the Reformation when Roman Catholicism constituted a political as well as a religious bond among European nations. Supranationalism in the West, too, has its geographic and cultural gradations. There is the narrowest level of Franco-German amity, a major popular and political concern of postwar West German opinion. Then there has been the Little Europe of the Six (now Nine), the Schuman Plan (ECSC), Common Market (EEC), and European Atomic Community. The addition of Great Britain to the original six produced the Western European Union, a common defense organization. Add another eight nations from Turkey to Iceland and the Council of Europe emerges, an organization for cultural exchange and standardization which considerably outruns current popular German feelings of European kinship. Germans would very likely include the Czechs, Poles, and Scandinavians before the Greeks (who recently withdrew) and the Turks. In the days of de Gaulle's greatest influence in West Germany, in the mid-sixties, there were in fact serious public discussions about a European confederation from the Atlantic to the Ural Mountains, which, among other things, would have achieved a German reunification of sorts among other East and West European member states. Finally, there is the North Atlantic Treaty Organization and the Organization for European

Cooperation and Development (OECD), which tie Europe to the North American subcontinent. This level of supranational identi-fication is very strong in the Federal Republic, both for reasons of military security and because of processes of acculturation to aspects of the American way of life. There is a weak parallel among East German elites who identify with the Soviet Union, but hardly on a broad popular level.

FROM GENERATION TO GENERATION

Political culture is transmitted from one generation to the next by complex processes of political socialization and encultura-tion which maintain patterns of continuity over the generations. However, when cataclysmic political and social changes occur, such as wars, defeats, and revolutions, the very mechanisms of socialization and enculturation may be disrupted. Families may lose their fathers to the wartime draft or even death. Schools may lose their male teachers to the same cause. Curricula are changed, images of authority demoted, and faculties may be purged and indoctrinated to ensure conformity with a new regime. All of these circumstances help to explain the notable generational conflicts and changes of political opinion which have marked German attitudes toward the world in the twentieth century.

Politically motivated youth revolt has long been a typical feature of German politics. From the nationalistic reaction to the Napoleonic conquest of German states until the revolution of 1848, young men and especially university students were in the forefront of nationalist activism in Germany. Their protests ranged from the poetic writings of the Young Germany of a Heinrich Heine or Ludwig Boerne in exile to political violence in pursuit of national liberation from Napoleon and revolution against the princes of the states. The youth of the Bismarckian Empire, by contrast, were quiet, conservative, and preoccupied with accom-modation to the aristocratic-military forces dominant in the *Reich*. The generations of adults who grew up during the half-century of the empire were too busy coping with the enormous social changes induced by massive industrialization, urbanization, and the shift from a local or regional to a national orientation to have much time and interest for politics. Only in the decade and a half before World War I were there once more two substantial movements of youthful protest, neither one of a pronouncedly nationalistic character. One grew from the working class socialist movement, which was chiefly preoccupied with domestic reforms but also espoused pacifism and international brotherhood among the workers of all countries. The other was the bourgeois Youth Movement, which was quite apolitical except for its intense distaste for power politics and the new industrial-urban civilization in which bourgeois youth found itself. Both were revolts against the older German generations of that period.

World War I and its aftermath constituted a watershed of political opinion in Germany. A whole generation of *kleindeutsch* patriots was determined to win from a hostile world a place in the sun for their growing country. They were bitterly chastened and hardened by the ordeal of the first great mechanized war, the murderous "thunderstorms of steel," as one of their poets called it. In the midst of death and destruction in the trenches of World War I, a substantial number of this generation of *Frontsoldaten* (soldiers of the trench) resolved more stubbornly than ever to fight to the bitter end, and to renew the fighting even after a temporary peace might be concluded. Another substantial fraction decided that Germany's future lay with internal reform in a democratic and socialist direction, which implied reconciliation with the enemy and international cooperation. This part of the war generation was instrumental in the establishment of the parliamentary democracy of Weimar (1919-33), the welfare state, and a foreign policy of accommodation and, as far as possible, nonviolence.

The nationalistic bitter-enders, however, were not prepared to accept the German defeat in World War I. They avidly used the weakness of their opponents and the vengeful indignities visited upon Germany by the victors, such as the Treaty of Versailles, territorial cessions, the demand for German reparations and, most of all, the French occupation of the Ruhr area in 1923, to plot their take-over of the republic. They were organized in several political parties, countless veterans' and patriotic organizations, vigilante groups, and voluntary army corps (Free Corps) which at first fought against left-wing insurrection within the Polish raids against the republic and then threatened the republican government itself. Their strident nationalism eventually became the vehicle for the Nazi electoral landslide of 1930-32 which accompanied yet another wave of youth rebellion, hundreds of thousands of young storm troopers marching and fighting for the creation of a Third Reich. The brown waves inundated all resistance, including the militant youth of the extreme left, and established the dictatorship which step by step undid the effects of the defeat of 1918: it remilitarized the Rhineland (1935), annexed Austria (1938), and proceeded from the annexation of the Sudetenland and further aggressions against the rest of Czechoslovakia and Poland to the resumption of all-out war against nearly all the enemy powers of World War I. Only in the vast destruction and loss of life of World War II, it seems, did the fires of German nationalism kindled in World War I burn out.

In order to understand German attitudes toward foreign policy since 1945, a knowledge of these feelings of the succeeding generations during the earlier decades is crucial. The first generation of German postwar leaders which emerged in West and East Germany with the blessing of the Western and Soviet occupations, respectively, was born around the turn of the century and often had been among the *Frontsoldaten* of World War I. For example, the postwar SPD leader, Kurt Schumacher, and the architect of West German economic recovery, Ludwig Erhard (CDU), were both wounded as soldiers in World War I. The Communist leader of East Germany, Walter Ulbricht, was born a decade earlier and grew up in the socially oppressive class society before that war. Konrad Adenauer was born even earlier (1876) and was socialized into the political subculture of the Catholic minority within living memory of Bismarck's *kleindeutsch* coup of 1870 and the subsequent persecution of German Catholics. No great flight of the imagination is required to link Adenauer's past with the promotion of a Catholic Little Europe and his aversion to Berlin and to (formerly Prussian and Protestant) East Germany. By the same token, the nationalistic undertone of Schumacher and Erhard despite their political differences was no surprise. Later echelons of leaders in Bonn and East Berlin grew up during the decline of the Weimar Republic and the rise of the Third Reich. Some such as Defense Minister Gerhard Schröder or Chancellor Kurt Kiesinger followed the Nazi banner when they were still rather young. Others such as several FDP leaders and East German generals of the 1960s served as officers in Hitler's army or were decorated in World War II. They all shared the activist's contempt for ideology, including that of nationalism, and a pragmatic concern for the concrete problems of the day. The new generation of economic planners and managers in East Germany was born in the 1920s or later and is likewise beyond the doctrinaire rigidity of the older Communist leaders.

As new generations grow into leadership roles, they are likely to mirror the deep disillusionment with all political faiths of the years of defeat and postwar occupation when they were in their teens or early twenties. The youngest generation of voters, born after 1945, will begin to reach positions of leadership in fifteen or twenty years. But it already promises to be less preoccupied with nationalism or patriotism than any previous generation of Germans. The decline of aggressive nationalism as an ideology since its absurd exaggeration in the Third Reich naturally increases the availability of German political elites for other loyalties, especially to European integration.[4]

The public opinion polls of the adult population of West Germany always show a notable differential according to age in measurements involving national pride or patriotism. The respondents under thirty years of age, as elsewhere in Great Britain or the United States, feel the least allegiance to the symbols and identity of their nation. They also show the greatest inclination to recognize the accomplishments of other nations and to identify with larger communities such as the Little Europe of the Six or an East and West European federation.

In a recent poll of youthful new voters of 1969, the Institut für Demoskopie at Allensbach found its young respondents out of sympathy with the idea that "young people should be given a patriotic education." Only 15 percent of the new voters agreed, as compared to 30-50 percent of the general public and the "old voters" identifying with the SPD, FDP or CDU, in this order.

The decline of German nationalism in the twentieth century is also related to the prolonged crisis of legitimacy of the political institutions. Beginning with the decline and fall of the monarchic state in the *Reich* and *Laender* of 1918, the crisis of legitimacy was by no means over. The successor state of the empire, the unhappy Weimar Republic, enjoyed broad popular support for only a few months following the end of World War I. After that brief period the backlash to the "red" uprisings and the reaction to the imposed peace treaty of Versailles robbed the republic of majority support and made it the prey of the anti-democratic forces of the right and the left. By 1932, the combined Nazi and Communist vote, not to mention the anti-republican conservative (DNVP) vote, already topped 50 percent and early in 1933 the Nazi *Führer* was appointed chancellor.

As far as legitimacy goes, however, the praetorian Nazi state did no better. The first German parliamentary republic never had the chance to establish its legitimacy in the public mind. Despite the well-manipulated mass support of the early Nazi years, the legitimacy of the "thousand years' *Reich*" was undermined from the beginning by the lawless and vicious conduct of the Nazi government itself. The suppressed opposition and the generations young enough to react to the postwar revelations about the abhorrent Nazi record denied the Nazi government all legitimacy at an early date, and the general population did so soon after the collapse of Nazi rule.

The Bonn republic has had the benefit of decades of relatively little internal criticism. Nevertheless it is no rock of legitimate authority either, because of the commitment to and expectation of reunification. Even the Bonn constitution ends with an article which looks forward to its own replacement by "a constitution adopted freely by all Germans." The lack of legitimacy did not stop a solid West German political establishment from forming and perpetuating itself. Nothing lasts like the provisional, as the French say. But it has denied the Bonn republic the affection and civic pride of its citizens. There is no reason to assume that East Germans would exhibit any more civic pride if they were interviewed by the pollsters. They feel a great sense of pride in their economic achievements in the face of considerable obstacles. And they would very likely rate their social legislation more highly as a source of pride than did the West Germans.[5]

SOCIAL CHANGE & FOREIGN POLICY

Both East and West Germany today have barely evolved from decades, if not centuries, of social maladjustment which was closely associated with German attitudes toward the world and the German position in it. Foreign policy attitudes long tended to reflect social classes, class ideologies, and the deep antagonisms among the classes of German society. These class points of view have waned in importance but still play a considerable role, especially in East German official attitudes. An overview of German foreign policies in the twentieth century can hardly ignore the perspectives of different social classes on the German situation at home and abroad.

The classical age of German foreign policy making, until about fifty years ago, was dominated by what may be called the aristocratic tradition. The crowned heads of the German states and their chancellors, ministers, and advisers were nearly all noblemen themselves. In spite of personal variations, they identi- fied with the traditional rule of other monarchs and aristocrats from the courts of Versailles to St. Petersburg. With rare excep- tions, these aristocrats had little sympathy for the wave of nation- alistic, bourgeois-constitutional, or democratic movements touched off by the French Revolution and a great deal less for the inter- national socialist and Communist movements. They felt an in- stinctive resentment not only of the domestic menace of these revolutions to their thrones and class privileges, but also of the disregard of the revolutionary movements for their dynastic borders and bailiwicks. Even German nationalism, not to mention Polish or other Slavic nationalisms, posed a mortal threat to the existing empires or the German states and their princes.

The Prussian Junkers from east of the Elbe river, for example, viewed their fellow Junker Bismarck's achievement of a German nation-state with deep distrust, refusing on occasion to cooperate with what was supposed to be Prussia's greatest coup, a Prussian- dominated German *Reich*. The new German *Kaiser* also had great personal difficulty understanding in 1871 why he could not be the ruler of all Germans in the same fashion in which he was the ruler of all Prussians. What the Prussian aristocracy understood very well, on the other hand, was the need to fortify Prussian overlordship in Germany, and eventually German claims in Europe, with military power and a web of alliances. The military establishment consequently became the backbone of the aristo- cratic ruling class and monarchy of Prussian-German power in Europe. The military's social role and military-aristocratic preju- dices continued, despite the passing of aristocracy in the Weimar Republic, within and without. By 1945, finally, the Nazi regime had milked the last drop of international power from German military prowess while socially demoting and effectively isolating the domestic power of the military. The Bonn republic and the DDR are the first regimes on German soil in a century in which the military is kept safely under civilian control, although it still plays a not inconsiderable role in the making of defense and alliance policies.

The emphasis on alliances and treaties of the aristocratic tra- dition manifested itself most admirably in the complex dealings of Bismarck until 1890. The Iron Chancellor knew how to pacify a continent wary of his new German nation-state with a web of treaties and alliances insuring the *Reich* against the menace of attack from all sides, in particular from Russia. After his demise, his system of European alliances and reassurances in the best aristocratic tradition was allowed to lapse by inept successors in an increasingly bourgeois age. Hostile alliances formed and encircled Germany and Austria prior to the fateful clash of World War I. Although men with aristocratic titles continued to dominate the German Foreign Office and military until 1945—and have not been unknown among the Bonn diplomats—the golden age of aristocratic foreign policies is obviously over.

To speak of a bourgeois tradition in German foreign policy in contrast to the aristocratic tradition can be somewhat misleading. In the nineteenth century and until 1918, in any case, "bourgeois foreign policy" had a fairly concrete content, namely that of liberal nationalism. The liberal revolutionaries of 1848, for example, were bent on national unification in the face of resisting princes and state borders. Their goals and objectives ranged from economic betterment and cultural nationalism to domestic democratization of the feudal remainders of the past. The German bourgeoisie later came to accept the new nation-state of its longtime enemy Bismarck only because it was the realization of the bourgeoisie's fondest dreams. To be sure, the German and Austrian bourgeoisie failed to exhibit much sympathy with the aspirations of other nations and nationalities. Nevertheless, even in 1918 their liberal nationalism still predisposed them to see merit in President Wilson's demand for "national self-determination" for all Europeans, just as the one-sided interpretations of this principle with regard to Germany's eastern borders offended their sensibilities.

In the Weimar Republic, the German bourgeoise was finally in a commanding position in which they could have realized their conceptions in foreign policy. By this time, however, the bourgeois classes were so badly split among several parties and, moreover, in progressive disintegration as a movement that they did not have a discernible common attitude toward the world. The spectrum of bourgeois foreign policies was nearly as broad as that of the whole party system, ranging from an internationalist and pacifistic liberal left over the economic nationalism of the entrepreneurial classes to the pseudo-bourgeois radical nationalists of the extreme right. If it had indeed a common denominator, it was that of private economic interests of bourgeois opinion leaders of all stripes, masquerading as sacred national rights and interests. There was also a succession of distinguished bourgeois foreign policy makers, ranging from Walter Rathenau to Gustav Stresemann, who tried to stabilize the precarious position of the Weimar Republic in a hostile world.

A proletarian or socialist tradition in German foreign policy is again rather nebulous outside of narrow limits. To be sure, early socialist writers such as Karl Marx himself followed international wars with avid interest, taking sides, for example, with "more progressive France" against the "reactionary Tsar." Only toward the end of the nineteenth century, however, did a basic proletarian foreign policy line win general acceptance among European labor movements and socialist parties, namely the brotherhood and common interest of the international proletariat against the nationalistic bourgeoisie of the different countries. Just before World War I, this proletarian internationalism assumed a dramatic form with the threat of French, German, and Russian Social Democrats to halt any bourgeois-capitalistic or nationalist-imperialistic war among the great powers with a general strike of the workers of these nations. War between capitalistic nations was presumed to be motivated chiefly by economic rivalry and competition for colonies. The workers did not relish the thought of serving as cannon fodder for the international clash of national capitalistic interests. Thus internationalism and pacifism became the foreign policy line of the underdogs of national societies even though the promised general strike never came off. The Social Democrats of France, Germany, and Russia in the end supported the war effort of their respective nations at least until years later when the toll of the war in death and hunger mobilized broad popular waves of socialism, pacifism, and internationalism in all three countries and elsewhere. Such a wave swept in the large democratic majority of the Weimar Constituent Assembly and produced transient soviet regimes in several parts of Germany.

The October Revolution and the Bolshevik take-over in Russia created an entirely new situation for a proletarian foreign policy in Germany or anywhere else. To begin with, it perpetuated the wartime split between workingmen and socialists loyal to their nations and those asserting pacifism among and proletarian revolution inside the nations. Internationally organized into the

Second International of Social Democratic parties and the Communist Third International, the two labor parties and trade union movements fought each other bitterly in every country. In the Weimar Republic, where the labor movement was the largest and best organized anywhere, this division was a fatal weakness at exactly the time when the republic and the cause of German labor needed solidarity most. In foreign policy, the two parts of the labor movement, as well as further smaller branches, disagreed fundamentally on many points. The Social Democrats generally supported the foreign policies of the government, while the Communists remained both more chauvinistic and more internationalistic than the republican government. At the time of the French occupation of the Ruhr (1923), for example, the Communists bitterly fought against the French when the government was ready to come to a compromise. On other questions of foreign policy, the German KPD closely followed whatever the Soviet leaders of the Third International proposed. A Communist revolution in Germany was one of the great expectations of the movement and, as an internal goal, it was far more important than any foreign policy issue. The German Communists' excessive dependence on the ludicrous policies of Joseph Stalin toward the rising Nazi threat was the final straw that broke the back of the Weimar Republic. The Communists were so busy fighting the Social Democrats (whom they called "social fascists") and collaborating with Hitler's destruction of the republic that it proved impossible for the divided labor movement to stem the brown tide.

Today, a foreign policy based on the alleged interest of the working classes and diametrically opposed to the foreign policies of "imperialistic-capitalist bourgeois states" such as the Federal Republic or any of the Western powers is claimed to be the East German stance in foreign affairs. Peter Florin, the East German ambassador to Czechoslovakia, wrote in his book on the foreign policies of the DDR:

> The working class has a historical mission, namely to abolish the exploitation of man by man and to build a new social order of socialism and of communism. . . . In the socialist DDR, the working class is the leading force of the people and exercises political power in league with the peasant class in the cooperatives, the socialist intelligentsia, and the other

working strata of the people. . . . The SED [Communist party], as the party of the working class, creates and formulates the socialist foreign policy of the DDR.

The first principles of a socialist foreign policy are to be found in the writings of Marx and Engels and in their actual revolutionary activities. They include proletarian internationalism, the ideology and policy of international solidarity among the workers of all countries in the struggle for liberation from capitalist exploitation and national oppression . . .[6]

Florin goes on to contrast bourgeois nation-states which are said to be internally divided by antagonistic classes, and socialist nations which are characterized by internal solidarity and a commonality of interests among each other. According to Florin, there are "just wars"—struggles of national liberation—and "unjust wars" that aim at the oppression and exploitation of foreign peoples. Soviet foreign policy, to Florin, is the model of a socialist foreign policy which is dedicated "not just to peace but to democratic peace." Lenin is credited with having first described a policy of "peaceful coexistence" between socialist and capitalistic states and to have spelled out the need to base such a policy on the military strength and security of the socialist countries.

The policy of peaceful coexistence is . . . a specific form of class struggle between socialism and capitalism. Its strategic goal is the victory of socialism and communism on a global scale, but by economic, political and intellectual-cultural competition . . . not by military clash.[7]

These principles require some comment in order to place them into the proper perspective and to help the student over the semantic pitfalls of the language of Communist propaganda. First of all, there is a fundamental difference between the use of a social class interpretation of historical developments in which political power changed hands from class to class, and Florin's claim to a proletarian class label after the social change has run its course. The very terms of class interest and class policy are predicated upon the presence of antagonistic classes which are no longer present in the DDR nor in the original form in Western countries. Secondly, Florin's "working-class party" should be distinguished from such working-class movements as the British

Labour Party, the West German SPD, or the Scandinavian Socialist parties. The East German SED obviously did not mean to express its solidarity with the "social democratism" of these socialist parties and the trade unions and workers they represent, but only with Communist parties, Communist workers, and their friends. Furthermore, it is hardly self-evident in what sense the SED can call itself the one and only representative of the working class in a country in which antagonistic classes have been abolished and in which no other party[8] is allowed to compete with it for workers' votes. There are also semantic difficulties in extending "proletarian solidarity" to revolutionary movements in the Third World whose members are by no stretch of the imagination industrial proletarians in the accepted meaning of the term.

As a third point, the peculiar use of the words "socialism" and "communism," which goes back to Marx and Engels, requires clarification insofar as it reflects Soviet terminology of the Stalin era. Stalin found it necessary during the long climb of the Soviet Union toward industrial modernization to distinguish between the far-off utopian goal of a communist society and the immediate goals of socialism which he hoped to achieve during his lifetime. This distinction was promptly used also to rationalize some glaring inequalities in Soviet society, such as between city workers and collective farmers, and in the burgeoning post-1945 Soviet empire in Eastern Europe. Thus, the new people's republics, including the DDR, were not accorded real equality with the Soviet Union because they were only "starting on the road to socialism," whereas Russian society was already on its way from socialism to communism. Communist interpretation rationalized the historic German guilt and error in order to claim that the East Germans in particular had shown themselves to be far from ready for communist democracy before 1945 and required therefore a period of intensive tutelage. The Soviet tutors used this rationalization for many years to cover an extreme degree of economic exploitation of East Germany which could hardly be described as an example of "proletarian internationalism." Today, with the economic bondage significantly reduced, the East German government evidently feels that the country has long since arrived at the stage of socialism and is entitled to a more equal partnership with the Soviet Union. At the same time, as in the Soviet Union, there is no more starry-eyed talk about the road to a true communist utopia, because Red China somehow managed to preempt this road and put the Soviet and East German ideologists on the defensive.

PAN-GERMANISM & NATIONAL SOCIALISM

The German bourgeoisie had fallen politically silent after the debacle of the national revolution of 1848-49 and the various dynastic efforts to create a German nation-state from the 1850s to 1871. Bismarck's success where they had failed further diminished the bourgeoisie's self-confidence and interest in politics. With Bismarck's fall (1890), however, a new wave of politicization seized certain parts of the bourgeoisie and found expression in a strong revival of *völkisch*[9] foreign policy images. Some of these ideas of German racial superiority and legitimate dominion over the "lesser breeds" can be traced back to earlier currents of German nationalistic thinking, especially in response to the challenges of unraveling the ethnic border questions at the time of the 1848 attempt to create a German nation-state. Wherever Danes, Poles, or Czechs were living together with German populations in the ethnic fringe areas, the political application of the principle of nationality naturally raised questions about where a given area belonged, to a future German or a Danish, Polish, or Czech nation-state.

After Bismarck's dismissal, a Pan-German Association was founded (1890) to promote the idea of going beyond his dynastic creation toward a true German national state which should at least include the German parts of Austria and perhaps also such other German ethnic areas as German Switzerland and parts of the Russian empire where ethnic Germans lived. Thinking along Pan-German lines, in fact, could lead to the discovery of more and more areas all around Germany and deep in the Balkans that either had German-speaking minorities or some sort of ethnic kinship, as with the Dutch and Flemings, or even the Anglo-Saxons and Scandinavians. Along the eastern borders, moreover, there were new ethnic shifts occurring during the late nineteenth and early twentieth century which made the question of German ethnicity more acute. In some places it was the rural exodus of German farmers and farm workers who left their places to Poles, which raised fears of a receding ethnic frontier. In Bohemia it was the rural-urban migration of Czechs who became effective competitors to German workers and artisans, driving the latter to organize the German National Socialist Workers Association, a pre-1914 predecessor to the Nazi party. Throughout the Austro-Hungarian empire and beyond, awakening Slavic nationalities tended to push aside the dominant German elements.

The dissolution of the Hapsburg empire into a number of new and ethnically heterogeneous nation-states and the substantial cessions of German territory such as Alsace-Lorraine, North Slesvig, West Prussia, Upper Silesia, and the Memel district under the Treaty of Versailles made the German ethnic problems even more painful. Before 1918, the Pan-Germans had wanted to support and defend against all challengers the traditional German dominance even in areas where the ethnic Germans constituted a very small minority. Now the Treaty of Versailles and the International Control Commission saw to it that the ethnic majorities got the upper hand and in some cases the results of the ballot box were forestalled or "corrected" ex post facto. Thousands of ethnic Germans fled to the *Reich* and further thousands accommodated themselves by changing, at least temporarily, their nationality and allegiance. Others led a bitter struggle against their alleged ethnic oppressors.

The National Socialists eventually appointed themselves the spokesmen and executors of the German ethnic legacy in Eastern Europe. They claimed, as had the Pan-Germans, that Germany needed more *Lebensraum* (living space), beginning with the eastern territories and colonies taken away from Germany and Austria by the Treaty of Versailles. To their minds the real identity of Germany was not the accidental boundaries of the Weimar Republic or the treaty-imposed boundaries of Versailles, but the extent of the German *Volk* (people) "from the Meuse to the Memel Rivers, and from the Adige [South Tyrol] up to the Belt [a Strait in the Baltic Sea]," as the German national hymn described it with borders all lying beyond the boundaries of Versailles. In Eastern Europe, in particular, there was almost no limit to the claims for ethnic dominion of the "Greater Germany" Hitler was going to build. Moreover, this ethnic empire was going to establish the rule of a master race over the "lesser breeds," a brutal racism whose nature only World War II and the German occupation of many of these areas began to disclose.

It was not always feasible during the years of the Nazi build-up to press the German ethnic complaints as much as Hitler may have wanted to. In the case of the South Tyrol, for example, a prudent regard for his fellow dictator, Mussolini, prevented any complaints being aired altogether. Therefore, the Nazi regime at an early point simply called on the ethnic Germans in the east and elsewhere to come "home to the Reich," an invitation followed by thousands. But it also used them as fifth columns to undermine foreign governments or to increase ethnic friction in order to supply a pretext for invasion. The interest of the Nazi government also extended to Germans living elsewhere, such as in Latin America and in the United States where attempts were made to propagandize them and to start a subversive movement, the *Bund*. The Nazis hoped thereby to fashion a world-wide political leverage which could reconcile public opinion in foreign countries to their plans at an appropriate time.[10]

These visions of racial imperialism were almost realized for a short, horrifying spell before the German war machine began to run out of steam. With the German defeat and division, they receded into the minds of the various sects of the radical right in West Germany which every now and then score a modest showing at the polls. Even among these splinter groups, the visions of racial superiority and dominion over other nationalities are expressed only with great reserve because there are criminal statutes and constitutional court proceedings in the Federal Republic by which individuals can be punished and groups outlawed for advocating hatred or war against other nations. Even the twelve millions of surviving refugees and expellees from the east, except for a small radical fringe, have long disavowed any revisionist claims with regard to Austria or the old ethnic German areas to the east. The radical right among the refugees speaks only of the area beyond the Oder-Neisse line, East Prussia, and Danzig, in other words, areas within the German boundaries of 1937 which were severed from Germany in 1945. A few diehards still speak of the Sudetenland and some others plant bombs in the South Tyrol.

The death and destruction visited by Hitler's troops upon Eastern Europe and the Soviet Union in pursuit of his visions of racial empire extirpated all willingness of the Eastern Europeans to tolerate ethnic Germans in their midst. In the first rage of liberation, an estimated 16.6 million ethnic Germans either fled or were expelled forcibly from their abodes, often under very violent circumstances. Some 3.2 million died or vanished without a record. Another 1.4 million of them who had been in Russia for centuries were resettled in Siberia or also disappeared without a trace. Twelve million reached West or East Germany and merged with the population there. This was the end of the dream of the racial empire of "the German *Volk* wherever it happens to live"; their non-German neighbors made sure the Germans would no longer be scattered all over Eastern Europe.

Notes

1 According to the "civic culture" study of Gabriel A. Almond and Sidney Verba, this differential also manifests itself in the much lower sense of political efficacy West Germans feel toward their national as compared to their local governments. In comparison to Englishmen and Americans, their political unity is evidently still rather new and distant to them (*The Civic Culture* [Princeton: Princeton University Press, 1963], pp. 191 and 203).

2 For the West German polls on these questions, see above, chap. 1, pp. 28-32. The question of an *Anschluss* of Austria has lost its saliency on both sides of the border.

3 *DIVO* 1960, p. 18. The higher "nationalistic" response came from the north and south ends of the Federal Republic, from Schleswig-Holstein and Bavaria.

4 The study of the political views of West German elites conducted by Rudolf Wildenmann in 1968 asked its 800 respondents to rank political goals of their government according to their urgency. They ranked Western European integration highest, above stable economic growth, educational reform, East-West cooperation, and even reunification. Thirty-three percent of Wildenmann's respondents were in their fifties, 28 percent were over sixty, and 29 percent were between forty-one and fifty years old (*Eliten in der Bundesrepublik*, unpublished draft manuscript, August 1968, pp. 161-62).

5 Hans Apel, *DDR 1962, 1964, 1966* (Berlin: Voltaire Verlag, 1967).

6 Peter Florin, *zur Aussenpolitik der souveraenen sozialistischen DDR* (East Berlin: Dietz Verlag, 1967), pp. 11-13.

7 Ibid., pp. 15-19.

8 The SED (Socialist Unity Party) originated in 1946 under Soviet occupation from a forcible merger of the East German KPD (Communist Party of Germany) with the SPD which was henceforth outlawed in the DDR.

9 The word denotes a mixture of populism, or faith in the common folk and its culture, with rank racialism, anti-Semitism, and anti-Slav sentiment.

10 Some observers and Allied war propaganda once claimed that this worldwide Nazi network was intended to bring about Nazi rule over the entire world, but such a claim would appear to be a little too extravagant even for the megalomania of an Adolf Hitler.

CHAPTER 3

German Foreign Policies

Surrounded by this plethora of visions and dreams about Germany's position in the world, German foreign policy makers have had to respond to the concrete challenges of their environment. Foreign policy is not made in a vacuum; it is determined by the exigencies of a state surrounded by other states, friendly or hostile, and by the ever-changing international situation at least as much as by internal conditions and attitudes of people. There can be little doubt that one of the foremost practical objectives of any body politic is its own self-preservation. If a state cannot preserve its existence as an autonomous state, all other questions of policy become illusory. Self-preservation runs like a red thread through all discussion of foreign policy goals although it has a way of masquerading under different colors. Some policy makers are satisfied with protecting their country from conquest by largely defensive policies or even a policy of neutrality among the powerful blocs. Others insist that external threats can only be contained with a policy of strength which may rely on alliances with strong friends or lead to a striving for the rank of a great power.

SECURING THE NEW NATION-STATE, 1871-90 & 1919-32

The foundation of the Bismarckian empire in place of a loose confederation of small and medium states in the center of Europe immediately presented Chancellor Bismarck (1871-90) with the

68

further problem of how to secure the new nation-state from external pressures. France, which had most strongly opposed the German consolidation, had just been decisively defeated in the Franco-Prussian war and was not by itself in a position to threaten German security. Bismarck, therefore, moved to placate the Austro-Hungarian empire which he had defeated in 1866 and shut out of his new state. He shrewdly decided to conclude with Austria and Russia the Three Emperors' League (1872). At the same time, he avoided offense to Great Britain by refraining from any challenge to its naval and colonial predominance. Thus France remained isolated from potential allies against Germany. The Balkan rivalries of Russia and Austria eventually brought on a German-Russian rift at the time of the Congress of Berlin (1878) but again Bismarck succeeded in forestalling its potentially dangerous consequences. He concluded a defensive alliance with Austria (1879) and, in 1882, added the kingdom of Italy, another new nation-state, to form the Triple Alliance. Russia, too, was soon persuaded to renew its ties with the German Empire in a series of treaties. Thus Bismarck not only maintained the peace, backed up by a strong army, but achieved a stable position for the new German state in Europe by his complex system of treaties and alliances which protected Germany from the East as well as the West. His mastery of "the game of the rolling balls" set itself limited objectives and achieved them without further bloodshed until his fall and replacement in 1890.

The Weimar Republic (1918-33) faced the problem of self-preservation on a much more difficult level following the defeat of the Central Powers (Germany, Austria, Bulgaria, and Turkey) in World War I. France had finally found allies in Great Britain, Russia (Triple Entente), and Italy and, with the help of the United States, won the war. Germany was not as badly off as Austria and Turkey which were reduced to small rump states, mere shadows of their former selves. But there was the Treaty of Versailles (1919) to face, which aimed at rendering Germany powerless to get back at her wartime enemies. For this purpose, the German army was limited to a defensive size of 100,000, the Rhineland demilitarized and partly occupied, the war fleet taken away and severe limitations were imposed upon any German rearmament. All the German overseas colonies were placed under foreign mandates. Substantial cessions of German territory in the east were motivated with the principle of national self-determination where Polish or Czech inhabitants formed a majority, a principle not easy to apply in the midst of impassioned agitation and armed clashes of irregulars on both sides. The Austrian desire, on the same principle, to join the Austrian rump state to Germany (*Anschluss*) was thwarted however at the instigation of France, which also claimed the Saar area and took back Alsace-Lorraine which it had lost in 1871.

The new Weimar government was presented with the grim choice of either accepting the popularly detested Treaty of Versailles or facing the threat of conquest and occupation of Germany by hostile armies. The government evidently decided that self-preservation demanded submission to the *Diktat* of Versailles and an earnest attempt at fulfillment of the allied conditions. This policy sealed its political fate with the electorate. Later on, throughout the Weimar era, the specter of the fulfillment policy was to be the Cain's mark of all republican governments in the view of the radical and the conservative right wing, regardless of the actual policies attempted or carried out.

The new government had to fight hard, both politically and with the Free Corps, irregular armed forces, against domestic revolutionaries and invaders from the East to assure its survival. At a later point, to secure Germany against external pressures the government also made several attempts to hark back to the policies of Bismarck. These began in 1920 with secret agreements with the Soviet Union regarding the forbidden training of German artillery, tank, and air force personnel in Russia. The policy of renewed ties to the East was highlighted by the agreement of Rapallo (1922), in which the German and Soviet governments agreed to drop all remaining mutual financial claims and to resume diplomatic relations. Although it had been preceded by trade agreements, the Rapallo treaty came as a surprise to the Western allies who had shown little cooperation or understanding for Germany's difficulties in meeting its enormous reparations imposed as the bill for alleged German aggression in World War I.

Due to German economic deterioration, France and Belgium in particular decided to take the lagging German payments by force in the form of coal and other goods, and invaded and occupied the Ruhr area in January 1923, touching off nearly a year of economic catastrophe and right-wing coups against the republic, including the beerhall *putsch* of Adolf Hitler. The Weimar government attempted to meet the external threat with a policy of passive resistance, which eventually had to be abandoned. Compromise proposals of payment by the German government were rejected out of hand by France.

At this point, a new cabinet was formed under Gustav Stresemann, whose influence on Weimar foreign policy was dominant from the crisis of 1923 to his death in 1929. Stresemann succeeded in gaining control over the revolutionary turbulence in the country and in stabilizing the German currency on a new basis. At the same time, he strove to establish a better bargaining basis for Germany to pursue its goal of revision of the severity of the financial and other strictures imposed at Versailles. The Dawes Plan (1924) of German payments, which proposed to adjust the demands made to the German capacity to pay, was the first major step toward agreement on the reparations. Further initiatives by Stresemann, who was now foreign minister, aimed at German admission to the League of Nations and the cessation of the occupation of the Ruhr and Rhineland. The Conference of Locarno (1925) confirmed the new understanding between Germany and France, and resulted in border guarantees and the renunciation of war among the signatory powers. In 1926 Germany was admitted to the League of Nations, a landmark on its way back to equal stature among European nations. Characteristically, the rapprochement toward the West established at Locarno was counterpointed promptly by the Treaty of Berlin (1926) with the Soviet Union, in which the two nations exchanged guarantees of friendship and non-aggression so as to allay Soviet suspicions of the German membership in the league.[1] In this fashion, both Bismarck and Stresemann interpreted the German role in Europe as a "bridge" or broker of both East and West, always looking in both directions rather than professing commitment only to one side.

The hopeful beginnings of Locarno were followed by relative stagnation in German foreign policy against a background of seeming economic recovery. In actual fact, however, the economic recovery of the middle years of the Weimar Republic, 1925 to 1929, was heavily dependent upon foreign credit, especially from the United States. The foreign investments were withdrawn in the great Wall Street crash of 1929, and Germany tumbled head over heels into the fatal economic and political crises which propelled Adolf Hitler into power. Much too late, the Conference of Lausanne (1932) yielded the fruits of years of endeavor to ease the reparations burden. The Germans won a three-year moratorium and a lump sum obligation in place of the long-term indebtedness of the Young Plan (1929) of reparations. Half a year later the internal political convulsions, the Great Depression, and the fourteen years of unrelenting pressure by the victors of World War I brought their nemesis to the helm of the German state, bent on fighting the war all over.

GERMAN IMPERIALISM, OLD & NEW

Historians and political scientists still argue over the proper definition of the term *imperialism*, whether it is a reflection of economic expansionism, the highest stage of capitalism (Lenin), or an atavistic drive for loot and political domination (Schumpeter). But it is easy to set off the imperialistic eras in the history of a people from those eras that were not imperialistic. Bismarck was not an imperialist, even though he used force and power politics to give permanence to the political edifice he was building. He was not an imperialist because his goals and objectives conspicuously eschewed limitless expansion and accepted the given boundaries and limitations without question. His successors and the young emperor, Wilhelm II, on the other hand, just as conspicuously set their sights beyond the voluntary self-limitations of Bismarck's political world. The dawning age of world politics made them yearn for Germany to become a world power. And in this fateful pursuit, they threw overboard one by one the careful arrangements by which Bismarck had safeguarded his new ship of state from foundering on the rocks of external reality.

First they allowed the important backstay of Bismarck's system, the security treaties with Russia, to lapse while they concentrated on a mutually advantageous settlement with the British. The Russians promptly approached the French and in 1892 concluded a military assistance pact with them against Germany. Later unsuccessful efforts to win back Russian support, moreover, alienated the British in turn, which reduced the German empire to reliance on the Austro-Hungarian and Italian monarchies amidst the growing hostile "encirclement." Wilhelm II, who had ebulliently taken on personal leadership, seemed not to mind the growing isolation of Germany, because of the surging feeling of economic strength which in the mid-1890s swept the country. The annual exodus of half a million emigrants died down to a trickle as industry and urbanism spread unprecedented prosperity throughout the empire.

A significant indication of the growing bourgeois appetite for a world political role for Germany was the Pan-German League which, beginning in 1890, spread the new gospel of social Darwinism, nationalism, and racist imperialism throughout the middle classes. There are many links of ideology and objectives between the Pan-Germans and the Nazi party of Adolf Hitler. The Pan-Germans are particularly notable for their interest in expanding German domination into Eastern Europe and their agreement with the newer versions of a greater Germany, including Austria, which the Nazis later adopted. Other organizations with imperialistic overtones promoted colonial expansion and mentality—in 1898 the Kaiser even added a Chinese colony to his African and South Pacific possessions—and the building up of a powerful imperial navy, an obvious challenge to British sea and colonial power. The indiscretions and provocations of Wilhelm II toward British involvements in South Africa and the Middle East alone were hardly designed to establish a good relationship between the two imperial rivals.

The naval buildup was a personal ambition of the young emperor as well as a necessity because of the rising export and foreign trade volume which by 1896 put Germany in second place behind Great Britain even though its navy was only in sixth place after the British, French, Russian, Italian and American fleets. The founder of the new Imperial Navy, Admiral von Tirpitz, con·sidered the possibility of a naval clash with the British, but in terms of deterrence rather than of a German victory. Nevertheless, this naval build-up was an important part of the arms race that led to World War I. The crisscrossing of far-flung colonial and economic interests and the missed opportunities of British or Russian friendship did the rest. In 1906-07 even Italy left the Triple Alliance, while England joined the hostile circle of powers. The German empire was solely dependent on Austria-Hungary which inevitably drifted into friction with Russia over conflicting territorial claims and nationalistic resistance in the Balkans. The last years before the outbreak of war saw a series of war scares and threats while the hard-liners on both sides stiffened their backs and the military brass polished its armor.

In the last resort, the roots of the great war were psychological. Born of repeated waves of war psychosis and the hysteria of "insulted national honor" on both sides, the psychology of the hour made it impossible for the political actors to back away from open clash. For the Germans, in particular, there was a mixture of social malaise, a yearning for "cleansing thunderstorms of steel," and a cocksure gamble for what they thought was the inevitable victory of German arms. As General von Bernhardi put it in his popular book *Germany and the Next War,* either Germany would become a world power or she would perish. This mentality also explains the detailed plans for vast German annexations which some German politicians and industrialists had made in anticipation of victory. As it turned out, Germany lost the war after a gruelling four years of mass slaughter. And no one was more belligerently resentful of the loss of the navy and the colonies, and the cessions of German territory under the Peace Treaty of Versailles than those who had been bent on massive annexations if Germany had won.

The years of the Weimar Republic again were hardly years of imperialistic drives, although it is a moot question to ask what certain Weimar leaders might have dreamed about or what they would have done had their country not been so defeated and held down by the Treaty of Versailles. In any case, when the most extreme of the party leaders of the Weimar Republic seized absolute power in 1933, Germany soon embarked on a new drive for empire with far less self-restraint or limitations than even the greediest phase of Wilhelminian Germany. Adolf Hitler arrived at the helm of state without any great knowledge of foreign countries, languages, or the extensive literature on international relations of his time. He was a rank amateur in governmental administration as well. Yet he had an encompassing ideology of foreign and domestic affairs, *völkisch* imperialism, which readily prescribed a course of action for every area of foreign policy. Moreover, his enormous drive and energy in a world situation marked by catastrophic depression and political weakness almost everywhere permitted him to shape the European world of the 1930s and early 1940s to his desires with startling rapidity. His was without a doubt the purest kind of imperialistic drive for expansion and dominion over others that the world has witnessed since the great khans led their horsemen across the steppes of central Asia.

At first glance, the earlier policies of the Nazi regime give the appearance of being merely rectifications of what the Treaty of

Versailles had done to the Germans and Austrians. But closer study reveals that Hitler had never meant to leave it at that.[2] As he set forth in his second, unpublished book (1928) and in a 1932 speech to German industrialists, the totalitarian reorganization of German society and massive rearmament were meant from the beginning to forge a powerful weapon for an aggressive foreign policy. The depressed German economy could be saved only by the conquest of *Lebensraum* in the East. The build-up for conquest would obviously take some time during which France or Poland with their large armies might intervene preventively in Germany.[3] Therefore, Hitler would have to dissemble and negotiate at Geneva for parity of arms, when in fact he was preparing a far superior force. The funds for rearmament were raised by deficit financing on a fantastic scale. And the bad impressions created abroad by the Nazi takeover were softened by a display of caution in the replacement of prominent foreign policy officials such as Foreign Minister Baron von Neurath and the ambassadors to the various posts. There had been a growing feeling abroad anyway that the peace settlement imposed on Germany had been too harsh and that some further concessions might well be in order.

Quite typically, the Nazi regime passed up a proposal of Mussolini in 1933 to solve some of the most pressing problems of border revision with Poland with a minor exchange of territory. The Nazis did not want to start any revisions until they had a more powerful army than Poland and other potential opponents. At the Geneva conference on the level of armaments the same year, they were similarly uninterested in obtaining minor concessions from the other powers. They just wanted to be sure that they made no commitments they would have to break too conspicuously, and that the conference would break up because of French intransigence rather than because of German demands. Even the July Concordate with the Vatican, Hitler's first major recognition from abroad, was concluded with such obvious intent not to abide by its terms that one can only wonder about the good sense of the Vatican in concluding it.

With regard to Poland, Hitler displayed similar caution in restraining his stormtrooper activists in Danzig, which had been left a free city amid Polish territory by the peace treaty. Early incidents had provoked a stern reaction from the Polish chief executive, Marshal Jozef Pilsudski, who even consulted with the French about a preventive strike against Nazi Germany. But the Poles, a middle power between rapacious neighbors, were quite ready for a rapprochement with Germany to forestall open conflict. Contacts with Hitler produced assurances that Germany would not resort to force in rectifying its territorial complaints. Hitler indeed overruled von Neurath and others who wanted to keep up the pressure on Poland, though hardly for reasons of sincere friendship. He ignored the German minority there for the time being simply because he knew how to wait for the vastly bigger stakes of his ambition. He even concluded a trade agreement that ended years of a trade war with Poland at the same time the Geneva conference collapsed and Germany pulled out of the League of Nations. Following this, Hitler attempted to draw the reluctant Pilsudski into a Polish-German alliance against the Soviet Union.[4] A treaty was signed instead in 1934 in which the two countries promised for ten years to solve all their problems by negotiations, not force. Hitler had succeeded in breaking up the ring of French alliances and in keeping Poland out of a Franco-Soviet-Czech alliance. He won peace in the East by soft-pedaling national minority issues[5] for several crucial years while building up his strength.

In contrast to the temporary settlement with Poland, Hitler exercised strong pressure on Austria, which he hoped to subvert and "coordinate politically" from within with the help of the Austrian Nazi party, just as he had "coordinated" the neighboring German *Land* government of Bavaria. The attempt misfired and led to Italian, British, and French pressure on Berlin. Austria drifted closer to the fascist regimes of Italy and Hungary and, at Mussolini's behest, permitted an internal proto-fascist upheaval while holding off the National Socialist pressures from Germany. A coup organized with Hitler's assistance in 1934 involved the assassination of the Austrian chancellor Engelbert Dollfuss but failed again to win power for the Austrian Nazis. The international reaction to this debacle finally persuaded Hitler to relent in his pressure on his native Austria until he would have the armed might to withstand international disapproval.

Hitler's policy toward Czechoslovakia, where three million Sudeten Germans were awaiting a national liberation of sorts, was again one of waiting until Germany would be strong enough to take what it wanted. In the meantime, the Sudeten German activists were told to simmer down and there was even some talk of a nonaggression treaty. By 1934, Berlin was no longer inclined to make any commitment to the Czechs that it knew it would break a few years hence. Hitler discussed his designs on Czechoslovakia in the frankest manner during a 1933 visit by the Hungarian premier Gyula Gömbös, whose country was another one of the revisionist forces of Eastern Europe just waiting to reclaim its areas from Czechoslovakia and other new states created by Versailles. The German minority in Hungary, on the other hand, was also instructed to hold back, just as the Germans in South Tyrol were given no hope of Nazi support against Mussolini. Germany prepared to exercise hegemony over southeast Europe by such means as trade treaties with Hungary, Rumania, and Yugoslovia, thereby undercutting Italian, French, and other regional influences there.

With the field for expansion in the East well prepared for the future, Germany concentrated on rearmament in violation of the Treaty of Versailles and other agreements, in part even while negotiating in Geneva over an agreed level of armaments. When the Geneva conference foundered, a plebiscite was held (November 12, 1933), the first of many, to demonstrate national solidarity with the government, which even undertook a publicity campaign of friendship for France, the one nation from which it still feared armed intervention. The other European powers were not unaware of Hitler's designs, but lacked the will, the popular support, and the means to stop him while he could still be stopped.

In the forefront of Germany's rearmament program stood plans for vast numbers of war planes and war ships including submarines, precisely the kind of arms the Treaty of Versailles had forbidden the Germans. Some of the naval buildup had the purpose of protecting the vital import routes of a country lacking in certain natural resources indispensable to arms production and war. At the same time, however, the Nazi government also moved early (1933) to develop synthetic gasoline and other synthetic products which would make it independent of foreign supplies. A policy of stockpiling important resources closed the remaining gaps. Finally, the building up of the German army to massive proportions was begun with the help of a new conscription law (March 1935) which again violated the Versailles limits on the German peacetime army. This buildup of a large conscript army was accompanied and preceded by the military indoctrination of the people, especially youth.

In 1935, after the Saar plebiscite in favor of a return to Germany, Hitler began to put his cards on the table. He made public announcements of Germany's air and naval rearmament, including submarines, and of the reintroduction of conscription. Since his plans for naval rearmament called for only one-third of the British strength, he even sought the sanction of a naval treaty with Great Britain. The Italian attack on Ethiopia at about the same time took some of the heat for violating various international agreements off Hitler and started the development of the Berlin-Rome axis. Germany continued to sidestep the friendly overtures of France and the Soviet Union and to avoid multilateral commitments guaranteeing the status of Austria or other Eastern European borders. Also in this year the first military plan for a surprise attack on Czechoslovakia appeared and was quietly shelved again. The time was not yet ripe.

The biggest challenge to the status quo, however, was the remilitarization of the Rhineland, whose demilitarization had been decreed in the Versailles Peace Treaty and solemnly reaffirmed by Germany at Locarno. As long as the left bank of the Rhine and a fifty-kilometer strip along the right bank of the river were kept demilitarized, Germany was not only unable to attack France or the Low Countries, but was also defenseless against any retaliatory strike by France in case of a German move against any of the Eastern countries who were the chief object of Hitler's designs. In view of the Franco-Czech-Soviet alliance and French objections to the *Anschluss* (annexation) of Austria, a demilitarized Rhineland effectively tied German hands by rendering vulnerable its most tender flank, with large population centers and the nub of German industry. And the French had shown their readiness to intervene in 1923 for much lesser causes than a German aggression. As Hitler had long been well aware, judging from his book *Mein Kampf* and his second book, the demilitarized status of the Rhineland was, next to German rearmament, his biggest stumbling block on the road toward revising the eastern boundaries of Germany. The remilitarization of the Rhineland took place early in 1936 and was preceded by legal maneuvers and complaints against the Franco-Soviet pact, which had not yet been ratified by the Chamber of Deputies in Paris. Why did not the French or the British at least threaten military intervention or sanctions such as Great Britain had imposed on Mussolini's Italy during the Ethiopian War? The French seem to have been overly impressed by the current military strength of rearmed Germany, while the British were undecided and debated various ways of appeasing Germany.[6]

Thus, Germany took the offensive and embarked on a course directed toward war, all the while assuring everybody that its action was an isolated act and unlikely to lead to further steps in the same direction. But the new theme had already been proclaimed in January 1936 when Propaganda Minister Goebbels launched a new slogan—"Guns instead of butter!"—to rationalize the serious foreign exchange difficulties brought on by the rapid rearmament of the country. On March 7, a Saturday, German military units rolled into the demilitarized zone with instructions to retreat without fighting if there were a French countermove. The Germans were careful to use minimal forces and to make clear that no attack on any other country was involved. In the end, neither France nor Great Britain responded to the collapse of the post-World War I security system. And in Eastern Europe, the dominoes began to fall in rapid succession as government after government sought accommodation with the aggressor.

Hitler's success in remilitarizing the Rhineland gave him the confidence to plunge further into the preparations for World War II. The pressure on Danzig, the Czechoslovak government, and Austria increased perceptibly. The German economy was increasingly mobilized for the war effort in spite of the foreign supply and exchange problems and the inflationary pressures this policy engendered within.[7] The Spanish Civil War provided both Germany and Italy with an opportunity to try out their new armaments and military skills on the Spanish Loyalists. It also helped along the development of the Berlin-Rome axis to which Japan was soon added. The three revisionist powers, fresh from aggression in the Rhineland, Ethiopia, and Manchuria, stood ready to challenge the tottering collective security system of the League of Nations.

Nazi Germany finally made its move into Austria in March 1938 and, in September of the same year, into the Sudetenland, after the Munich Conference sanctioned the German seizure of large parts of Bohemia. The ease with which Great Britain and France gave in at Munich whetted Hitler's appetite for the rest of Bohemia and Moravia, which he annexed in March of the following year. The Memel district was also taken and at the same time the German pressure grew once again on Poland to hand over Danzig and the Polish Corridor.[8]

During a brief lull in Nazi aggression the Poles felt safe with French and British assurances, when all of a sudden the unexpected Nazi-Soviet Non-Aggression Pact (August 23, 1939) removed the last barrier to an all-out German thrust into Poland. On September 1, German tanks and airplanes invaded Poland in the first of Hitler's *Blitzkrieg* moves, subduing Polish resistance in 2½ weeks. The Soviets moved in, too, and the two totalitarian states divided Poland between them. As Hitler had said privately, referring to the three historical partitions of Poland, "There'll be only one more division of Poland." But this time at least, the Western powers no longer let him get away with his aggressions, even though they were far from adequately armed to meet his challenge. On September 3, both Great Britain and France declared war on Germany. World War II had begun.

Much of the action of World War II, of course, was designed to defeat the enemy rather than to reveal the long-range intentions of Nazi policy. Thus the lightning invasion of Denmark and Norway and the *Blitzkrieg* on France in 1940 did not necessarily denote a German intention to annex these areas.[9] In the East, however, the German appetite grew right along with the military successes. Hungary, Rumania, and Bulgaria had already joined the Axis powers in 1940 while Mussolini was engaged in an abortive effort to conquer Greece. In April 1941, German troops invaded the lone holdout, Yugoslavia, in yet another *Blitzkrieg* and went on to Greece and Crete. And on June 22, 1941, the European Axis powers plunged into the Soviet Union and quickly overran the Ukraine, another item on the list of potential German annexations.

Exactly which territories Hitler would have kept or annexed had he won the war is, of course, anyone's guess. There seemed to be no limit to his ambition, not even limits suggested by the distribution of ethnic Germans. Just as he had quickly gone on from claiming the Sudeten Germans to the rest of Bohemia and Moravia, he went on from Danzig and the Polish Corridor to solidly Polish areas, and even began to speculate about including blond and blue-eyed Russian children into his Aryan racist empire. After all, he had expressed his contempt for the idea of the nation and nationalism as early as in *Mein Kampf* and his obsession with the pseudo-scientific concept of race had proved flexible enough when it was a matter of welcoming other fascist brothers-in-arms in Brussels, Rome, or Tokyo. It was unlikely to limit his territorial appetite anywhere that German arms could carry him. And the German national potential in Europe, at least, was formidable enough to dominate the continent in the service of Hitler's mania until such extra-European powers as the United States and the Soviet Union joined forces to meet the challenge.

Next to the Russians, the Germans were by far the largest ethnic group in Europe, "forty millions too many" as the French liked to say, and as the Peace Conference at Versailles had evidently forgotten when it decided to replace the multinational empires of Eastern and Central Europe with nothing but nation-states and their petty national interests. The debacle of nationalism, and especially of German nationalism, was something which the Europeans did not soon forget after the final defeat of the Nazi empire in 1945.

SECURING THE FEDERAL REPUBLIC

The final defeat of German imperialism by the Allied armies in 1945 signifies a major turning point in the evolution of both German and the European roles in world politics. There had already been indications of the waning of the central position of Europe following World War I, even though both America and Russia were too preoccupied with themselves to make their weight prevail over the exhausted old European powers. For the first two decades after 1945, however, there was no real doubt about the fundamental bipolarity of the postwar world, which proceeded to form two antagonistic camps, each collecting allied states around itself much as two magnets might attract metal filings. This bipolar world and Germany's utter defeat, conquest, and occupation by the victorious Allies were the point of departure of German postwar policies.

In the beginning, there were even some Allied plans to dismember Germany into several smaller, independent states, or to turn it back into an agrarian society stripped of industrial capacity (Morgenthau Plan).[10] Germany's western neighbors proposed to annex parts of German territory and the Soviets were preparing to indemnify Poland for the Polish territories they had acquired under the Nazi-Soviet Pact of 1939 with the German territories beyond the Oder-Neisse line. Except for this last-mentioned *fait accompli*, however, neither dismemberment nor annexations took place. Instead, the worsening relations between Moscow and

Washington in response to the Communist coups in Eastern Europe, and most notably in Czechoslovakia in 1948, brought about the fateful split between East and West Germany. The German territory had been divided into four zones of occupation for the British, French, American, and Russian armies, but these boundaries were not meant to be permanent. There were plans for reestablishing a national German government. And Berlin had been jointly administered by the four powers rather than integrated into the Soviet zone of occupation. But the rapid deterioration of East-West relations led to the breakdown of the Allied Control Council and to the Soviet blockade of Berlin, which the West countered with the famous airlift of 1948. Hence the reestablishment of German government above the *Land* (state) level took place separately in the Soviet zone and in the combined Western zones.

What seemed at first a crushing legacy of the German division and weakness was turned into the great West German opportunity by a man whose stature and influence overshadow the first decade and a half of the Federal Republic. As the late West German historian and political scientist Waldemar Besson put it, "In the beginning there was Adenauer."[11] Konrad Adenauer, the former mayor of Cologne, had recognized as early as 1945 that the German defeat of that year had little in common with that of 1918, and that the future lay with a Western-oriented German state. The East-West split and German division proved him right. As he rose to the leadership of the Christian Democratic Union (CDU) and in 1949 became the first chancellor of the Federal Republic, his notions came to prevail over older, more nationally oriented images of foreign policy within his own party and those of his great early rival, Kurt Schumacher of the Social Democratic Party (SPD). More important still, Adenauer's ideas increasingly coincided with the views of the incoming Eisenhower administration in Washington as well as with those of members of influential circles in London, Paris, and Rome whom he persuaded to support his policies. It was this lucky coincidence of views and situation and Adenauer's political skill in international negotiations which enabled him to rehabilitate and reintegrate Western Germany into the Western family of nations against seemingly impossible odds.

As Adenauer saw the world in 1945, Eastern and Western Europe had broken asunder and the Soviet Union was secure in its new sphere of influence. The West German rump state was destined to be the "integrating core" of Western Europe for the mutual benefit of Germans, Englishmen, and Frenchmen. The French, Dutch, and Belgian desire for security from German aggression was better satisfied by close economic ties among these countries than by cutting off the Rhineland and Westphalia from Germany and giving these territories to its Western neighbors. The latter policy would only push the rest of Germany into the arms of the Soviet Union, which Adenauer then regarded as the biggest threat to the security of Germany and Europe. His great antagonist Schumacher and other Social Democrats shared his pronounced anticommunism, especially after the clumsy attempt of the East German Communist party to merge with and take over the SPD in 1946. But Schumacher took a dim view of the capitalistic and Catholic-clerical overtones he perceived in Adenauer's plan for Western European integration. His was a vision of socialism and democracy within and national self-determination and equality among the other nations for Germany.[12]

Adenauer's earlier notions were laid down in the official declaration of policy of his newly inaugurated West German government in 1949. The Federal Republic was by no means a sovereign state at that time, but was dependent on the Allied High Commissioners in every decision, according to the Occupation Statute. The new government was not even permitted to conduct its own foreign relations through a Foreign Office until much later. Nevertheless, Adenauer pursued his goal of German integration with Western Europe step by step through the High Commission. It was typical of Adenauer's mode of operation to turn vestiges of occupation control such as the continued removal of German industrial equipment or the creation of the Ruhr Authority into tokens of German cooperation with the Allies' interest in securing themselves against renewed German aggression. The Petersberg Protocol late in 1949 was a landmark of this process of widening German freedom of action in proportion to demonstrated German loyalty to the West.

In 1950, Adenauer faced perhaps his gravest test, avoiding a direct confrontation of interests with France over the Saar area, which France wanted to maintain as a kind of economic protectorate. Instead of insisting on German interests, Adenauer suggested putting the Saar under an international or European authority. The ensuing negotiations and contacts ultimately led the French to propose the establishment of the supranational

European Coal and Steel Community (Schuman Plan) with West Germany as an equal member, a giant step forward on the road to German rehabilitation. The London conference of foreign ministers of the same year promptly responded by promising a revision of the Occupation Statute. The outbreak of the Korean War and the camouflaged rearmament of Eastern Germany made pressing the deliberation of the next fateful step along the road: West German membership and rearmament within NATO. How else could the occupation of Germany be phased out under the shadow of the Soviet Union or a Korea-like East German threat? Again the bitter pill[13] could be swallowed only because it was elevated to the European rather than the national level, and because the cold war had turned into a hot war in Korea. Neither the Germans nor their allies would have found a national German army an acceptable solution. And the implication of a German contribution to NATO was, of course, that West Germany would advance a major step along the road to equality.

Again the French came up with a proposal, to form a European Defense Community (Pleven Plan). But this time, the obstacles were greater than ever. The military of all the Allies were skeptical of the workability of a joint army based on small national units. The German SPD and other oppositional elements found German rearmament a better issue than any other in their campaign against the coalition government of Adenauer. The French opposition was even stronger and eventually defeated the ratification of the EDC treaty in the National Assembly. But most discouraging were the small concessions offered to the Germans by the Allies. They granted the Bonn government the right to speak for all Germans, including those in East Germany, and promised to guarantee the security of West Germany and Berlin. There were also promises of permitting German consular representation abroad, of ending Allied restrictions on science and industry, of allowing the establishment of an equivalent to the massive East German police forces, the Readiness Police (*Bereitschaftspolizei*), and of stationing substantial numbers of Allied troops on West German soil to protect West Germany against a surprise attack.

At this point the Soviet Union and the newly established East German government also got into the act. Moscow invited the East Berlin government to join the Council of Comecon, the Soviet bloc economic organization, and to attend as a full-fledged member government the Eastern Bloc conference in Prague, which pointedly demanded a return to the Potsdam agreements on the status of Germany. The conferees in Prague proposed an all-German council on which both Germanies would be equally represented. East German President Otto Grotewohl wrote a letter to Adenauer calling on "all Germans to sit down at the same table." The underlying intent was obviously to neutralize both Germanies and to keep West Germany from integration with the West. This may have been the last major opportunity to achieve a German reunification of sorts. Adenauer, however, rejected the proposal and, with the full support of the SPD and most of the German public, demanded "free elections in East Germany for a national constituent assembly as the preliminary to any rapprochement.[14] This demand, which of course touched the vital difference between the democratically elected government of Bonn and the Communist dictatorship in East Germany, henceforth became the adamant basis of the West German stance toward East Germany. However righteous it may have been, it was an unlikely beginning for any understanding between Bonn and East Berlin.

In March 1952, the Soviet government made a further all-out effort to prevent the consolidation of a West German state integrated with the Western alliance. In identical notes to the three major powers, the Soviet Union again proposed a four-power conference on Germany and offered as the reward for abandoning West German integration with the West "German reunification within the boundaries of 1945," the withdrawal of all occupation troops, a German national army, and membership in the United Nations. Grotewohl once more added his acceptance of free elections to a constituent assembly. This was without question the most generous offer ever made on this subject by the Soviet Union, disregarding for the time being the question of good faith. The SPD and some CDU leaders for once found the Soviet proposal worthy of further exploration. Adenauer, however, was unmoved by the Soviet offer, which he evidently interpreted as a clever way of thwarting the Western policy of containment. Neutrality alone and even a national army did not strike him as a sufficient guarantee of German security.[15] He preferred making West Germany the chief instrument of American consolidation policy in Europe. He hoped, moreover, that the Soviet offer and the positive reaction of many West Germans would put pressure on the Western Allies to make good their promises of

German advancement and equality.[16] The die was cast, and in spite of Adenauer's rhetoric of how the "policy of strength" would eventually produce reunification of the two Germanies, such a development was more remote than ever.

The international squeeze play was expensive to Adenauer in terms of the growth of a national and pacifistic opposition in his own country.[17] His party, the CDU, had already suffered grievous losses in the state elections of 1951. The approaching federal elections of 1953 promised a showdown on the major issues of West German foreign policy and rearmament. Beginning with the London conference of foreign ministers early in 1952, the quid pro quo of the West German membership in the European Defense Community and the final revision of the amended Occupation Statute were under debate. Since the EDC was indirectly tied in with NATO, which would have to respond to any attack on non-member West Germany, the French feared that German territorial demands such as reunification would change the defensive character of NATO. Adenauer quickly volunteered German assurances that the Federal Republic would never employ any but peaceful means to obtain reunification. To the Allies, and especially to Great Britain and France, the question was essentially one of securing German cooperation in the common defense without according full equality to West Germany. This discriminatory intent also had to be faced in such questions as the remaining limitations on German armaments, the status of the Saar, and the pending prosecution of German war criminals, a particularly sensitive issue in an election year.

Regarding the Saar, incidentally, Adenauer showed none of the zeal for "free elections" or plebiscites he had displayed toward the question of reunification. He could not afford to jeopardize French cooperation with such insistence on the self-determination of the Saar population.

In the end it was the American and British assurances of maintaining troops in continental Europe which calmed French suspicions of Germany and cleared the way for the success of Adenauer's policies.[18] The ensuing close relationship between John Foster Dulles and Adenauer signaled the height of the Adenauer era. In March 1953, the treaties were approved in Bonn and the following parliamentary elections vindicated Adenauer's policies with an astonishing landslide of popular support.[19] The domestic opposition had already been impressed by the cordial reception of Adenauer in Washington before the election and was now cowed by the popular verdict.

As it turned out, the coincidence of Adenauer's efforts with the prevailing international trends had already begun to decline in 1953. Stalin had died and been replaced, for the time being, by a rather unstable leadership in Moscow. The Korean war had ended in an armistice. In East Germany a workers' revolt had broken out against the regime in June and the American reaction had proved the pronouncements of Foreign Secretary Dulles on "rolling back the Iron Curtain" were mere campaign rhetoric. Most ominously, the Soviet Union had just exploded its first hydrogen bomb. At this juncture, the new Conservative administration in Great Britain called for a four-power conference on Germany which might reopen all the painfully settled issues of German integration into the Western alliance. When this conference was finally convened in Berlin in January 1954, Asian issues such as the new role of Red China and the collapsing French position in Indochina also intruded upon the debate on Germany. British Foreign Secretary Anthony Eden proposed his plan for elections, the formation of an all-German government, and a peace treaty, leaving no doubt that a reunified Germany would be at liberty to join the Western alliance. The Soviet government was adamant in its insistence on restrictions upon the foreign ties of a reunified Germany, which made it clear once more that the price of reunification would be neutralism. This was unacceptable to the Western allies, who viewed a reunified, independent Germany between the power blocs with as deep a suspicion as the Soviets viewed a European army that included Germany with its aggressive past and its unrenounced territorial claims.

Under these circumstances, the German problem remained insoluble in spite of the strong desire of both East and West to reduce the tensions in Central Europe. The logical consequence of the competing interests was to keep Germany divided and for the Soviets to build up their part of Germany while the Western Allies proceeded with the integration of West Germany into the Western alliance. France, however, was at this point under the painful pressure of its humiliating defeat at Dien Bien Phu, which occurred in the middle of the Geneva Conference and toppled the government in Paris. The successor government under Pierre Mendes-France strove to liquidate the French position in Indochina as painlessly as possible and, for this purpose, welcomed Soviet support in obtaining a peace settlement. The price of a reasonable settlement in Southeast Asia, it turned out, was the abandonment of EDC in Europe. The loss of this stepping stone toward a united Europe was never completely remedied even though a substitute arrangement was found shortly with British help. A Western European Union on the model of the defunct Brussels Pact of 1948 was formed to include Great Britain, France, the Benelux countries, Italy, and the Federal Republic, which was thus again joined to NATO. The United States and Great Britain promised once more to maintain troops on the continent and Adenauer pledged that the Federal Republic would not engage in the production of atomic-biological-chemical (ABC) weapons, warships, rockets, or bombs above a certain capacity. Bonn's compliance could be supervised by the WEU.

With the defeat of EDC, the progress toward European integration, upon which much of the German advance had been built, slowed down considerably although Adenauer still succeeded in bettering his understanding with France. In place of the boost received from European development by the Federal Republic, there now came close cooperation between Bonn and Washington, which had reason to view Adenauer as a more reliable and pliable ally than France or Great Britain in their postcolonial agonies. A Franco-German agreement placing the Saar under a European commissioner and provisionally under WEU pending popular ratification was the last obstacle to West German sovereignty.[20] In February 1955, the *Bundestag* approved the Treaty on Germany, which embodied both the West German obligations and West German sovereignty. In May the treaty went into effect, signifying among other things the end of the occupation and the establishment of German diplomatic relations abroad. A foreign secretary, Heinrich von Brentano, was appointed and Defense Commissioner Theodor Blank became Bonn's first minister of defense. A few days later, WEU was established and a German representative attended Germany's first NATO meeting.

With this day, the evolution of the postwar role of the Federal Republic had reached a landmark. The Soviet Union, in response, was quick to solidify the situation behind the Iron Curtain, where Nikita Khrushchev had emerged as the new leader after years of "collective leadership." The *fait accompli* in the West was countered with the foundation of the Warsaw Pact and the admission of the DDR as a full-fledged, presumably sovereign member. The USSR had evidently abandoned its hopes for a re-unified, neutral Germany and reoriented its policy according to the presence of two German states. At the same time, the Western allies also could not be persuaded, in spite of Adenauer's efforts, to include German reunification on the agenda for the next summit meeting at Geneva, which was devoted mostly to the relaxation of tensions between the superpowers. On the other hand, there was also the conclusion of a peace treaty with neutralized Austria in the first half of 1955, as if the Soviets were trying to demonstrate what a good bargain Bonn could have had for the asking. There was also a noticeable tendency of the two power centers, Moscow and Washington, to turn to new problems such as the penetration and development of the Third World and neutralist camp rather than to the problems of Central Europe. Almost imperceptibly and obviously contrary to Adenauer's sense of his own importance, Bonn had begun to slip from the center of the world stage to the position of a rather minor sideshow.

THE EAST GERMAN SEARCH FOR SECURITY

The rapid advance of West Germany toward economic prosperity and full acceptance among the Western family of nations left the Soviet zone of occupation, and later the DDR, conspicuously behind. It is not correct to say, as some observers insist, that the West German advance was won at the expense of the East Germans, for there was nothing the West Germans could have done except join the East Germans in decades of all-German misery. More likely, the eventual East German advance and even the Soviet offers to allow the creation of a reunified, neutralized Germany were triggered chiefly by the spectacular successes of the West Germans, which caused the Soviets to abandon their earlier policies. But the rise of the Federal Republic also had pervasive negative consequences for the DDR.

East Germany was, perhaps, not notably different in the amount of destruction suffered during the war, but it had to endure a much harsher occupation, beginning with the day the Soviet troops made their brutal entry into the lives of German civilians.[21] In June 1950, the Institut für Demoskopie asked a

TABLE 5   German Reactions to Occupation Troops (%)

Reaction Reported	British troops	U.S.	French	Soviet
Bad experiences	37%	49%	65%	95%
Pleasant experiences	16	15	7	1
Noticed little	47	36	28	4
Totals	100%	100%	100%	100%

representative sample in the Federal Republic and in West Berlin, presumably including refugees and expellees from Eastern Germany, about their experiences with the coming of the occupation troops.[22] As Table 5 shows, the Soviet occupiers were thought to be by far the most unpleasant, which may reflect the savagery of the German occupation of Russia and the cruelties of the last phases of the Eastern front when neither side was inclined to give quarter or to take prisoners.

The Soviet occupation regime also was economically exploitative in the extreme, going far beyond the industrial reparations measures exacted by the Western occupiers. The Soviets proceeded to squeeze every last penny in equipment and skilled labor out of their German colony prior to 1949, and even after that date, they were quite efficient in obtaining their pound of flesh.[23] And there was, of course, no Marshall Plan to pump capital back into the depleted industrial capacity of East Germany. The Soviets, after plundering the country, have rendered only very limited assistance designed chiefly to restore crippled industries which might produce something of interest to the Soviet Union. In spite of this enormous handicap and its unfavorable international situation, the DDR has since grown into the second most potent industrial state in the Soviet bloc and one of the ten strongest industrial powers in the world, a remarkable achievement for a country which ranks only about 92nd in population size in the world.

East German foreign policy for many years has been ignored by Western scholars[24] and even journalists on the assumption that it was unlikely to be much more than a mere instrument of Soviet foreign policy. The East German government has indeed been a most loyal ally to the Soviet Union, as Bonn has been to Washington, but without Bonn's leverage and without Bonn's recurrent periods of sulking. It still cannot be said that the DDR has an autonomous foreign policy. But this is not to deny the major underlying problems the DDR has had to face and the evident desire of its government to cope with these problems. The DDR foreign minister, Otto Winzer, in a 1968 speech, laid down five principles of East German foreign policy that are worth closer examination:

(1) The creation of the most favorable international conditions for building up socialism in the DDR.

(2) Increasing the political and ideological unity, solidarity, and power of the community of socialist countries by working further on our close and friendly collaboration with the Soviet Union and other members of the socialist family of states, especially of the Warsaw Pact, on the basis of socialist internationalism.

(3) Support for peoples struggling for liberation from the colonial yoke and cooperation with those already liberated, especially if they followed a noncapitalistic path of development.

(4) To develop normal relations with the capitalistic states according to the principle of peaceful coexistence, with the goal of contributing to a European system of collective security and to a stable order of peace in the whole world.

(5) To fight the evermore aggressive and dangerous policies of West German imperialism and its arrogant claim to represent all Germans (*Alleinvertretung*).

As many as four of these principles refer to aspects of East German security. The emphasis on favorable conditions for internal socialist development, East German integration with the Soviet Union and the Warsaw Pact, European collective security, and the reference to West German imperialism all stress the underlying quest for security. Most revealing, despite the timing of the speech a few months before the Warsaw Pact invasion of Czechoslovakia, is the last principle, and especially the reference to Bonn's claim of *Alleinvertretung.*

The West German claim to represent the East Germans as well as the West Germans was from the beginning a painful thorn in the side of the East German government. To begin with, it accorded East Berlin the status of a revolutionary regime which is not being recognized in a civil war situation because it will probably not survive the civil war. Until recently West German official pronouncements, especially under Adenauer, always stressed this intent not to recognize the "illegitimate regime over there" for fear of giving legal permanence to what was considered merely a provisional arrangement under Soviet occupation. Official Bonn for many years insisted on referring to the formally sovereign DDR as "the zone (of occupation)" as if it were still an occupied country. There is a hint of physical threat in this state of affairs even though the substantial Soviet military presence and Western restraints made a West German attack on East Germany most improbable. But the threat was not lost on the East German regime, especially not after the workers' uprising of June 17, 1953, when only the intervention of Soviet tanks saved the Communist government from its own people. Hence there is an authentic note of concern for East German security audible underneath the propaganda line about West German imperialism despite the absence of any aggressive West German action in over two decades.

As a second point, the DDR has been seriously handicapped and held back in the development of its international relations as a result of the refusal of Bonn and the Western allies to recognize and establish normal diplomatic relations with it. For many years, West Germany intensified this boycott with its policy of threatening to withdraw recognition from other countries that recognized the DDR (Hallstein Doctrine), which the Soviet Union and the people's democracies of the Communist orbit had already done. This policy was quite effective until Bonn became aware of how West German withdrawal in a neutralist country tended to leave the scene of action to the other Germany, and how governments of the Third World could use this strange recognition game to blackmail Bonn. The strong interest in the developing countries naturally led to many a contest over recognition of the DDR there and the DDR was no less concerned about possible blackmailing pressure than Bonn had been.[25] Until the wave of international recognition in 1972-73, the DDR had diplomatic relations with only about one-fourth of the countries of the world and any kind of representation in less than half of them, and hardly for lack of trying.

It is worth dwelling on East Berlin's early recognition efforts for a minute. The first country to recognize the DDR upon its foundation in October 1949 was the Soviet Union, followed by Poland and Czechoslovakia after the East German government had specifically recognized all the Eastern European boundaries, including the Oder-Neisse line. Red China and the other people's democracies soon followed suit. Several years later, the Soviet Control Commission was turned into the High Commission (1953) and the Communist states renamed their "diplomatic missions" in East Berlin "embassies." The Soviet Union announced East Germany's graduation to formal sovereignty in 1954 by putting their mutual relations on a footing equal to that of other Soviet relations with sovereign states and by solemnly according the DDR "the freedom to decide its internal and external affairs including its relations to West Germany." A solemn treaty the following year between Moscow and the DDR ended the state of war and once more proclaimed East German sovereignty, reserving however "all international obligations referring to Germany as a whole." It remained to be seen how much of a free hand East Germany would actually possess.

The invitation to the non-Soviet bloc nations to enter diplomatic relations with the DDR, meanwhile, was followed at first only by Yugoslavia (1957) and Cuba (1961), in both cases with the immediate repercussions threatened by the Hallstein Doctrine. Trade missions, nevertheless, were exchanged with the United Arab Republic (1953), Syria (1955), Iraq (1958), and the Sudan and Yemen (1956), as well as with India (1954), Ceylon and Burma (1955), Indonesia (1958), Guinea (1959), Colombia and Uruguay (1954), Brazil (1958), Finland (1953), Belgium and Greece (1955), Norway (1954), the Netherlands (1955), Denmark and Sweden (1957), France (1957), Turkey (1955), Austria (1954), and Italy (1958), in the great wave of expansion of East German commercial relations in the 1950s. Another wave aimed at consular relations began at the end of the fifties—United Arab Republic (1959), Syria (1961), Iraq (1962), Burma (1960), and Indonesia (1960) —and at the beginning of the sixties, when trade relations were also established with Mali, Morocco, Tunisia, and Great Britain. A second push for full diplomatic relations in the second half of the sixties netted the United Arab Republic (1969), Syria (1969), Algeria (1970), Iraq (1969), Sudan (1969), South Yemen (1969), Cambodia (1969), Ceylon (1970), Somalia (1970), Congo-Brazzaville (1970), Central African Republic (1970), and the Maldives. At the same time, consular relations were established with Guinea (1969),

India (1970), and Tanzania (1965), and trade relations extended to Libya (1965), Kuwait (1970), Zambia (1967), Cyprus (1965), Chile, Ecuador, and Mexico (all 1967). The DDR representation in West Germany had been limited to two offices of the Foreign Trade Ministry in Düsseldorf and Frankfurt.[26]

This was hardly a record of stifling isolation even though there were some conspicuous gaps, such as North America, Australia, Japan, Pakistan, Iran, Kenya, Ethiopia, Argentina, and South Africa. State visitors of the DDR in India, Iraq, and Egypt were always received with due pomp and circumstance, as were the special envoys the DDR preferred to send after the erection of the Berlin Wall. And the DDR in turn received its share of official visitors and delegations and engaged fully in cultural exchanges from all over the world.

In its attitude toward the question of a reunified Germany, the DDR government has undergone a good deal of change since 1949. In the manifesto of the National Front of the Democratic Germany of 1949, the SED leaders called on all "patriotic forces of the German people to fight against the division of Germany and the colonial enslavement of the Western zones" and added:

> The purpose of the separatist Bonn government is to integrate West Germany into the war bloc of the Atlantic Pact. Thereby, the divisive and colonial policy of the imperialistic powers is threatening the peace and, at the same time, the existence of the German nation."[27]

Among the goals of East German foreign policy,[28] this initial statement also mentioned the "restitution of the full sovereignty of the German nation with a recognized right to an autonomous foreign policy and foreign trade." The Bonn government was depicted as "militaristic," "undemocratic," and "revanchist" in most of the early official pronouncements. The charge of revanchism was usually connected to the refusal of the Adenauer government to recognize the Oder-Neisse line, which East Germany had solemnly recognized, along with the German-Czech borders of 1937, as "an integral peace and friendship boundary" in mid-1950.

In October 1949, the DDR also presented to the Prague conference of Eastern European foreign ministers a proposal on the German question which demanded a peace treaty with Germany pursuant to the Potsdam Agreements and the withdrawal of all foreign troops from Germany within one year. An all-German constitutional council was to be formed from an equal number of East and West German representatives to prepare the formation of a provisional all-German government and for consultation on the peace treaty. This proposal became the basis of Soviet and DDR policy for years to come and reappeared in particular in the March 1952 Soviet note to the Western powers. Bonn and the Western powers, however, regarded it with deep suspicion in view of the Korean War and the existence of some 70,000 East German "garrisoned people's police" behind the demands for a withdrawal of foreign troops.

With the onset of the 1960s and, in particular, after the erection of the Berlin Wall, the DDR suddenly lessened its interest in German reunification and began to speak increasingly of an East German state and an East German national consciousness. The Soviet Berlin ultimatum of 1958 and the rejection of the Soviet proposals for a peace treaty the following year may well have been chief events triggering this change of policy. As recently as 1957-58, the East German People's Chamber still proposed the idea of a confederation of East and West Germany, a form of government which would have forestalled any central government interference with the Communist dictatorship in East Germany.[29] The new line of emphasis, to be sure, was still accompanied by references to reunification in a specifically Communist form, namely to "demilitarize" West Germany and to bring the blessings of the East German kind of government to all of Germany.[30] As recently as 1965, in fact, the DDR government was augmented with a State Secretariat of All-German Questions.

A typical example of the emerging duplicity was a talk by the SED central committee member and ambassador Gerhard Kegel in 1966 which reinterpreted the right of national self-determination exclusively as the right to establish a "socialist order" of society and denied all legitimacy to any government that derived its authority from other sources such as democratic elections. The "people of the DDR and its national German workers-and-peasants state have realized their self-determination . . . The bearers of the German right of self-determination are two rather different, independent German national states, each with a German national population of its own. There is, furthermore, the territory of West Berlin, also with a German population." Thus the "abstract idea of one German nation" was a matter of the past,[31] except for wishful thinking about making the Federal Republic more like the Communist society of the DDR.

The social background of the change from waiting for reunification to the proud assertion of East German statehood and national identity includes several heterogeneous elements. Politically, the softening of Soviet rule over the Eastern European satellite empire since 1953 had evidently shifted more autonomous weight to the DDR leadership in spite of its loyalty to the Stalinist line. The Soviet maneuvers in the 1950s to entice or cajole Bonn away from NATO and into a neutral course that might lead to reunification had obviously left East Berlin in limbo and gainsaid any definite planning for an East German future. At the same time, the development of the East German economy visibly quickened in the benign climate of the post-1956 thaw and with the benefit of the foreign trade expansion described above. The economic progress at first remained hidden behind the conspicuous success of the West German "economic miracle," which continued to drain away skilled and professional young manpower by the thousands every week. The loss of these refugees became so critical and embarrassing to East Berlin at a time when the waiting game for changing the course of Bonn had come to an end that the Communist leadership in Moscow and East Berlin decided to take action. Despite the anguished protests of the West and ominous rumblings inside the DDR, the Berlin Wall was built and the entire borderline from East to West Germany made so impenetrable with "death strips," land mines, and guard dogs that hardly anyone succeeds in escaping from the DDR anymore. Thus, the DDR regime forced its own population to focus their personal ambitions and energies on building up the DDR.

Western observers at first expected the wall to produce an internal explosion as in 1953, speculating that the great migration in the preceding years had acted as a vent syphoning off the most dissatisfied elements, thus reducing the pressures and discontents. Observers reasoned that these dissatisfied people, unable to leave the DDR, would now vent their discontent on the SED regime. There was probably such a transitional period of smoldering discontent although an efficient totalitarian state with its spy apparatus and repression has little to fear from such rumblings. In any case, there has been a noticeable settling down of opinion since the building of the wall and some of the friends of the SED

regime even claim that a new feeling of identity or "state consciousness" has emerged in the DDR. Whatever may be the answer
to that, there also were other social upheavals in the DDR at the
time, such as the determined drive for agricultural collectivization
and the long period of scarcities following it. The building of the
wall was not the only contemporary event which could explain
such internal transformations.

In the second half of the 1960s, further steps followed that
stressed the concept of the "socialist fatherland DDR." The State
Secretariat for All-German Questions was renamed. A new DDR
citizenship was proclaimed (1967) in place of the legal fiction of an
all-German citizenship. And the visitors' permits for West Berliners to East Berlin to keep in contact with their relatives there
became harder and harder to obtain. The separatist emphasis became particularly pronounced at the time of the debate over the
exchange of speakers between the SED and the West German
SPD. Some observers have suggested that it was Leonid Brezhnev
who vetoed the speaker exchange and induced the DDR leaders
instead to stress their own identity.[32]

Walter Ulbricht, in a speech of April 1966, reiterated the
confederation proposal of 1957 together with a number of further
conditions for West Germany to meet. They included the renunciation of any West German claims to *Alleinvertretung*, diplomatic
recognition of the DDR and its borders, including the Oder-Neisse
line, the rescission of the new West German legislation for a state
of emergency, a "parliamentary reform" along the lines of the
DDR, control over the West German economy and the press, and
a purge of the West German administration and military of
"militaristic, revanchist, and ultrareactionary forces."[33] As Ulbricht said later, at the fifth anniversary of the erection of the
wall, the disarmament and neutralization of the Federal Republic
were taken for granted as another precondition. The "democratic
and socialist revolution" in West Germany described earlier would
require "the cooperation of the labor unions and progressive
elements" there. The severity of these conditions left no illusions
in Bonn about East Berlin's interest in German reunification. If
anything, the nationalistic rhetoric retained alongside the emphasis on the "socialistic fatherland" hinted at the intention of
forming a "national liberation front" with the help of the then
outlawed West German Communists (KPD) rather than at bona
fide reunification in any form.[34] These conditions, of course, form

the background to later exchanges of letters and offers such as the letter of Premier Willi Stoph of May 1967 and similar memoranda.

The 1968 constitution of the DDR finally put the twofold policy toward the concept of a unified Germany into the appropriate legal formulas. The new constitution dropped the phrases of 1949 which pointed out the continued existence of one German state and nation and carried instead the following preamble:

> Guided by the responsibility to point the way into a future of peace and socialism, and in consideration of the division of Germany by American imperialism in league with West German monopoly capital, for the purpose of making West Germany an imperialistic base against socialism and in defiance of the vital interests of the nation, the people of the DDR gives itself this socialist constitution.

Other passages refer to the DDR as "a socialistic state of the German nation" and call for peaceful coexistence and normal relations between the two German states.[35]

As in the case of the Federal Republic, the role and conduct of the DDR in foreign policy is also the product of its position among the other states of the Soviet bloc and especially its close alliance with the Soviet Union. The relationship between the DDR and the Soviet Union takes place on four different levels. First and foremost, there are the close links between the two Communist parties, the CP (USSR) and the SED, which each thoroughly dominate their own respective systems and assure the political dependence and conformity of the DDR to the Soviet Union. Secondly, there are the military relations which place the DDR National People's Army (NVA) into the context of the Warsaw Pact, the thin veneer over Soviet military domination, and maintain a large army of Soviet troops in East Germany. The purpose of the Soviet military presence is both to defend East Germany against the West and to protect the SED regime against the East German people, as turned out to be necessary in the workers' uprising of 1953. A third level is composed of the many links at a state or administrative level which coordinate administrative and especially economic policies through Soviet consultants and organizations such as COMECON, the Communist Common Market. Last, but not least important, there are mass organizational contacts between such groups as the two countries' trade unions and organized youth, via cultural exchanges, and through German-Russian friendship societies.[36]

The original Eastern European treaty system of 1947-49 did not include the DDR but was aimed at a German resurgence, in analogy to the Brussels Treaty of 1947. But in 1950 the newborn DDR was admitted to COMECON and in 1955, just having won sovereignty, it became a cofounder of the Warsaw Pact of consultation and mutual assistance, the Eastern answer to the inclusion of Bonn in NATO.[37] Further multilateral agreements on nuclear research, railroad and postal cooperation, and credit, and bilateral arrangements on transportation, customs, and aviation have added to the ties with various Eastern European countries. The most important political treaty, however, was the Friendship and Assistance Treaty between the DDR and the Soviet Union of June 1964 which may have been in reaction to the new *Ostpolitik* of Bonn Foreign Minister Schröder. The DDR and Moscow probably suspected that the purpose of Bonn's wooing of Eastern European countries was the isolation and undermining of the DDR regime. Similar bilateral agreements with Poland and Czechoslovakia followed in 1967, and with other Eastern European countries since, except Rumania and Albania.

The relations between the DDR and the other Eastern European countries, however, have not been as friendly as the official pronouncements from East Berlin would lead one to assume. To begin with, there has always been a strong residue of Eastern European distrust of Germany, of which the DDR for reasons of proximity has received far more than its share. Poland and Czechoslovakia were not at all pleased to see East German rearmament and integration with the Warsaw Pact. The burgeoning economic growth and consequently more assertive posture of the DDR in Eastern Europe intensified the distrust and dislike for the DDR, at times in contrast to the relatively friendly reception for West German delegations. Rumania, of late, has been the country most at odds with the DDR, especially since the establishment of diplomatic relations between Rumania and Bonn. Partisan differences such as the East German reactions to liberalization in Prague and Budapest also introduced friction into the DDR's relationship with its neighbors. But the most hostile reaction was reserved for the East German troops who participated in the invasion of Czechoslovakia in 1968, when the Czechs often went out of their way to brand the East Germans as Nazis. It is inconceivable now that East German troops would ever be called into Czechoslovakia again, or for that matter into Poland. During the Polish food riots late in 1970, national resentment against a possible Soviet intervention was so strong as to suggest extreme reactions against any invader, but most of all against German troops.

The DDR government, on the other hand, could hardly have been expected to view with equanimity the West German overtures to Eastern Europe and especially the negotiations between Bonn and Warsaw or Moscow. Thus tension continued to smolder under the surface of Eastern bloc amity and cooperation. The DDR, it would seem, did well to rely for security mostly on the Soviet Union.

BONN'S UNEASY ALLIANCE

Adenauer's prodigious efforts and the favorable international situation had brought West Germany her sovereignty and deep involvement in the Western alliance. However, West German relations with France were less than cordial after the defeat of EDC and the British likewise seemed to view with skepticism the new Phoenix-on-the-Rhine, risen so suddenly from the ashes of World War II. In this predicament, Bonn naturally attached itself as a junior partner to Washington, even though the unequal partnership was bound to create many a disappointment.

One of the first such disappointments grew from the coincidence of the German parliamentary debates of 1955-56 over the reintroduction of German conscription with the American plans to reduce U.S. conventional forces and increase the nuclear striking capacity (Radford Plan) for purposes of deterrence. NATO was changing its function from all-around defense to the sword-and-shield concept,[38] and the hopes of Adenauer to use NATO as an instrument of his policy of strength toward the East were not supported by Washington. Adenauer began to have visions of a partial American withdrawal from Europe and of the resultant isolation of the Federal Republic in the world. But his resistance soon gave way to an attempt to seize the new opportunities, rather than accepting an unequal role in NATO for Germany. One of his junior ministers, Franz Josef Strauss, became the new West German defense minister and soon undertook to obtain some participation in the nuclear side of the sword-and-shield concept for his new West German army, the *Bundeswehr*.

The German uncertainty was compounded by the headless confusion in NATO at the time of the Hungarian revolt and Suez invasion of 1956. The Soviet move into Hungary to quell the revolt demonstrated that the post-Stalin thaw in Eastern Europe and the slogans of peaceful coexistence and detente still did not denote a Soviet willingness to abstain from the use of military force. And the Suez invasion witnessed two major NATO powers, Great Britain and France, in a neocolonialist military adventure with no prior consultation of the other NATO members whatsoever. The Federal Republic felt more exposed than any other country to attack from the East. Bonn felt more insecure because of its recent reemergence from the doghouse of Europe and also therefore felt more isolated and abandoned. To make these feelings more acute, there were several proposals under debate in Europe and America to effectuate a relaxation of tensions in Europe by nuclear disengagement. The most prominent of these plans was that of Polish Foreign Minister Adam Rapacky, who in 1957 proposed a central European area composed of Poland and the two Germanies which was to be kept free of nuclear weapons of any kind. George F. Kennan and other prominent Americans had similar ideas and so, of course, did the leaders of the Soviet Union and some NATO circles. But the West German leadership saw in these proposals yet another attempt to neutralize their country and cut it off from the Western alliance.[39]

The nuclear armament issue became the subject of an extraordinary campaign by Adenauer's internal opposition prior to the 1957 elections. The SPD and the trade unions as well as pacifistic groups escalated their agitation "against atomic death" in a very effective manner including massive demonstrations with signs showing, among other things, a dinosaur with the caption: "Too much armor—too little brains: extinct." They also attempted to hold plebiscites on the question, although the courts tended to hold these unconstitutional. The Adenauer government campaigned instead with the defensive slogan "no experiments." Adenauer was, indeed, on the defensive at home and abroad. His spectacular postwar career was past its peak and his famous capacity for adaptation to changing circumstances seemed to have left him, with one notable exception: his discovery of Gaullism.

Actually, there were a good many hopeful signs for some of his long-term objectives in spite of the seeming reverses. The European Economic Community (EEC), or Common Market, went into effect in 1957, promising to join and interlace the economies of France, Italy, and the Benelux countries with the burgeoning West German economy over a period of a dozen years. Bonn had perhaps greater political expectations for the EEC than did the other members. Adenauer even expressed the hope that German reunification might come out of this step toward the Europeanization of the German question. But the gradual waning of bipolarity and the reemergence of national interests throughout Europe, if not the world, tended to give a specious character to this line of reasoning. Nevertheless, the new momentum of the "relaunching" of European integration was a great help in the final solution of the Saar question when the French agreed, simultaneously with the EEC negotiations, to allow the Saarlanders to rejoin West Germany with some safeguards for French interests.

Adenauer's progress toward German reunification was, by all accounts, a dismal failure. He is often accused of not having advanced reunification for selfish, partisan reasons or for lack of patriotism. With the benefit of hindsight, it is indeed easy to see that his policy of German integration with the West automatically rendered unlikely a reconciliation with the East. It would not be too far amiss to say that Adenauer de facto effected a final peace settlement with the West, but that the high cost of this settlement, considering the German circumstances in 1949, made it quite impossible at the time to pay off the East as well. It is, of course, not possible to say with confidence that a similar settlement with the East rather than the West could have been carried out without sacrificing once and for all German internal freedom and external autonomy, given the Soviet intent to add all of Germany to the Communist orbit.

Whatever may have been the consequences of an alternative course of action, there can be no doubt about Adenauer's assessment of the situation at the time of Khrushchev's offer of reunification and all-German elections at Geneva in 1955 and Adenauer's subsequent invitation to visit Moscow. On his return from Geneva, Khrushchev stopped off in East Berlin and reportedly said to the East German leaders in a blunt manner that under no circumstances would there be elections in the Western sense. Adenauer in turn had never taken the offer very seriously but feared that the Soviets would try to pillory him as an archenemy of the relaxation of tensions in Europe. He started his journey with no thought of attempting to negotiate substantive West German concessions or of achieving even the beginning of a settlement with the East. German reunification, he announced, was the responsibility of the victorious powers and their representatives at Geneva to arrange, not his. Any rapprochement with the Soviets, and even any "national" autonomy or neutralism exhibited by the Federal Republic, he feared, would run the danger of alienating his Western allies. Thus the visit in Moscow only produced the establishment of diplomatic relations between the two countries and the Soviet assurance that the surviving 10,000 German prisoners of war still languishing in Soviet camps would be permitted to go home, ten years after the end of the war. No one could accuse Adenauer of having staged another Rapallo.

And, once more, the DDR got the worst of the bargain. Although Soviet policy now increasingly gave "the state that no one wanted" a chance to live and develop, Bonn insisted on pretending it did not exist. Adenauer's foreign policy advisers, Walter Hallstein, Wilhelm Grewe, and von Brentano, the foreign secretary, had already taken a dim view of his Moscow visit. Now they persuaded the West German government to adopt the Hallstein Doctrine, presumably to avoid the awkwardness of having two German embassies in foreign capitals, each claiming to be the sole representative of Germany. The Soviet Union and its satellites, of course, had already recognized the DDR and the Western powers were unlikely to do so for the time being. The chief objects of this ban, then, were neutral governments of the Third World which might prize trade relations with Bonn higher than with the DDR. It amounted indeed to a formidable barrier to the recognition of the DDR by the developing countries while it lasted. The Communist states of Eastern Europe, on the other hand, had recognized the DDR anyway and thus Bonn was kept from establishing relations with them. Bonn had entered a dead-end street of its own making. However, this state of affairs complemented all too well Adenauer's aversion to any contacts with the East such as his internal opponents in the SPD and FDP were advocating at the time.

Adenauer's stubborn perseverance against all disengagement plans began to bear fruit by 1957 in a strong NATO alliance with nuclear warheads and middle-range rocket launching pads all over the Federal Republic. But the Soviets had not been kept napping either. Their Sputnik rocket of late 1957 signified a delivery capacity for intercontinental missiles almost on a par with that of the United States. Instead of the overwhelming presence of the United States in Europe, there now was a mere standoff between the two giants while various national centers began to stir and to pursue their own separate interests.

The most spectacular development of this kind was the birth of the Fifth Republic of France in 1958 and the reemergence of its towering president, Charles de Gaulle. Adenauer hastened to establish a good personal relationship with the new French president even though he was aware of the latter's nationalistic attitude toward European integration and NATO. He hoped to stress instead their common fear of the extra-European superpowers, in his case especially of the Soviet Union. The Soviets on their part had once more stepped up their pressure on Berlin, possibly to test the new French president whom they expected to return to the old Franco-Russian understanding of the days before 1917, at the expense of Germany. In November 1958, Khrushchev addressed an ultimatum to the Western powers to negotiate a new Berlin statute within six months, or else he would simply turn over the authority of the Soviet Union there to the DDR, which occasionally voiced claims not only to East Berlin but to West Berlin as well.

Under the challenge from the East, Adenauer was once more at his best, counseling the Allies not to yield and to avoid any permanent settlement in Berlin. He also sought contact with the Soviet Union, offering among other things increased trade. In January 1959, Khrushchev presented the draft of a German peace treaty in which the Soviet policy toward the Germanies showed a further progression from assuming the presence of two German states to adding a third, Berlin. At this point, the United States and Great Britain simply ignored Adenauer's advice and sought extended discussions with the Soviets. An estrangement set in between Bonn and Washington which henceforth drove Adenauer more and more into the arms of de Gaulle. The grave illness and death of John Foster Dulles in April-May 1959 severed the last personal link on which Adenauer had relied in Washington.

Khrushchev's ultimatum laid bare the relative weakness of the Western alliance in comparison with the new strength of the Soviet orbit. British Foreign Secretary Selwyn Lloyd went to Moscow to discuss plans of disengagement. The general position of the Western Allies seemed content with securing West Germany and West Berlin, rather than pursuing German reunification. Even

Adenauer seemed to give in to the inevitable when he began to say that the relaxation of East-West tensions did not need to be tied to a solution of the German problem. The very nature of the nuclear standoff made it nearly impossible for the West to meet a local threat or fight the Communist "salami tactics" (i.e., one slice at a time) over Berlin.

The Geneva conference of foreign ministers of 1959 began with a cautious reiteration of the Western proposals of 1955 by the new U.S. secretary of state, Christian Herter. They were promptly rejected by Soviet Foreign Minister Andrei Gromyko, who was no longer interested in linking German reunification with a settlement. The West still attempted to come to an understanding at least on Berlin and then the conference adjourned *sine die*, having accomplished nothing. With this last defense of the confused status quo, the activities of the four powers to settle the German question came to an untimely end, which once again dropped the problem into Adenauer's unwilling lap.

BONN BETWEEN WASHINGTON & PARIS

The Soviet challenge had found the Anglo-American allies wanting. Only de Gaulle gave Adenauer the support he desired. There consequently ensued a close relationship between the two statesmen in which the French president turned out to be stronger and more capable of manipulating Bonn for his own designs than vice versa. Adenauer and his hard-liners evidently never grasped the fundamental differences between de Gaulle's hard line on Berlin and their own. France had no desire to see Germany reunified. It welcomed the opportunity to alienate German affections from the Anglo-Americans and to dismantle the same NATO alliance which Adenauer had so far considered the only real security for West Germany. France was in favor of European integration, but only insofar as it was profitable for France and could be used to run off and keep out the American interlopers. The French supported a tough stand in Berlin but chiefly to discourage some of the new West German voices that called for direct negotiations with the East. And Adenauer believed de Gaulle when the latter said that America would be unlikely to live up to its assurances of protection in any real crisis under the conditions of a nuclear standoff. Why should Washington risk American cities over the question of access to Berlin? Would it not be safer to rely on a European nuclear deterrence such as the "force de frappe" planned by General de Gaulle, which would at least be next door rather than thousands of miles away?

The failure of Camp David and of the Paris summit meeting of 1960 seemed to prove the French and West German hard-liners right. And yet de Gaulle's enmity for the supranational features of EEC and NATO eventually alarmed even Konrad Adenauer, who unexpectedly found himself groping for the role of a mediator between the diverging trends of European integration, Gaullist plans for a European "third force," and American global policies toward the Soviet Union. The major changes in President John F. Kennedy's new defense posture of "flexible response" (in contrast to Dulles' emphasis on massive nuclear retaliation) finally brought the confrontation with the plans for a French "force de frappe" to a head. The United States in 1962 withdrew its intermediate range ballistic missiles from various European countries, replacing them with Polaris submarines, which further tended to centralize nuclear control in American hands at the precise moment many NATO members were clamoring for the decentralization of the nuclear command. And Washington furthermore urged the Europeans to build up their conventional strength for all eventualities in order to avoid the awesome choice between capitulating in local conflicts such as the lingering Berlin crisis or all-out nuclear confrontation. The logic of "flexible response" could not but raise European doubts about American reliability as well. What if the United States chose not to strike the decisive blow when the chips were down? Was a build-up of conventional defense not an open invitation for Soviet aggression?[40] The common aversion to "that brash young man," John F. Kennedy, again united the two old men governing West Germany and France as late as 1961.

The Soviet ultimatum of 1958 over Berlin had been neither carried out nor entirely dropped. The DDR carried on the war of nerves with continual harassment of the Western access roads to the city and of other vulnerable aspects of the life of West Berlin. The Soviet government sent another note to Bonn in February 1961, calling for a peace treaty and proposing to make Berlin "a free city," while hinting that the four great powers would come to an agreement on Berlin anyway with or without the cooperation of Bonn. President Kennedy met Khrushchev in Vienna in June 1961, and was handed a Soviet memorandum which unmistakably warmed over the ultimatum of 1958. Two months later, the hasty construction of the Berlin Wall between East and West Berlin presented the Western Allies with yet another *fait accompli* which tended to give irrevocable form to the status quo in Central Europe.

The Communist move followed immediately upon a televised speech of the American president which announced a drastic increase in American military preparedness and hinted at the American will to defend the military presence in West Berlin. The North Atlantic Council responded with a statement setting forth the essentials the West intended to defend there: the Western military presence, free access, and the indispensable economic links between the city and Western Germany, of which Berlin is not de jure a part. Thus, the building of the wall constituted a direct challenge counterpointed by the Soviet and American tanks rolling up and facing each other muzzle to muzzle at the Friedrichstrasse crossing, although the three essentials had not been violated and token rights of access by Western military to East Berlin were maintained. The building of the wall in itself guaranteed the viability of the DDR by choking off the exodus of refugees to the West. Needless to stress, it shocked and alarmed the Germans on both sides of it far more deeply than it did the Western Allies, who accepted it reluctantly and with token protests. They were relieved that the test of strength between East and West was, for the time being, over. The Germans were deeply angered by what appeared like collusion among the great powers at their expense.

The Berlin crisis of 1961 also coincided with the West German federal elections which witnessed the nadir of Adenauer's postwar career. His party was deeply divided and came close to ousting him after it had lost its majority in the Bundestag. Only his political skill and the reluctance of his rivals to play Brutus to the octogenarian Caesar saved him for two last years in office during which he further moved under the spell of the great Frenchman.[41] Oddly enough, his opposition parties, the SPD and FDP, had by this time abandoned much of their opposition to his original foreign policy, and especially the SPD had come to embrace what it had fought for a decade and a half. The real opposition to Kennedy's reorganization of the faltering Western alliance, and thereby to Adenauer's earlier commitment, came precisely from de Gaulle who saw in the multipolar softening of the East-West balance a unique opportunity for France to assert its historic interests and autonomy in spite of all the European and Atlantic ties that had developed over the years.

As he went about carrying his policies to fruition, de Gaulle was by no means merely obstreperous and destructive, as the American press tended to see him. He earnestly set out to reform NATO by proposing a tripartite council of France and the United States together with Great Britain, which had long enjoyed the benefits of its "special relationship" with the United States. France's expectations of American assistance with its nuclear development and with the liquidation of the rest of its colonial empire were disappointed. When Kennedy attempted to tighten the reins of the Western alliance in American hands, then, it was quite logical that France would resist and that it would seek to broaden its leverage wherever it could, but most of all in Europe. West Germany in its momentary disorientation in the Western alliance was a most likely ally, even though it had been a fear of West German objections, among other things, which made Washington shy away from de Gaulle's tripartite proposal.[42]

Inside Adenauer's CDU/CSU, there were now also new forces who welcomed the close entente between West Germany and France and envisioned the emergence of a Franco-German-led, continental European great power which would balance the weight of the United States in NATO. But this new European power center was to develop not from the Common Market or other supranational institutions but from the direct political cooperation of the governments. It was to be not a supranational European federation, as the European federalists had hoped to create, but a "Europe of fatherlands," which would cooperate politically among the governments of sovereign states.

The dreams of German "Gaullists" such as the Baron von Guttenberg[43] outran by far the willingness of de Gaulle to consent to any increased European cooperation and especially to the admission of Great Britain to the EEC. European federalists such as Walter Hallstein, however, were not especially keen on British admission either as long as Great Britain showed interest only in the economic advantages of membership, and not in the prospects of political integration.[44] On the other hand, free traders such as Foreign Minister Schröder and the architect of the West German "economic miracle," Ludwig Erhard, were avidly for the inclusion of Great Britain in the EEC because they favored a reduction of the protective trade barriers which had grown up around the Little

Europe of the Six—France, West Germany, Italy, and the Benelux countries.

It was a supreme irony of history that Adenauer's idealistic hopes for a united Europe thus were aborted with his own cooperation. A summit conference of the chief executives of the EEC countries in Bonn still made believe that everything was in motion toward European integration as of July 1961, when even de Gaulle's oracular pronouncements created the impression that he favored the election of a European parliament and British admission to the EEC. Half a year later France changed its tune, and de Gaulle in a televised speech held up the "enduring reality" of the European nation-states over and above supranational ideology and technology. He indicated as the purpose of his policy "breaking of the net of earlier agreements which assign to us the vote of an extinct nation integrated in a larger whole." In mid-1962, after de Gaulle had shown his true colors and after Adenauer's relations with Washington had reached a nadir, *der Alte* paid an official visit to de Gaulle, hoping to find there the support against Soviet pressure which the Americans had denied him. De Gaulle responded with a visit to Germany which turned into a campaign of popular acclaim, and resulted in the Franco-German Friendship Treaty of 1963, a few months before Adenauer's resignation from office.

The grand old man of West German postwar politics had started out with the bold assumption in 1945 that the old Germany and the old Europe of quarreling nation-states had died. A new European community superseding the national identities of his youth and middle age was to ease also the identity problems of the West German rump state. West Germany's salvation lay in European integration and in never again having a national politics of its own. The Gaullist challenge, however, was clearly a challenge to pursue the "national interest" of Germany, or at least of the Federal Republic. It was this challenge of resurgent nationalism, not the feeble French substitute for American protection, which eventually got the better of the old man's policies.

Notes

1 The German admission had already been tied to a qualifying clause regarding Article 16, the enforcement paragraph of the League of Nations covenant. Germany wanted no part of any enforcement action against the Soviet Union.

2　　See especially Gerhard L. Weinberg, *The Foreign Policy of Hitler's Germany* (Chicago: University of Chicago Press, 1970), chap. 2, and the sources cited there.

3　　No such intervention occurred, of course, but the German military nevertheless was instructed to prepare mobilization plans for such an eventuality during the early years.

4　　Although the close economic and military relations of the Weimar years had turned into a noticeable cooling off between Germany and Russia, punctuated by provocative incidents on the German side, Hitler did not then intend to go directly after Russian territory, as he and other Nazis clearly hoped to do at a future point.

5　　The nationality issues included not only Danzig, but also the Memel Germans in Lithuania and the Ukrainian nationalists who mistakenly expected him to help them against the Poles. More likely, he might have traded their Ukraine upon conquest for the Polish Corridor. His reversal of the traditional German alliance with Russia against the Poles alone pointed significantly into a future German conquest of Eastern Europe.

6　　See Weinberg, *Foreign Policy of Hitler's Germany*, pp. 241-45, and the sources cited there.

7　　As the growing literature on the Nazi economy has demonstrated, the economy never reached a fully mobilized state until the last years of the war. Hitler instead preferred to create merely a substantial economic headstart and, on this basis, to knock out the enemy with a *Blitzkrieg* rather than with a prolonged war of matériel.

8　　In April 1939, Fascist Italy again joined the fray and seized Albania. By this time the Western powers had finally dropped their policies of appeasement and belatedly stepped up their armaments within the context of a new antiaggression front.

9　　Parts of eastern France and the Benelux countries were on the list of areas for annexation which frequently appeared in Hitler's table conversations and on other occasions.

10　　See also this writer's *Origin of the West German Republic* (New York: Oxford University Press, 1963), pp. 4-8. Some of the plans for industrial disarmament, stripping of plants, decartelization, and international controls over German industry were carried out.

11　　Waldemar Besson, *Die Aussenpolitik der Bundesrepublik* (Munich: Piper, 1970), p. 55.

12　　On the different foreign policy currents of the period in question, see especially Hans-Peter Schwarz, *Vom Reich zur Bundesrepublik* (Neuwied: Luchterhand, 1966), pp. 501 ff.

13　　It was as bitter to the Germans as to the other Europeans. An extraordinary amount of political opposition and street demonstrations in West Germany concentrated their efforts on defeating all plans for rearmament.

14　　This approach had first been taken in the Declaration on Germany of March 1950 by the Adenauer government. In a note of September 1951, Grotewohl even accepted the call for free elections but neither Adenauer nor the Allies believed his offer was more than a delaying maneuver. The offer was later withdrawn when a UN Commission undertook to investigate the conditions for free elections in East Germany. Why should the Communists have surrendered their hold on power?

15 He stressed the weak economic foundation for maintenance of a German army and the need for economic integration with the Western Allies. There was also the question of Communist East Germany inside the proposed new state.

16 The Allies responded to the Soviet vote, at Adenauer's urging, that prior to any steps for reunification, the "social preconditions for free elections would have to be created" and that the elections would have to take place under UN supervision. These conditions were unacceptable to the Soviets.

17 The opposition of the SPD was presently reinforced by bourgeois spokesmen such as FDP leader Reinhold Maier and historian and journalist Paul Sethe, who both would have preferred a neutralized, reunified Germany.

18 The domestic political struggle over the EDC and the revision of the status of Germany was also fought before the Federal Constitutional Court, which was called upon to rule on the constitutionality of the treaties and on whether the cabinet needed a simple or a constitution-changing two-thirds majority of the Bundestag to pass them.

19 The electoral victory in turn enabled Adenauer to remove the last constitutional doubts by changing the relevant clauses of the Basic Law with the two-thirds majority of his new coalition government.

20 The Soviet Union continued in 1954 and 1955 to address notes with further concessions to the Allies, including Soviet acceptance of international supervision of all-German elections, if only West German rearmament were stopped. The Allies paid no heed, evidently considering the Soviet moves a tactical maneuver to delay matters.

21 See, for example, the account of occupation violence by Zoltan Michael Szaz, *Germany's Eastern Frontiers* (New York: Regnery, 1960), pp. 92-94 and the sources cited there.

22 *JOM 1947-1955*, p. 146.

23 For details, see especially J. P. Nettl, *The Eastern Zone and Soviet Policy in Germany, 1945-1950* (New York: Oxford University Press, 1951), and Wolfgang Stolper, *The Structure of the East German Economy* (Cambridge, Mass.: Harvard University Press, 1960).

24 There has been a growing literature in recent years which was surveyed most recently in a paper on DDR foreign policy presented by Manfred Rexin of the Free University of Berlin to the Conference Group on German Politics at the International Political Science Association Congress in Munich in 1970.

25 See, for example, Peter Florin, *Deutsche Aussenpolitik, zur Aussenpolitik der souveränen sozialistischen DDR* (East Berlin: Dietz Verlag, 1967), pp. 67-68.

26   Even where the DDR had only a trade mission, its functions and diplomatic privileges were often expanded so as to blur the distinction between official and unofficial diplomatic contacts. Following the Basic Treaty of 1972 between the two Germanies, the ice was finally broken and, one after the other, the Western NATO powers dropped their reserve and, except for the U.S., granted diplomatic recognition.

27   *Dokumente der SED* (Berlin, 1950), vol. 2, pp. 268 and 327-55.

28   Unlike the Federal Republic, the DDR had a foreign policy section in its Council of Ministers from the beginning. It was headed by Georg Dertinger until his arrest in 1953, when first Ackermann and then the better known Lothar Bolz succeeded him. Bolz was an old Communist who belonged to the NDP, one of the "bourgeois parties" of the multiparty façade of the DDR.

29   Ulbricht also presented a number of prior conditions which West Germany would have to meet in order to obtain a confederate reunification. They included the replacement of West German labor codetermination with the East German "workers' rights" and "workers' controls" in large enterprises, the liquidation of private monopolies, a plebiscite on the nationalization of key industries, the replacement of the "privileges of owners of large estates" with the "democratic rights of worker-peasants," expropriation of all holdings above a certain acreage (100 hectares), and "democratic school reform."

30   See especially the "national document" of June 17, 1962, the SED party program of January 21, 1963, and the Manifesto to the German People and the World of May 5, 1965.

31   See *Neues Deutschland*, January 16, 1966. This was the culmination of a brief wave of nationalistic propaganda in the DDR, which expressed itself in an East German claim of *Alleinvertretung*, a "national mission" of the DDR to forge ahead into the socialist future of Germany.

32   See, for example, Fritz Kopp, "Doppelgleisige Deutschlandpolitik der SED auch nach April 1966," *Deutsche Fragen* 12 (July 1967), pp. 121-25.

33   *Neues Deutschland*, April 22, 1966. The seventh SED convention in 1967 reiterated the demand that West Germany would have to become "socialistic" before a confederation was feasible.

34   See also the formulation of Walter Ulbricht in *Neues Deutschland*, April 18, 1967, that German reunification was possible only when the working-classes of DDR and Federal Republic had joined in united action. See also *Neues Deutschland*, April 29, 1967; May 3, 1967; and December 20, 1967.

35   For the text, see *Neues Deutschland*, March 27, 1968.

36   See also Florin, *Deutsche Aussenpolitik*, pp. 35-37, who goes to great lengths in tracing German-Russian ties back to the nineteenth century and to the treaties of Rapallo and Berlin, a remarkable reference to historical traditions from such an antihistorical source.

37   According to Florin, *Deutsche Aussenpolitik*, pp. 46-47, the DDR retained the right to drop out of the Warsaw Pact at will, unlike the Federal Republic with regard to NATO. However, the consequences of the Hun-

garian attempt to leave the pact in 1956 and similar considerations with respect to Czechoslovakia and Rumania in recent years make this contention most questionable.

38   This concept assigns only a holding or trip wire action to the conventional troops of the alliance until the nuclear sword can be applied to an aggressor.

39   For a full discussion of these fears and sentiments, see especially Besson, *Die Aussenpolitik*, pp. 203-8.

40   See also Ernst Majonica, *Deutsche Aussenpolitik*, 2d ed. (Stuttgart: Kohlhammer, 1965), p. 233, and the discussion in Henry A. Kissinger, *The Troubled Partnership* (Garden City, N.Y.: Doubleday, 1965), pp. 107-25.

41   For details, see this writer's "Equilibrium, Structure of Interests, and Leadership: Adenauer's Survival as Chancellor," *American Political Science Review* 56:3 (September 1962), pp. 634-50.

42   See also Kissinger, *The Troubled Partnership*, pp. 41-65.

43   See especially Karl Theodor von Guttenberg, *Wenn der Westen will*, 2d ed. (Stuttgart: Seewald, 1964) and Franz Josef Strauss, *Herausforderung und Antwort* (Stuttgart: Seewald, 1968).

44   See also Ruediger Altmann, *Das deutsche Risiko* (Stuttgart: Seewald, 1962), p. 64 ff.

CHAPTER 4

A New Departure

The end of the Adenauer era, as could be expected, did not immediately produce a new foreign policy orientation. The postures and commitments of this era were too deeply rooted for such a sudden death. At the same time, there had been attempts at new departures all through the Adenauer era and especially during his declining years. The SPD in its opposition, of course, had offered alternatives and criticisms all along although they tended to be halfhearted and frequently undistinguished. Paradoxically, the SPD leadership first had to free itself of its old shibboleths of opposition and to take over Adenauer's policies of European and Atlantic integration and defense before it could come up with promising innovations and alternatives. The landmark of this process was the Bundestag speech of Herbert Wehner of June 30, 1960, in which he dropped the reservations the SPD had hitherto expressed about Adenauer's policies[1] and turned the eyes of his party to the future. The coalition partner of Adenauer's CDU, the FDP, had already been holding out for a more nationalistic departure in foreign policy under such leaders as Reinhold Maier, Karl Pfleiderer, and Thomas Dehler since the mid-fifties. More nationalism inevitably meant contacts with the Soviet Union and other Eastern European states and attempts to bargain for German reunification in one form or another.

Germany's foreign policy under Bismarck and Stresemann had always looked both ways, East and West, much as the two-faced Roman god, Janus. Adenauer had resolutely confined his gaze to the West and turned his back on the East, knowing all too well what he would find there. His successors and opponents, however, began to peek, even to stare toward and to importune the East, safe in the knowledge that, owing to his efforts, they could turn their back to the West without fear.

THE PARADOXES OF TRANSITION

After the electoral defeat of 1961, the last Adenauer cabinet also exhibited its share of internal dissent on foreign policy, especially with the replacement of Foreign Minister von Brentano by Gerhard Schröder. Brentano was, like Hallstein, an arch-supporter of European union and a rigid, Catholic anti-Communist in his foreign policy. Schröder, a Protestant, by comparison sought new departures of West German foreign policy somewhere between the goal of the integration of the Federal Republic into a European union and the pursuit of German reunification at any price. Unlike both Adenauer and the fervent advocates of reunification, Schröder evidently thought in terms of a recognizable "national" identity and interest of the Federal Republic and sought to provide for its future even if neither European nor German unification would ever come to pass. He had no intention to dissolve any of the European and Atlantic ties that had served West Germany so well in her recovery. But he would pursue them for their present, pragmatic uses rather than for ideological or nostalgic reasons.

Another bellwether of the new direction of West German foreign policy was the remarkable career of the West German ambassador to Moscow, Hans Kroll, in the early sixties. Bonn's purposely one-sided adherence to the West had condemned the Moscow embassy to inactivity. But this was not Kroll's temperament nor was it his interpretation of his mission in the Soviet Union. Remembering the turnabout at Rapallo in the 1920s, he managed to establish a good personal relationship with Nikita Khrushchev. Just as the Soviet pressure was heaviest and the relations between Bonn and Washington were poorest, late in 1961, Kroll broached some of his own views to the Soviet premier, to the consternation of the Western Allies. The ambassador suggested that Bonn could recognize the DDR de facto, though not de jure, in exchange for Soviet guarantees of the status of Berlin. Khrushchev promptly responded with a confidential conciliatory memorandum on Germany to Adenauer which proposed direct negotiations, since none of the Western Allies, it was averred, was likely to favor a settlement in the interest of the Germans. *Der Alte* probably relished the competition between East and West for West German cooperation, although he abstained from premature responses, while FDP leaders and Bundestag President Eugen Gerstenmaier (CDU) were eagerly calling for further contacts with Moscow. Only Schröder strongly opposed the venture for fear of upsetting his current efforts at improving German-American relations. Nevertheless Kroll's proposals went under in a maze of intrigues and false press commentary in the Springer press, which led to his retirement in 1962.[2]

Foreign Minister Schröder indeed made some headway in persuading Washington not to jeopardize the security of Berlin by making its disposition a part of the general German questions under debate between Moscow and Washington. Instead, as Adenauer's declaration of policy in November 1961 proposed, a treaty renouncing the use of force between Bonn and Moscow could demonstrate at least the good intentions of West Germany, which Moscow and East Berlin never tired of accusing of warmongering and belligerent imperialism. Otherwise, the declaration contained nearly all the old Adenauer formulas—about reunification and nonrecognition of the DDR—with the American blessing that Adenauer had once more brought back from Washington. In spite of all the apparent changes, everything still seemed to be the same. But within a few months, there was already new cause for friction between Bonn and Washington.[3] The seeming unity of foreign policy making in Bonn once more fell apart into antagonistic camps, chiefly Adenauer versus Schröder and the FDP in the government and the SPD in the opposition. The latter camp soon emerged as the most likely collaborator with Washington's plans for an East-West settlement and the relaxation of international tensions.

The new Atlanticist camp around Schröder, the FDP, and the SPD also turned out to be the basis of many West German politicians' angry reaction to de Gaulle's rude rejection of British admission to the EEC in January 1963. The new foreign policy leaders had no understanding for de Gaulle's reaction to Britain's earlier decision not to develop its own nuclear forces[4] and refused to separate the Franco-German Friendship Treaty from the chief object of their anger. Adenauer's days as chancellor were obviously numbered. The powerful Gaullist, Franz Josef Strauss, had just been thoroughly discredited and ousted as defense minister because of his high-handed conduct in the affair involving the news magazine *Der Spiegel*. In the end, the Friendship Treaty was ratified by the Bundestag only after a preamble had been added which brought it into harmony with NATO and the EEC. The final ratification took place with sentimental speeches about Franco-German reconciliation and the crowning of the lifetime efforts of the departing chancellor, when in reality the ratification denoted neither de Gaulle's nor Adenauer's original intent, nor was it really an outgrowth of Adenauer's earlier policies. More telling perhaps was the ensuing battle over the West German signature of the Nuclear Test Ban Treaty, which once more pitted the German Gaullists against Schröder and his foreign policy allies. De Gaulle refused to sign what he considered an attempt to cripple the development of a French or European nuclear force. Schröder, however, feared that Bonn would become isolated if it did not sign and he won out.

But the paradoxes of the transition continued through the years 1964 and 1965, even though Schröder's hand was strengthened by Adenauer's successor, Chancellor Ludwig Erhard. De Gaulle's insistence that the bilateral cooperation intended by the Friendship Treaty be in fact consummated triggered bitter struggles among the West German Christian Democrats. Strauss and the other Gaullists, including ex-Chancellor Adenauer, bitterly attacked Erhard and Schröder, the Atlanticists, and only the approaching elections of 1965 persuaded them to bury the hatchet. The personal rivalries between Adenauer and Erhard and between their would-be successors Strauss and Schröder helped to build up the issues of Gaullism beyond their true significance. The German Gaullists by no means shared many of de Gaulle's views on the German question, such as on reunification, or on anti-Communism toward the Soviet Union. Hence Erhard's electoral success in 1965 for a while silenced these controversies.

THE BEGINNINGS OF *OSTPOLITIK*
UNDER SCHRØDER & KIESINGER

Adenauer's policy toward the East had been an encapsulated refusal to enter contacts or negotiate a settlement. Schröder, on the other hand, began to advocate an improvement of West German relations with Eastern Europe as early as 1962. The final settlement of Germany's World War II legacy in the East, indeed, was a Gordian knot that had resisted Adenauer's "policy of strength." As it turned out, it failed to yield also to the blandishments of Schröder's *Ostpolitik* and later to the *Ostpolitik* of Willy Brandt, the foreign minister of the grand coalition (1966-69). Only the *Ostpolitik* of Chancellor Willy Brandt (1969-) has shown any real breakthrough so far, and even there the indications of a successful consummation still remain to be seen.

Schröder's new *Ostpolitik* was a modest attempt to establish trade relations with Eastern Europe without automatically negating the Hallstein Doctrine of diplomatic nonrecognition of states that had recognized the DDR. West German trade missions or treaties were indeed established after some initial difficulties[5] in Poland, Hungary and Rumania (1963), and a year later with Bulgaria, though not with Czechoslovakia. These trade contacts involved a certain duplicity toward the common organs of EEC in Brussels, which were not consulted, although Bonn strove to avoid formal violations of its obligations under the EEC treaty. Schröder hoped thereby to contribute his share to the relaxation of international tensions, although he had to endure much domestic criticism from the hard-liners of old. De Gaulle, who had long ago blazed a trail of contacts with Eastern European countries and Washington too, favored Schröder's new departures, which promised to bridge over the irremediable chasms of European realities. The government also had its allies, such as the FDP leadership and important academic and journalistic opinion leaders. Its initiatives had already been preceded by prominent Protestant and Catholic spokesmen who had advocated recognition of the Oder-Neisse line and other gestures of German reconciliation with Eastern Europe.

It was rather odd that Schröder's domestic critics should accuse him of confirming and accepting the status quo in Eastern Europe, which they still hoped to be able to revise. The Soviet Union at the same time was alarmed at how he was threatening by his *Ostpolitik* to change the status quo of twenty years of Soviet dominance and monopolistic control. Neither Moscow nor the DDR overlooked the significance of the omission of East Germany from Schröder's policy of conciliation, which gave his *Ostpolitik* the appearance of a sly maneuver to isolate the DDR. The telltale answer of East Germany to the *Ostpolitik* was the

Mutual Assistance and Friendship Treaty of 1964 between the DDR and the Soviet Union.

Schröder was not discouraged and proceeded to the next logical step, an attempted rapprochement with Moscow, beginning with a visit of Khrushchev's son-in-law Adzhubei to Bonn. Unfortunately, Khrushchev's fall put an end to this promising start. New efforts at strengthening the EEC were frustrated by de Gaulle's one-sided preoccupation with French agrarian interests. In mid-1965, France even withdrew from the EEC Council of Ministers and stipulated the following conditions for her return: (1) concessions to French agriculture, (2) an end to the supranational ambitions of the EEC Commission in Brussels, and most consequential, (3) the retention of the French veto in the EEC.[6] Nine months later, after his demands had been met, de Gaulle pulled his representatives out of NATO, withdrew French troops from the organization, and told NATO headquarters to leave France. Then he went on a state visit to Moscow, seemingly free of Western ties, while the Federal Republic had to remain tied to Washington for better or for worse.

Schröder's *Ostpolitik* and his other attempts at a reorientation of West German foreign policy in the end got no further than signifying a reorientation toward the forgotten or frozen Eastern aspects of the concrete interests of the Federal Republic. Most telling perhaps was the Peace Memorandum of 1966 in which Bonn proposed to exchange renunciation-of-force agreements with all the Eastern states save the DDR and to enter agreements to freeze the nuclear potential of Central Europe at present levels. This memorandum pointed the way for Schröder's successors.

Erhard's chancellorship came to an untimely end in 1966 when he was overthrown for various domestic failures. He also had some foreign policy crises in his record which further underlined his popular image of weak leadership. One of these was the Middle East crisis over the supply of German arms to Israel in 1964-65, which had led to Egyptian protests. The foreign aid policies of Bonn had always had a strong component of competition with the DDR. Now the Soviet Union made its economic support for Egypt dependent on better Egyptian relations with the DDR. President Nasser thereupon invited Walter Ulbricht for an official visit to Cairo and, upon West German protests, threatened to recognize the DDR unless the arms shipments to Israel were terminated. There ensued an agonizing debate in Bonn, which since 1952 had already paid Israel some 3.5 billion marks in restitution for the Nazi crimes against the Jews. Erhard and even Hallstein were of a mind to call the Egyptian bluff. But in the end Bonn capitulated ignominiously to Nasser, and the whole Third World took notice of how easily the Hallstein Doctrine could be used to blackmail West Germany. Israeli Prime Minister Levi Eshkol in turn reacted with anger and the pomp and circumstances of the Ulbricht visit to Cairo deepened the West German embarrassment. Bonn was sorely tempted to break off relations with Cairo and finally decided instead to take the long-delayed step of establishing diplomatic relations with Israel, whereupon nearly all Arab states withdrew their recognition of Bonn without, however, recognizing East Berlin. The DDR was probably the only actor in this charade who had any reason to feel a sense of triumph.

While Chancellor Erhard was caught in a deepening crisis of authority, the opposition SPD waxed strong in a foreign policy sally of its own, the plan for public debates between SPD speakers and representatives of the East German SED. The latter had originally proposed discussions at the forthcoming SPD convention and was soon persuaded to cooperate in two such debates, one in Essen, West Germany, and the other in Karl-Marx-Stadt (Chemnitz) in the DDR. Herbert Wehner (SPD), who had also played a role at the conception of the Peace Memorandum, intended to take over the initiative in the intra-German negotiations, now that all hopes for an Allied solution had become a matter of the past. The speakers' exchange never came off because the East Germans had second thoughts, but one by one the other West German parties fell in line. FDP chairman Erich Mende eagerly reiterated his plea for all-German technical commissions and endorsed diplomatic relations with Eastern Europe. And even CDU parliamentary leader Rainer Barzel eventually made a statement endorsing the technical commissions and opining hazardously that the economic and military interests of the Soviets in the DDR could also be maintained in a reunified Germany. This latter suggestion met an icy reception from Chancellor Erhard in Bonn, who for obvious reasons refused to give it the official imprimatur. The idea of agreeing in advance to stationing Soviet troops in a reunified Germany was indeed rather startling, to say the least. Still, the ice seemed broken between official Bonn and East Berlin at the same time that the American, British, and French military presence in West Germany was becoming more and more a matter of whether Bonn was willing to pay for the stationing of troops there.[7]

Erhard's cabinet was followed by a "grand coalition" of CDU/ CSU and SPD under the leadership of Kurt Kiesinger, whose Nazi past raised a storm in the world press.[8] The new government in its declaration of policy of December 1966 followed the example of President Johnson, who in a much-publicized television address in October 1966 had stressed the idea of building bridges to all the Eastern European countries. The SPD, and even the FDP, which was now in the opposition, intended to take the initiative in also seeking contacts with the DDR, though short of diplomatic recognition. Chancellor Kiesinger himself called "a German contribution to the maintenance of peace" the foremost aim of the foreign policy of his administration, thereby committing Bonn to the relaxation of tensions in Europe,[9] and devoted a good deal of attention to German-Soviet reconciliation and to the renunciation-of-force agreements offered earlier. Diplomatic relations with Eastern Europe and particularly a reconciliation with Poland and Czechoslovakia—including a denunciation of the Munich Agreements of 1938—were other notable items of the declaration of policy of the new government. The DDR was no longer exempted from the proclaimed willingness to build bridges to the East. However, Kiesinger only spoke of seeking contacts, human, economic, and cultural, "so that the two parts of our people do not become strangers to each other during their separation."

Whatever legitimate doubts the grand coalition may have raised in many minds,[10] in foreign policy it made sense, since the Christian Democrat Kiesinger and his Social Democratic foreign minister, Willy Brandt, at least initially seemed to speak the same language and to share the same goals of *Ostpolitik*. Within two months, in fact, the new government managed to achieve agreement with Rumania to establish diplomatic relations. This quick triumph was possible not only because the Erhard administration had been working on it for some time but also because the resulting communiqué simply ignored the problem of East German recognition and of the Hallstein Doctrine. At the same time, Kiesinger and Brandt met with de Gaulle and emerged from the meeting speaking of a common Franco-German *Ostpolitik*. This echo of the Gaullist and, more recently, Johnsonian pronouncements about healing the breach between Western and Eastern

Europe pulled the rug out from under the German Gaullists and other enemies of Schröder's *Ostpolitik*.

Unfortunately, the congruency of verbal formulae was not enough to solve the real problems posed by the situation. De Gaulle was still as far from endorsing German reunification as the Russians were from relinquishing control over their satellite empire. The Warsaw Pact countries, in fact, had pledged to make their solidarity with the DDR the test of their Communist loyalty as recently as July 1966. The price for West German diplomatic relations with Eastern Europe had gone up. Now it would take at least the abandonment of the Hallstein Doctrine and of the claim to speak for all Germans, the formal recognition of all de facto borders, and the end of West German nuclear ambitions. This was the reason why Eastern Europe had been rather reserved in its reaction to the new *Ostpolitik* of Kiesinger and Brandt.

The following months of 1967 soon were to demonstrate the limitations of the new *Ostpolitik*. Rumania had been an easy mark because it had long been on a path of emancipation from Moscow. Yugoslavia was another easy gain because it had already maintained diplomatic relations with Bonn until 1957 when the Hallstein Doctrine motivated Bonn to withdraw its representatives from Belgrade after Tito recognized the DDR. But the increasing Soviet pressure on Prague, Budapest, and Warsaw held these countries in a solidary ring against the wooing of Bonn. The Karlsbad Conference of April 1967 gathered all the Eastern European Communist parties except those of Rumania and Yugoslavia to debate on how to meet the West German threat to their solidarity. Western Communist parties, including that of France, were to help with discrediting the "revanchism" of Bonn. The conference issued a resolution calling for a European security conference exclusive of the United States, a proposal which must have pleased de Gaulle. At the same time, of course, the Soviet Union also strove to get American support for the Nuclear Non-Proliferation Treaty, which to de Gaulle was a prime example of the collusion of the great powers against the national independence of the European powers.

Bonn also had misgivings about the high-handed manner in which Washington neglected to consult its allies about its compromises with the Soviet Union. There must be some secret quid pro quo, the West German press suggested, possibly involving Soviet noninterference in the Vietnam conflict. And America's European allies were supposed to pay for it by accepting nuclear limitations while the great powers themselves undertook no disarmament steps. This issue now allowed the German Gaullists to rally their forces around Strauss and Adenauer in opposition to the leaders of the grand coalition and their policy of relaxation of international tensions. What better argument could be used against the new *Ostpolitik* but that the Soviet Union wanted nothing more than Bonn's signature on the Nuclear Non-Proliferation Treaty? More sober criticisms pointed out that the treaty would also bar West Germany from access to the peaceful uses of atomic energy. And the issue was also a divisive one for the grand coalition, because Kiesinger was more inclined to agree with the critics and with de Gaulle's advice not to sign than was Brandt.[11]

In place of the West German offer of bilateral renunciations of force, the Karlsbad Conference came up with the Gomulka Plan for a collective renunciation-of-force agreement to be signed by all European states, including the DDR, whose international discrimination in any case was to cease forthwith. The DDR, furthermore, concluded Friendship and Mutual Assistance Treaties with Poland and Czechoslovakia to complete the regional integration of the DDR in case the Warsaw Pact should lapse following the security conference. And to draw the final line under the years of evolution toward a separate state, the DDR also moved to abolish the last remaining legal fiction of commonality, the all-German citizenship, and replaced it with its own nationality. Ulbricht would have liked to make the establishment of diplomatic relations between Bonn and the East European countries dependent on Bonn's recognition of the DDR in a reversal of the Hallstein Doctrine, but he did not succeed in winning the support of the conference.

The Federal Republic attempted to break into the northern tier of Eastern European states but met a good deal of resistance even in Prague, which had welcomed the Kiesinger statement about abrogating the Munich Agreements of 1938. Instead of diplomatic relations, Bonn only achieved the conclusion of a trade treaty and the establishment of trade missions. Warsaw still showed no signs of giving in to the German wooing. Bonn had to settle down in patience for the long waiting game, all the while assuring the East that it had no intention of isolating the DDR or any other state. And, once more, it attempted to advance the idea of mutual renunciations of force with each Eastern European state, which amounted to a West German admission that Bonn could not but accept the state of things as they were anyway.

On the reverse side of the coin of a renunciation of force were. Bonn's nuclear ambitions. The original position of the Adenauer administration and its Defense Minister Strauss in pursuing a "policy of strength" had led them down the garden path of demanding participation in NATO nuclear defense. Failing this, they wanted to be a part of an independent European or Franco-German "force de frappe." Despite their ritualistic assertions of the primacy of German reunification, they apparently did not seriously consider the possibility of renouncing nuclear arms as part of a reunification settlement for fear that any such settlement might be a Communist trap or might jeopardize the freedom and independence of West Germany. This was a gamble of sorts considering the extremely exposed position of Germany in case of open hostilities, nuclear or conventional.[12] The Erhard-Schröder team was more inclined toward accepting the idea of stopping the proliferation of nuclear arms, at least with the support of the FDP and the opposition SPD. Nevertheless, Erhard kept open the options of trading a renunciation of nuclear arms for reunification, Bonn's participation in a European "force de frappe," and sharing in the planning and operation of a NATO nuclear force. The latter idea for a time took the form of a multilateral atomic force (MLF) mounted on surface ships manned by multinational NATO teams as a device of decentralizing nuclear control from Washington. The MLF turned out to be popular only in Washington and Bonn[13] and was quietly forgotten by the mid-1960s.

The Kiesinger-Brandt team could no longer hope for the trade-off of reunification and nuclear arms, but was reluctant to drop its interest in Western nuclear planning and in peaceful uses of atomic energy. Kiesinger, moreover, wanted to maintain the West German stake in a future European "force de frappe," while Brandt stressed the willingness of the Federal Republic to agree to nuclear nonproliferation, provided it was going to be a first step toward general nuclear disarmament or effective international controls on the nuclear arms race between the great powers. This argument found strong support also with India, Japan, and Sweden at the Geneva Conferences of 1967 and 1968, and it was obviously in better harmony with the *Ostpolitik* than were the fulminations of the German Gaullists and the Springer press.

Until 1967, Chancellor Kiesinger had succeeded in avoiding the highly divisive impact of the Gaullist issues on his party and policies by skillful maneuvers and gestures by which he professed to be rather in sympathy with the general and with Franco-German friendship. During 1967, however, de Gaulle himself tarnished his image so substantially in West German public opinion that even former leading German Gaullists such as Strauss turned against him. Convinced Europeans had long seen through his scheme of advocating European unity and independence only in order to ward off American influence. His renewed rejection of British admission to the EEC and the European celebration of the fusion of EEC, Euratom, and the Schuman Plan (ECSC) in 1967 only added fuel to their disgust. De Gaulle's evermore intense relationship with the Soviet Union at a time of increased anti-German Communist propaganda did not endear him to the newspaper-reading West German public. The Middle East war of July 1967, in which he plainly sided with the Arabs and the Soviet Union against Israel, broke the back of the Gaullist sympathies in the Federal Republic. He had finally struck the sensitive nerve of German guilt feelings toward the Jews and even the hard-lining Springer press turned wrathfully against him. A wave of pro-Israeli sympathies swept West Germany and other European countries including France, leaving de Gaulle isolated and his cause deserted. His plea for a European security system from the Atlantic to the Ural mountains during the Franco-German consultations of July 1967, moreover, sounded so much like an echo of the Karlsbad Conference that Kiesinger must have been cured of any remaining shred of Gaullist feelings.

THE ROAD TO KASSEL

The most significant aspect of the *Ostpolitik* of Kiesinger and Brandt was the interaction, or rather the lack of it, between Bonn and East Berlin. In April 1967, Bonn presented a list of sixteen proposals to ease relations between East and West Germany with respect to traffic, transportation, trade, scientific and technical exchanges, and the like. Much of the initiative in this direction came from the new minister of all-German affairs, Herbert Wehner, who strove for contacts with East German officialdom from the bottom up and hinted that there would be no need for reunification if the DDR would turn from its hard-lining Stalinism to a quasi-Yugoslav form of socialism. The Ulbricht regime, however, understandably shied away from any such emasculation of its dictatorial control. Instead of a rapprochement from the bottom up, Ulbricht wanted the legitimacy of his regime recognized first. Only then, he suggested, might intra-German relations be improved. Why was Bonn so particular about whether the Ulbricht regime enjoyed popular approval, he implied, when it had no such reservations about the legitimacy of other Communist regimes with whom it tried to establish diplomatic relations?

Ulbricht finally responded by proposing a meeting of Premiers Kiesinger and Stoph either in East Berlin or in Bonn. At the same time, the postal and traffic ministers of the DDR offered to negotiate other details. The Bonn leadership was so surprised to find open doors where they had evidently expected a rebuff that the cabinet was in a tizzy of internal consultations on how to respond. Wehner was prepared to seize the opportunity for a meaningful dialogue and a demonstration of West German good will for the consumption of all Eastern European states. The CDU, however, began to worry about some of its internal dissent and the approaching state elections of Lower Saxony. Only after these elections had brought the CDU a minor triumph over the SPD and FDP did Kiesinger reply to the East German proposal in a form which stressed the unity of the German people on both sides of the Iron Curtain. Now it was Stoph who delayed his answer until September 1967. Then he sent a draft treaty for mutual diplomatic recognition and demanded that a normalization of intra-German relations would require Bonn to drop out of NATO and the EEC and to become a socialist country. East Berlin had again raised the price of better relations to the point where Bonn was sure to refuse. After this a large majority of the CDU insisted that further negotiations be broken off for fear of bringing about a de facto recognition of East Germany.

Toward the end of 1967, the Soviet Union and the DDR once more heated up the international climate with threats toward the status of West Berlin and any West German government conferences there. Moscow sharply demanded that Bonn recognize all existing borders and renounce all its nuclear ambitions and "designs on West Berlin," and pointed to the increase of right-wing radicalism in West Germany as a sign of Bonn's untrustworthiness. In spite of protests by the Western Allies, the East Germans with Soviet approval prevented Bonn government officials and members of the NPD from getting to Berlin. The Western Allies have always held that West German government organs could meet in Berlin and that the four-power status applied to East Berlin as well as to West Berlin. In June 1968, the DDR also introduced the requirement of passports and visas for travel from West Germany to West Berlin, again over Allied and West German protests. While the Kiesinger government reiterated once more its willingness to negotiate practical details of intra-German relations, East Germany's ability to start a Berlin crisis at any moment of its choosing served to keep the approaches of Bonn at arm's length.

On August 21, 1968, the tanks of the Warsaw Pact forces, led by the Soviet Union and including East German units, rolled into Czechoslovakia to snuff out the liberalism of the "Prague Spring." There were reports of clandestine protest actions inside East Germany, but by and large the East German troops were as surprised as the Russians that the Czechs tended to compare them to another armed invasion they had suffered thirty years earlier. They fiercely resented the swastikas which Czech youths and some of their own countrymen painted on their tanks and rolling stock. The Soviet desire to rein in its wayward satellites with a harsh hand had been evident for some time.

The implications of this action for the West German *Ostpolitik* were ominous. Bonn's negotiations toward a mutual renunciation of force with the Soviet Union had run aground on the hard demands of the Soviet government at the time of the Berlin crisis of November 1967. In the meantime, Moscow further added a reference to certain clauses of the Potsdam Agreements of 1945 and the UN Charter which justified hostile intervention on the part of the original signatories in case of a revival of fascism in any of the erstwhile enemy nations of World War II. This right of intervention could presumably be construed to refer to the NPD or any other neofascist splinter party of postwar Germany and West Berlin, or, for that matter, to the Bonn government itself, which Communist propaganda had been calling "fascist, imperialist warmongers" since its beginnings in 1949. The Soviets indicated that they would maintain this right of intervention even after a renunciation-of-force treaty was signed and, to add insult to injury, published the content of the confidential negotiations for all the world to see. The Czechoslovak invasion, which the Warsaw Pact justified as such a "suppression of fascist elements and foreign agents" (Brezhnev Doctrine) presumably coming from West Germany, finally revealed that a fascist Bonn was a functional prerequisite to maintaining Soviet control over the satellite empire. The West German government had still tried to reason in a note that a renunciation of force would have to be based on equal conditions for both partners and could not be modified with any one-sided right of intervention. The Soviets replied in the strongest language that the Federal Republic had no claim to equality with other European states and that its renunciation-of-force proposals left untouched its "revanchist platform with regard to all the main questions of European security."

An article by Brezhnev in *Pravda* (September 1968) now set forth the Brezhnev Doctrine. Leonid Brezhnev contradicted the claim evidently abroad in some satellite capitals that the Soviet intervention violated the principles of national self-determination and of Marxism-Leninism. He rejected an abstract concept of national sovereignty which was not related to the class struggle. The sovereignty of a socialist state could never be in contradiction with the interests of international proletarian socialism.[14] The Soviet interpretation that there had been a fascist and Bonn-inspired counterrevolution in Prague, of course, was unlikely to impress anyone in Western or Eastern Europe. But the Soviet tanks did and the tremors could be felt in Bucharest, Belgrade, and Budapest as well as in West Berlin and Bonn. The Brezhnev Doctrine could justify armed intervention whenever a satellite country ventured along a path of its own.

When at the time of the invasion Soviet troops began to mass across the border from West Germany in the Bohemian Woods, moreover, Bonn urgently called for strengthening NATO and appealed to the Western Allies for a change in the uncertain status in Central Europe. At West Germany's urging, also, the Western Allies forcefully rejected the Soviet interpretation of the UN Charter and the Potsdam Agreements. Washington bluntly announced that any Soviet invasion of West Germany would bring immediate military retaliation. This finally cooled down the ardor of Soviet belligerence.

The crisis of the *Ostpolitik* in 1968 was matched by other failures of that year. The completion of the customs union of the EEC countries was due in mid-year, but the French veto of the admission of Great Britain and the Scandinavian countries and possibly Austria was still as certain as ever. The Benelux countries, Italy, and later Bonn attempted to break through the barrier with various proposals stressing the "technological community" of

Europe vis-à-vis America, but to no avail. Not even the revolutionary upheaval in France in May 1968 could budge French
recalcitrance. The pressure for regional cooperation beyond the
EEC and beyond the dead hand of Paris grew both among the
other European states and in West Germany. At the same time, a
lingering currency crisis of the weak U.S. dollar, English pound,
and French franc pressed on the West Germans to increase unilaterally the value of the mark. They resisted at first and then
gave in a year later.

Notes

1   The SPD plan for Germany of 1959 had still stressed German military
     disengagement and reunification by stages, although the Soviet Union had
     long abandoned its earlier offers in this direction.

2   At about the same time the German ambassador to Washington, Wilhelm
     Grewe, one of the original hard-liners of Adenauer's Western-oriented
     policy, was also retired because he had exceeded the reserve normally
     expected of diplomats and pleaded in the American press against the
     "sell-out" of the American commitments by the Kennedy administration
     to the Soviets.

3   The cause was an American package of proposals on an international
     control authority for the access route to Berlin and the inclusion of the
     DDR in this authority and in a series of nonaggression pacts. The State
     Department insisted on an immediate answer, whereupon the package
     was leaked to the press in a defensive maneuver likely to wreck the
     project in the general uproar.

4   See Henry A. Kissinger, *The Troubled Partnership* (Garden City, N.Y.:
     Doubleday, 1965), pp. 66-89.

5   Poland, for example, at first insisted on the establishment of normal
     relations and on West German recognition of the Oder-Neisse line.

6   The Rome Treaties had specified that after a certain period, decisions
     would be made by majority vote rather than unanimity. France insisted
     on continuing the unanimity rule, which none of the other states wanted.
     The Luxembourg Accords of January 1966 signaled that, in substance,
     France had been successful.

7   The Erhard regime's final crisis was financial in nature, and Erhard went
     to Washington to seek a more favorable modus of payment for the sta-
     tioning of U.S. troops and purchase of American equipment by West
     Germany. The failure of this mission toppled him from power.

8   Kiesinger had joined the party back in 1931 and served during the war in
     the propaganda section of the Foreign Office. After 1949 he played an
     important role in the CDU in the Bundestag and was minister president
     of his home state, Baden-Württemberg.

9   The standard formula of past administrations had always begun with the call for German reunification.

10   The chief criticism of the coalition of the two largest parties, who together accounted for some 90 percent of the seats in the Bundestag, circled around its effect on the two-party system and its preemption of an effective opposition. The last-mentioned feature, furthermore, was frequently blamed for the growing strength of the radical right, the NPD, and the New Left, the Extra-Parliamentary Opposition (APO).

11   The protest in Bonn led to several financial concessions (the same concessions President Johnson had denied to Erhard) and to a more conciliatory approach than had been used by Defense Secretary Robert McNamara before.

12   There is abundant evidence in USIA polls that the West German population in the 1950s and early 1960s feared nothing more than being exposed to nuclear bombardment, possibly in reflection of the pitiless bombardment of German cities in World War II.

13   As one high German NATO officer frankly told this writer during the interviews of the Deutsch-Edinger-Macridis-Merritt study of disarmament views in 1964, "The MLF is of dubious workability from a military point of view, but if the Americans want it, we'll support it too." See also Karl W. Deutsch et al., *France, Germany and the Western Alliance* (New York: Scribner's 1967), pp. 147-49, 192-95, 265-66 and 296-300. Kissinger, *The Troubled Partnership*, also has a chapter on the MLF.

14   In Communist parlance, "socialism," of course, does not refer to the democratic socialism of the British or Scandinavian labor parties or the SPD, but only to the movements sanctioned by the Communist International and its successor organizations.

CHAPTER 5

An Opening to the East

The parliamentary elections in September 1969 became something of a watershed in postwar West German history in that they finally retired the Christian Democratic Union/Christian Social Union (CDU/CSU) as a government party of twenty years' standing. The chief issues were of a domestic nature, although the differences between the two largest parties also had significant foreign policy overtones. Strauss and his adherents conducted themselves as "the national opposition" against the Nuclear Non-Proliferation Treaty and the *Ostpolitik*. The Soviet claims to a right of intervention in Germany and the nonproliferation treaty were seen by many to be made of the same discriminatory cloth, and some hard-liners even spoke of a "super-Yalta" or "super-Versailles." Kiesinger insisted on polemicizing against a "party of recognition" (of the DDR) in a willfully crude distortion of the issues. Thus he and his party had retreated far from their position at the outset of the grand coalition. Brandt held out the hope that signing the nonproliferation pact would avoid Bonn's falling into isolation. Waiting for the Soviet ardor to cool off might yet produce an advance in *Ostpolitik*.

The coming electoral upset was heralded by the selection in March of a new federal president by the Federal Assembly[1] in Berlin, when the FDP threw its electoral votes behind the SPD candidate Gustav Heinemann, who thereby won the contest. The FDP had already developed a draft "general compact" for orderly relations between East and West Germany and thus was obviously ahead of even the SPD.[2] Again there were bitter anti-Bonn propaganda campaigns and harassment of the access routes to Berlin, but mysteriously both the DDR and the Soviet Union softened their approach again suddenly and began to make counteroffers relating to the access of West Berliners to their friends and relatives in East Berlin. There were two potent reasons for the change in approach. As Ambassador Tsarapkin of the Soviet Union informed the West German government, Chinese and Soviet troops had clashed bloodily at the Ussuri River halfway around the world. And the steadying hand of the Nixon administration had appeared on the scene with President Richard Nixon's personal visit to Berlin. Europeans had great confidence in Nixon's foreign policy adviser, Henry Kissinger.

The SPD and FDP together won a narrow majority of the seats in the Bundestag, thus winning a popular mandate for their *Ostpolitik* initiatives over the Kiesinger and Strauss line, which had conjured up the Communist menace and the "national sell-out" by their opponents in a manner going even beyond the rhetoric of Adenauer in his prime. The new government of Chancellor Brandt and Foreign Minister Walter Scheel (FDP) was regarded with greater favor by the East than the Kiesinger government. It took office amid new signs of an Eastern willingness to negotiate, although the terms had hardly changed. The recognition of the DDR and of the existing borders and West German renunciation of nuclear ambitions were still the first order of business. And there was also the renewed proposal of a European security conference without the United States, in which Brandt professed some interest.

In May 1969, Poland's Wladyslaw Gomulka also had expressed his willingness to discuss the normalization of the relations between the two countries, which immediately led to a sharp partisan squabble over the recognition of the Oder-Neisse line. Moscow invited the FDP leadership, and later also the SPD Bundestag leaders, for a visit in the middle of the election campaign which understandably led to charges of Soviet attempts to influence the German elections, even though eventually the CDU was also invited but did not go. Increased economic interaction and a plan to deliver Soviet oil to the Federal Republic also accompanied the resumption of the negotiations over the mutual renunciation of force.

Willy Brandt tackled the objectives of his *Ostpolitik* with a dispatch born of years of observing the ups and downs of Soviet-German relations. After a mere five weeks in office, the chancellor had already put an end to the debate over the Nuclear Non-Proliferation Treaty by attaching the West German signature to the treaty. A billion-dollar deal with the Soviet Union followed in which Bonn obtained Russian gasoline by trading pipes for a huge pipeline through European Russia. A platoon of diplomatic emissaries from Bonn descended upon Warsaw, Prague, Budapest, and Bucharest with other favorable credit and commercial arrangements as well as assurances about the peaceful intent of the Federal Republic.

The whirlwind of activity focused in particular on Moscow, where Brandt's special ambassador, Egon Bahr, met with Foreign Minister Gromyko about forty times between January and August 1970 alone to prepare the renunciation-of-force agreement with the Soviet Union. Foreign Minister Scheel also met with his Soviet counterpart some seventeen times during the same period for this purpose.

Still more surprising, Brandt maneuvered the reluctant East German government into two widely publicized encounters between himself and DDR Premier Willi Stoph, one in the historic East German city of Erfurt, the other in Kassel, West Germany, to demonstrate to the whole world an intra-German understanding of sorts. And at the same time, Brandt also got the four great powers, who had neglected for so long their responsibilities for the status of Berlin, together once more to work out a permanent solution for the beleaguered city. Events moved so rapidly in 1970 as to take Brandt's opponents in East and West Germany rather by surprise. The interpretation and analysis of what happened is only now beginning to catch up with the decelerating flow of events.

The element of surprise, to begin with, could be maintained in large part only because of the air of unreality and hopeless entanglement which had long surrounded the relationship between Bonn and the East. Twenty-five years after the end of World War II, the tensions in Europe were still unrelieved, with nearly one-third of a million American troops and half a million Soviet troops stationed in various Western and Eastern European countries. West Germany had made its peace with the West, but never really with the East, pretending the DDR did not exist and ignoring the border questions and de facto losses of territory. Twenty years of hard-lining CDU governments and certain refugee and right-wing groups had been talking as if Germany had not lost the war in the East and as if the Western alliance could be used to win back in the long run the rightful spoils of war of Poland, Czechoslovakia, and the Soviet Union, which had suffered so grievously from the German invasion in World War II. These right-wing elements and parts of the West German press rose in righteous wrath against Brandt's *Ostpolitik* initiatives. Ironically, they found their best allies among hard-liners in the East German SED who fought tooth and claw against any rapprochement with Bonn. The vested interests in the status quo from both Germanies joined hands in manufacturing propaganda, provoking and magnifying incidents, and leaking confidential documents and reports in order to wreck this unconscionable intra-German and Eastern rapprochement.

THE RENUNCIATION-OF-FORCE TREATY
WITH THE SOVIET UNION

In spite of all the bitter sallies and incidents of that eventful year, the Renunciation-of-Force Treaty between the Federal Republic and the Soviet Union was signed (but not ratified) August 12, 1970. It was published together with a letter on German unity and supplementary notes and documents which gainsaid the earlier alleged reports and agreements leaked by the opposition to create the public impression of a "sell-out" or "betrayal of the fatherland" to Communism, or of German ethnic interests to aliens. The two contracting parties solemnly pledged "to maintain international peace and achieve détente [and] . . . to further the normalization of the situation in Europe and the development of peaceful relations among all European states, and in so doing [to] *proceed from the actual situation existing in this region*" (italics added). They agreed to be guided in their mutual relations by the United Nations Charter and "to refrain from the threat and use of force." For this purpose they declared their acceptance of all present frontiers and disavowed "any territorial claims against anybody," with the reservation that a final peace treaty conference or mutual consent (e.g., between East and West Germany) might still produce changes.[3] The treaty was to be submitted for ratification to the Bundestag only upon a satisfactory result of the four-power negotiations on the status of and access to West Berlin.

In supplementary agreements, Bonn promised to conclude similar renunciation-of-force treaties with the DDR, Poland, and

Czechoslovakia. Regarding the DDR, in particular, the Federal Republic agreed to treat East Germany as "a second German state within German territory," on a basis of equality and non-discrimination, and no longer to claim the right to represent all Germans (*Alleinvertretung*). Since the "two-state" theory presumed that the two Germanies were not foreign countries to each other, their mutual relations did not need to be of a diplomatic character.

The treaty drafters made sure to cover also the points raised by the opposition spokesmen of the CDU/CSU and the refugee and expellee organizations. They left undiminished the German right of self-determination and reserved the final disposition of the frontier questions to a peace conference which would very likely be some years off in the future. Most important for the West German side, they made ratification of the Renunciation-of-Force and Cooperation Treaty dependent on a "satisfactory settlement" of the status and access to West Berlin, a point creating considerable controversy at home and abroad. This was the quid pro quo of West German acceptance of the status quo in Eastern Europe. In May 1970, the negotiations with Moscow nearly collapsed when the Soviets reportedly wanted to separate the linking of the two subjects since the four-power negotiations on Berlin after many a meeting had not produced agreement on vital points. But Bonn remained adamant and asserted in a June note that there would be no renunciation of force without progress on Berlin. If it had not been for this pressure on the Soviets and the Western powers, the four powers would very likely have never made the effort. There is at least some evidence that West German public opinion was very favorably impressed by this feature of the Bonn-Moscow negotiations.

Another important aspect of the treaty was its portent for the threat of Soviet intervention as made in 1967 under articles 53 and 107 of the United Nations Charter.[4] The Soviet note of December 1967 spoke of West German "attacks on Berlin" and "the aggressive nature of the policy of the Federal Republic of Germany as directed against the socialist German Democratic Republic and other socialist states." The Soviet Union had terminated the state of war unilaterally in 1955 at the beginning of its diplomatic relations with Bonn. The present treaty, despite some opposition comment to the contrary, was presumed to have the effect of invalidating the Soviet threat. To be sure, as the hard-liners in

West Germany and elsewhere were quick to point out, no conceivable guarantee of this nature can ever be expected to bar a totalitarian state from aggression under all circumstances. But the American and NATO assurances could always be depended on to protect the Federal Republic in the event the Soviet Union made an abrupt about-face and turned to aggression again.

Foreign Minister Walter Scheel put the rationale of a renunciation of force succinctly when he wrote in July 1970 that the nature of military tensions in Central Europe inexorably imposed certain necessary attitudes upon West German policy. It had to be a policy of peace, and free from the unrealistic illusions and emotions of yesteryear. It must work to inspire confidence and trust in German intentions and not "feed on existing distrust." And it had to be based on Bonn's alliance and the support of its Western friends.[5] The earlier policy of ignoring the East permitted the Soviets for twenty-five years to cement their empire by playing on the Eastern European fears of Germany. The "imperialist," "aggressive" nature of the Bonn regime was a functional prerequisite of Communist policy and cohesion. What a triumph, then, to get Moscow to acknowledge the peaceful, nonaggressive intentions of West Germany and its willingness to leave the border settlement to negotiations rather than strong-arm tactics! And as for the support of the Allies, this aspect of the *Ostpolitik* was quite in keeping with the Allied goal of relaxing international tensions, as a long line of prominent American and other international visitors testified, with rare exceptions. In fact, the renunciation of force in Central Europe was likely to serve as an essential foundation on which to base the next step of the relaxation of East-West tensions, perhaps the mutual balanced force reductions (MBFR).

The CDU/CSU opposition struggled valiantly but by and large unsuccessfully to assail the government's position on procedural and substantive grounds. After several last-minute attempts to scuttle the negotiations by sensational revelations and charges, the parliamentary CDU leadership finally attempted to clutch at the mantle of statesmanship before it might be too late. They offered a temporary truce to the government during the actual negotiations late in July 1970. In the first days of August, there were still press reports that the negotiations had bogged down again and might have to be adjourned until some time in the fall. But then, suddenly, the last disagreements were ironed out. The treaty was initialed August 7 and signed August 12.

The West Germans returned in triumph and the Soviets, too, appeared very pleased. In fact, half a year later, Party Secretary Leonid Brezhnev in addressing the 24th Party Conference made it clear that the Soviet Union would regard nonratification of the treaty by West Germany as a breach of confidence and with the gravest concern. As for the West German electorate, an INFAS poll conducted before the final signature demonstrated strong support for Brandt's *Ostpolitik* and, in particular, the renunciation-of-force negotiations with Eastern countries. Seventy-nine percent of the respondents considered the negotiations an opportunity which should not be missed, against only 8 percent who advised the government to drop the matter. Twenty-seven percent were hopeful of achieving agreement most easily with Moscow, 23 percent with Warsaw, but only 2 percent with the DDR.[6] Small wonder that the CDU/CSU began to give the negotiations some support.

THE DDR ON THE DEFENSIVE

The public assessment of the chances for agreement with the DDR was not far from the mark, as the encounters of Erfurt and Kassel, held in the spring of 1970, had demonstrated. The preparations for the meetings also began with Brandt's proposal to conclude a renunciation-of-force declaration although there were broader overtones of reviewing other questions as well. The DDR was reluctant to be wooed on this issue when Ulbricht had long been sending messages and even a draft treaty on taking up "relations of equal status" and diplomatic recognition, but Willi Stoph, presumably under pressure from Moscow, finally suggested a public encounter with Willy Brandt in Erfurt. The meeting took place in a setting fraught with nostalgia and symbolic meanings for both sides. The West German expectations had been rather modest as long as it seemed likely that East Germany would cancel the meeting at the last minute just as it had backed out of the speakers' exchange four years earlier.[7] There was even some speculation that if Brandt were to come to East Berlin, as originally planned, his official visit would reaffirm the alienation of East Berlin from its four-power status or be considered tantamount to international recognition by some countries of the Third World. Or, at the very least, it was said that the DDR was hoping to gain international prestige by prolonged negotiations between the two chief executives.

Premier Stoph opened the Erfurt meeting on March 19 with a long speech in which he predictably insisted on the recognition of the DRR and demanded, among other things, 100 billion marks of "reparations" for the pre-1961 loss of East German refugees to West Germany and for the "economic discrimination" suffered at West German hands. He also rejected any claim of four-power control over East Berlin or the DDR. But despite the expected clash of opinions, some agreement was discovered between the two sides. Brandt and the West German negotiators, for example, agreed to accept the recognition of the DDR by third parties, i.e., to drop the Hallstein Doctrine. They also dropped the claim to *Alleinvertretung*. Both parties agreed to sign a renunciation-of-force agreement, to each apply for United Nations membership, and to meet again for further discussions on their mutual relations and cooperation, though without agreeing on specific topics to be discussed. Stoph called the building of the Berlin Wall, the "death strips," and killing of refugees "a humanitarian act" and acknowledged Brandt's "two-state" theory as a pale substitute for diplomatic recognition.[8]

On the morning of March 19, in Erfurt, the Communist stage management almost lost control when thousands of common people dramatically broke through the police lines to greet Willy Brandt. But the government quickly recovered the stage with the usual massive and well-drilled official demonstrations with slogans, shouts, and banners attacking the Federal Republic and praising the DDR.

Two months later in Kassel (Hesse), on the other hand, the return meeting, to the embarrassment of the West German hosts, turned into a fiasco of disorder which would have repelled even a glutton for the democratic freedoms of the streets. Thousands of demonstrators of the newly licensed DKP (West German Communists) and of various right-wing organizations including the CDU Youth (Junge Union), the NPD, and refugee groups appeared, brawled with each other, and outdid each other's shouts, placards, and symbolic happenings. An attempt was made to stop the limousine in which Brandt and Stoph were riding. The DDR flag was taken down and torn to pieces by three right-wingers with forged press passes which enabled them to get close to the official activities. During the night, the East German wreath was defaced which had been placed after turbulent scenes during the day at a monument to the victims of fascism. The local police were rather ineffectual and the official SED newspaper *Neues Deutschland* complained of "unheard-of provocations."

The two conferees parted without having come any closer to agreement and proposed to let a long "thinking pause" go by before another meeting. The "thinking pause" was the formula to hide the evident failure of the negotiations behind the pretense that they were still to be continued. The thinking pause evidently applied only to the large political questions, while on technical problems some patterns of cooperation soon came to be developed.

In any case, the DDR's expectation of inducing the Federal Republic to grant it diplomatic recognition rather than "recognition by the installment plan" (the "two-state" theory), as the East German propaganda chief Eduard Schnitzler put it, was doomed from the start. Brandt had already made a commitment to non-recognition in his government declaration of policy in 1969, and it was unlikely at the time that the voters would stand for recognition.[9] More important, the Western Allies indicated they still intended to exercise their four-power authority over Germany and Berlin, a reservation which was contained in the 1955 Treaty on Germany as a limitation on West German sovereignty. Thus, diplomatic recognition was not even Bonn's to give and the United States hinted that it would oppose both DDR recognition and a DDR application for membership in the United Nations. It should be noted, in any case, that the quest for contacts and administrative cooperation between the two Germanies at the ministerial and subministerial level survived the debacle of Kassel to a modest degree in fields such as transportation and postal services—*Postpolitik* instead of *Ostpolitik*.

Viewing the developments through the eyes of East Berlin, the DDR leadership in a way had once more successfully managed the hazardous game of getting its way without Soviet support or even contrary to Soviet intentions. Once before, in 1964, the Khrushchev initiatives toward better relations with Bonn had very nearly upstaged East Berlin. On that occasion, Khrushchev reportedly called both Ulbricht and Mao Tse-tung "war-mongers" and advised Czechoslovak leaders to seek contacts with "anti-revanchist" elements in West Germany in spite of Ulbricht's opposition. But Nikita Khrushchev was deposed and East Berlin' had its way. This time, the climate for Bonn-Moscow relations was even more favorable, but the DDR had also won a good deal more de facto autonomy in the years from 1964 to 1970.

There can be little doubt that the DDR was not prepared to come to any agreement at Kassel[10] or even to present new proposals that might have had a chance of acceptance. Moscow, on the other hand, was not all that insistent on an intra-German rapprochement either. Judging from the frosty reports on the Kassel meeting in *Pravda*, the Kremlin was not particularly impressed by Brandt's proposals,[11] but stressed instead the symbolic significance of the official reception given Stoph in Kassel and the recently completed diplomatic recognition of the DDR by Algeria. The suspension of the intra-German dialogue for the time being clearly shifted the public attention back to the more important stage of East-West and also Bonn-Moscow negotiations in mid-1970, when the Renunciation-of-Force Treaty was about to pass the last hurdles.

To understand the defensive attitudes of the DDR leadership, one cannot ignore the obvious defects, in the East German view, of the negotiations between Bonn and Moscow. Bonn had declared its intent to organize its relations with the DDR "on the basis of complete equality, nondiscrimination, respect for the independence of each of the two states in matters of internal competence within their respective boundaries," and renounced the claim to *Alleinvertretung.* But these concessions were not an integral part of the Bonn-Moscow treaty, nor did they indicate a promise of real international recognition instead of the suspicious "inner-German" relations on Willy Brandt's program. The Soviets not only refused to force East German demands upon Bonn, but had even stated their readiness to bring about, on the basis of residual occupation rights, a Berlin settlement to Bonn's liking and presumably at East German expense. The assertion of the occupation rights meant a severe setback to East German pride and self-confidence. The DDR leaders honestly could not tell whether they were being taken to the altar or down the garden path. The nightmare of agreement between Bonn and Moscow had ever been East Berlin's *cauchemar des coalitions.*

The DDR had little choice but to accept the new situation, although not without attempts to undermine it. At first the leadership seems to have adopted a strategy of reinterpreting the Moscow treaty in the light of its own needs while pretending that the Federal Republic had merely been forced to conclude this "Soviet accord" and was not in fact the author of the policy. Thus East Berlin in August 1970 issued a statement approving of the treaty while denouncing Bonn for not ratifying it immediately and, in particular, for still withholding East German recognition.[12] At a later point, Ulbricht sought to shift the initiative in the Berlin question from the Allied negotiations back to a dialogue between the two Germanies. Bonn did not cooperate with this stratagem, but for a while, at least until the 24th CP (USSR) congress in Moscow, the willingness of the Soviet Union to come to terms with Western negotiators seemed to be noticeably slackening under the impact of pressure from the DDR.

The leadership in East Berlin also strove to defend its position with a determined campaign of "demarcation against imperialist West Germany" and against the "Social Democratism" emanating from Willy Brandt's SPD, a tool of "the monopoly, capitalist bourgeoisie." The tough new East German stance crystallized under Ulbricht's successor, Erich Honecker, the former security chief and Ulbricht's protégé, at the 8th SED party conference in mid-1971.[13] Unlike Ulbricht, who still felt some nationalistic tugs on his heartstrings, Honecker and his followers have been preoccupied with asserting the absolute border and separation (policy of demarcation) between the two Germanies rather than favoring peaceful competition, cooperation, and exchanges or relations of persons as intended by Wehner and Brandt. The choice of language used by Honecker and his Defense Minister Heinz Hoffmann, in referring to the "imperialistic mortal enemy" in the West and the "class enmity" between East and West Germany eloquently spoke for the hardness of their line.[14] The persistence of Stalinism in a country of such great potential bodes ill for the future of the foreign policy of the DDR. Given the liberalization of Polish, Czech and Soviet relations with West Germany and the common desire for further relaxation of East-West tensions in Central Europe, the DDR can only sink further into a defensive posture, isolated even from the other socialist states who dread its militancy and, since the Czechoslovak invasion, hate its armed forces from the bottom of their proud hearts.

With its striving for autonomy from Moscow, the DDR is of course in the best of company of all the other Eastern European states. But therein lies also a paradox of the East German situation. The nationalist Communist tendencies abroad in Eastern Europe tend to undermine the Warsaw Pact and Communist solidarity with insidious, Dubcek-style liberalization at a time when the Soviet Union is increasingly preoccupied with its conflict with

Red China. The mere thought that the nearly 200,000 Soviet troops in East Germany might be withdrawn because they are needed in the Far East, or for budget reasons, chills East Berlin at least as much as the thought of U.S. troop reductions induces panic in Bonn. On the other hand, in spite of Moscow's evident desire for a relaxation of tensions, the Soviet interest really cannot afford to permit a great deal of softening in the East German stance toward Bonn, as much as the Sino-Soviet conflict makes a settlement in Europe attractive to Moscow. The DDR is for the Soviets a strategic bridgehead in Central Europe, a very reliable partner not only against the West but also against the East European hankerings for greater independence. Nowhere else in Eastern Europe has the Soviet Union been able to maintain a larger army than that of the native country, and with the full consent of the native government.

TOWARD A EUROPEAN SECURITY CONFERENCE

For the DDR, long-range security seemed no longer to be found in bilateral agreements, but only in multilateral pacts and conferences, where its links to the Warsaw Pact nations would become less dependent on momentary internal problems or external expediencies on the part of its Eastern partners. The intense desire of East Germany for Western diplomatic recognition has been, at least covertly, also a desire for greater autonomy from Soviet hegemony, a desire to lessen the dependence of the DDR on the East. As a truly autonomous partner of the Communist bloc, the DDR could play a double-sided game of security politics, analogous to the role of the Federal Republic in the Western alliance, in which the Communist alliance would still guarantee its security without smothering it in its powerful embrace. Proletarian internationalism and socialist brotherhood need not be limited to the Russian bear hug. The Soviet inclination to contribute toward a relaxation of international tensions between East and West, on the other hand, has been viewed by East Berlin with the same alarm with which Adenauer used to regard similar tendencies expressed by President Kennedy. The East German attitude is also somewhat self-contradictory but understandable even when it may border on a quixotic sense of insecurity or paranoia.[15] East Germany's foreign policy, therefore, has looked toward the European security conference envisaged by the various Eastern European countries and the Soviet Union at Karlsbad (1967) and Budapest (1969), and debated also by the Western foreign ministers at Rome (1970)—with an immediate echo in Budapest—and by the smaller European nations in 1972 and 1973.

This European security conference, as originally proposed by the East,[16] would have excluded the United States, which was sure to provoke not only American apprehensions but also those of Western Europe and especially West Germany. Bonn cannot afford to go into the lion's den of what East German sources once described as "a conference for the taming of the imperialistic, tension-provoking West German *Ostpolitik*" without the protection of the United States, which is presumably at the origin of Bonn's troublesome initiatives.[17]

Originally, the DDR also rejected vehemently any attempt of Bonn or Washington to make their assent to the security conference dependent on prior agreement on the relations between the DDR and the Federal Republic or on Berlin. In 1972, Finland took the initiative in inviting thirty-three other states to prepare for the conference, which thereby took on a typical neutralist, small-country emphasis. Indeed, since it has been planned as a multilateral gathering of states on a formal level of equality, the seven Warsaw Pact states and the nine Common Market countries, and even the fifteen NATO states would not enjoy a dominant role.[18]

The subjects of the conference as proposed by the Prague Conference of Foreign Ministers in October 1969 would be a multilateral renunciation of force, and economic and political cooperation among *all* European countries, an idea that echoes the late French President de Gaulle. If the particulars reiterated in Moscow in December 1969 and once more in August 1970 are to be taken literally—noninterference in internal affairs, respect for each other's sovereignty, reduction of military forces, West German renunciation of nuclear arms, formation of a common consulting agency, territorial integrity, and inviolability of borders—the Soviet Union may have more reason to be concerned than the Federal Republic.[19] A country like Rumania would obviously welcome the conference. The expansion of trade, scientific, technical, and cultural relations is very important to the East Europeans. NATO has also expressed interest in discussing the principles that should govern the relations among states, including the renunciation of force. But it would like more to contribute to cooperation in the economic, technical, and cultural spheres, and to the free movement of people, ideas, and information between East and West, which is not quite the same as what the East Europeans have suggested. NATO circles also have expressed a desire to link MBFR with the conference.[20] The draft agenda adopted by the Common Market members and accepted by NATO in January 1973 proposed two subcommittees on security concerns, one on principles and one on appropriate measures. Other subcommittees would deal with (1) trade, industrial cooperation, energy, raw materials, and environmental protection, and (2) with the free flow of persons, ideas, and information. During this preparatory phase, representatives of Bonn and East Berlin frequently met on a relaxed, social basis and without the customary fears of what political significance might accrue from minor questions of protocol.

The Soviet Union and the DDR, on the other hand, also would gain from the announced goals. A multilateral renunciation of force would lend legitimacy to the territorial status quo and, perhaps, decrease the Eastern threat perceived by Western European states, which makes for the cohesion of the Western alliance as well. It would probably weaken somewhat the politico-military ties between Western Europe and the United States and might in the long run—but certainly not in the next five years—lead to the decline of NATO. It would certainly facilitate economic and technological exchange between Eastern and Western Europe and might secure Russia's Western flank in case of a Sino-Soviet conflict. For the DDR and other Eastern satellites, it would promise protection against the effect of the Brezhnev doctrine and increased independence to develop each in its own way. It was these benefits, undoubtedly, that moved the Soviet Union and the DDR to agree to a satisfactory Berlin settlement in 1972 and to significant concessions in the Strategic Arms Limitation Talks (SALT) as their contribution toward the coming about of the conference.[21]

The non-Communist small countries of Europe, judging from their role at the preparatory talks in Helsinki, also hope to get involved in building the new international order of Europe, an order which ought to give them, too, more freedom from the dominance of the superpowers. The United States, on the other hand, has shown great reluctance, even apprehension, about the European security conference, fearing evidently that it may be used as a propaganda circus, or that it may give comfort to its enemies. Neither the Soviets nor the Americans quite share the eagerness of their European allies for increased trade and contacts, but they are both interested in a mutual, balanced reduction of forces (MBFR) and other measures of disarmament and détente.[22] The preparations for an MBFR conference also began in January 1973 with hopes of convening the conference the same year as the European security conference.

There is a contradiction of sorts between the likely continued cohesion of the two military blocs at the same time that something like a vastly enlarged West-and-East European community of nations is beginning to gather. The NATO Council clearly welcomed the European security conference at its 1967, 1970, and 1971 meetings, but with no thought of dissolving its own bonds. The Warsaw Pact, as the instigator of the great coming together of thirty-four nations, likewise has no intention of disappearing in reality, regardless of gestures and promises. It could hardly afford to disappear, as long as NATO is not inclined to do so. In spite of the prominent concern with security, no collective security arrangement is being planned. Neither is the new all-European community going to signal a dissolution of the Common Market (EEC) or of Comecon in favor of the desired new economic, technological, and environmental patterns of cooperation. Instead, the vision seems to be merely one of a larger community superimposed upon well-established partial communities which in turn rest on the duopoly of the two superpowers. To the superpowers, this arrangement reduces friction and signals détente. To the smaller states, such as the DDR, it promises all kinds of incremental benefits in addition to a modicum of security both from their friends and their enemies.[23]

RECONCILIATION WITH
POLAND & CZECHOSLOVAKIA

The most significant aspects of a West German reconciliation with the East were the attempts to reach agreements with Poland and Czechoslovakia. At the heart of the *Ostpolitik* are historical questions reaching back into the Middle Ages when Otto I (936-73 A.D.) began to extend German control into eastern Central Europe, and the large kingdom of Poland included not only the Oder-Neisse areas of today but also Bohemia, Moravia, and vast areas now part of Soviet Russia. In the sixteenth century, the city of Danzig still had a much larger population (77,000) than Berlin (6,000) although German settlers had already filled up much of the territories that later became the core of Brandenburg-Prussia. In the late eighteenth century, Poland was divided up among Russia and the expanding Prussian and Austro-Hungarian realms, which extended German dominion far beyond the German ethnic settlements into areas increasingly restive with Pan-Slavism and their own national movements.

The racial imperialism of the Pan-German and Nazi movements, as will be recalled, strove to roll back the tide of Eastern European nationalism which had torn apart the Austro-Hungarian empire and, at the end of World War I, created a series of new nation-states such as a revived Poland and multinational Czechoslovakia. The Nazi state, in particular, embarked on a crusade for a German ethnic empire which "liberated" German minorities everywhere, joined Germany and Austria together, divided Poland once more with the Russians, and sought to establish German dominion over vast areas inhabited by Slavs and other non-Germans. Nazi rule in occupied Poland, for example, was characterized by the most barbarous racism which showed no regard for human life or dignity. Systematic plundering, forced labor, and genocide as well as wholesale deportation and shifting around of populations were standard policies. An estimated 5.5 to 6 million Poles and Jews lost their lives under Nazi rule in Poland.[24]

Stalin's plan for the Soviet Union to keep the eastern part of Poland, which it had received as a result of the Nazi-Soviet Pact of 1939, and to give the Poles the German areas east of the Oder-Neisse line was first presented at the Teheran Conference of 1943. Roosevelt, Churchill, and Eden agreed in principle without accepting the particulars, but had considerable difficulty in persuading the Polish government-in-exile in London of the merits of this transaction and the expulsion of the German population within the area now designated as Poland. But the Soviets eventually had their way since their victorious armies were present on the spot, and their Committee of National Liberation rather than the Polish exiles in London became the new Polish government.

There ensued the expropriation and expulsion of those German families who had not already fled before the Red Army in anticipation of the dreadful reckoning. Altogether, of about 9.5 million Germans living in 1939 in East Prussia, East Pomerania,

East Brandenburg, and Silesia and another 1.5 million from Danzig, the Memel area and other parts of Poland, only an estimated 1.2 million were left within the new borders of Poland in 1950. Nearly half of these people had fled before the Red Army, while about 5.6 million were expelled in several waves between 1945 and 1947. The rest were generally retained because of their skills and upon declarations of loyalty to Poland. Under the auspices of the Red Cross, moreover, another 367,000 ethnic Germans left Poland after 1955 to join their families in East or West Germany.

The Oder-Neisse line was immediately recognized by the Soviet Union and Poland while the French provisional government declared its agreement in principle. The United States and Great Britain, on the other hand, withheld their consent pending a peace conference. Even the SED in its early days referred to it as a "provisional boundary," as did all the West German parties. The Polish government confirmed its legitimacy with a plebiscite after the expulsions and urged the Allies at every opportunity to make the border final. Poland also insisted that German refugee and expellee organizations be outlawed and prevented from demanding a revision of the de facto border. The outbreak of the cold war gained Poland the immediate support and recognition of its borders by all the Communist satellites, including the newly founded DDR. But at the same time, the cold war also intensified Western opposition to the final recognition of Poland's Western border.

In the Federal Republic, in particular, with the end of the occupation the millions of refugees and expellees were free to organize and to express themselves without restraint. They became voters, joined all the major parties, and temporarily had a party of their own, the BHE, in addition to the various regional associations (*Landsmannschaften*) harking back to their homeland. Foreign observers watched the enfranchisement of the expellee interest with alarm. Nevertheless, the refugees and expellees were generally more interested in jobs, compensation, and special credits than in foreign policy or the revision of the status quo. In 1950, the refugee groups solemnly declared that they were willing to forego all revenge and retribution in view of the immense suffering which all mankind had been subjected to in the last decade. But they also postulated a universal human right to one's homeland and demanded the distribution of the economic burdens of expulsion among all of West German society.

The CDU/CSU, SPD, and FDP leadership, including of course their respective expellee spokesmen, all refused to acknowledge the Oder-Neisse line until quite recently. They generally adopted the legalistic objection that the DDR lacked the legitimacy to recognize any changes in the borders of 1937, which would have to be left to a future peace conference as stipulated in the treaties of 1952 and 1954 with the Western powers. At the same time, considerable public and private funds were expended to keep alive and study the legacy of the ethnic Germans in various Eastern territories, probably with the ulterior motive of insuring a favorable public opinion for the day when these matters would have to be decided. The Poles for their part pointed out that a whole new generation had grown up meanwhile in the disputed territories, including many expelled by the Russians from East Poland, and had made the land their own with hard work. There was no longer a German majority or even a sizeable minority living there and the refusal of Bonn amounted to rank revanchism. John Foster Dulles' "rolling back of the Iron Curtain" thesis and West Germany's NATO membership gave a hollow sound to Adenauer's protestations that West Germany would never use force to modify disputed borders. The West German "no" to the Rapacky Plan and other plans for neutralization was also related to the refusal to recognize the Oder-Neisse line.

The earliest indication of a softening of Bonn's posture came after a 1958 visit to Poland by Carlo Schmid (SPD), who proposed closer cultural, diplomatic, and economic relations with Warsaw. The Berlin ultimatum of that year and the draft peace treaty of the Soviet Union, which included the recognition of all borders, once more put the freeze on the question. In 1963, finally, a trade pact and an exchange of trade missions were agreed upon as part of Schröder's abortive *Ostpolitik,* but they produced no real understanding between Warsaw and Bonn. Slowly West German public opinion also began to change and to consider Bonn's earlier position an anachronism. In 1965, a memorandum of the Evangelical Church Council (EKD) on the question of the expellees hit the card houses of Bonn politics like a bombshell. The Oder-Neisse question, the memorandum argued, was not so much a legal as a moral problem and it was about time the Germans faced up to their moral debt toward the Poles.

The next way station was a turning point in Bonn's official policy. Foreign Minister Brandt proposed in March 1968 to "recognize or at least respect the Oder-Neisse border" until a peace conference would have the final word. German Catholic circles likewise showed their willingness to recognize the facts. The gradual change of responses to West German public opinion polls illustrates the evolution from 1950, when 80 percent of a national sample said they were against recognizing the Oder-Neisse line. Nine years later this percentage dropped to 67 percent, in 1966 to 54 per cent, and in 1967 to 33 percent. Since 1967 more than half the respondents have indicated their support for recognizing the Polish-German border.

This was a broad enough basis for the new *Ostpolitik* of Brandt who had still been committed to the borders of 1937 as recently as 1966. The West German signature on the Nuclear Non-Proliferation Treaty and on the Renunciation-of-Force Treaty with Moscow went a long way toward clearing out major obstacles between Bonn and Warsaw. The Poles wryly observed the intra-German dialogue at Erfurt and Kassel. Nevertheless, the negotiations proved difficult, since the Poles were not content with West German guarantees of their territorial integrity and a renunciation-of-force agreement. Among other things, Warsaw asked for a half billion marks in credit although it had renounced any claims to German reparations back in 1953. A specific formula recognizing the Oder-Neisse line pending the reserved rights of the four powers, such as had already appeared in the Moscow treaty, broke the ice. Still, it took another two months of negotiations to reconcile the conflicting concerns of the two sides. The West Germans wanted mostly a renunciation-of-force agreement and certain humanitarian concessions allowing ethnic Germans to leave Poland. The Poles wanted first of all the unconditional recognition of their border. They disagreed about the number of ethnic Germans still there and considered this a matter entirely under their domestic jurisdiction. In the meantime also, the CDU/CSU opposition organized a concerted campaign against the recognition of the Oder-Neisse line, buoyed up by the defection of three FDP deputies which reduced the government majority in the *Bundestag* to a mere six seats. The Permanent Council of East German *Landsmannschaften*, representing the expellees in the West, was even more adamant against "legalizing the expulsion of Germans from one-fourth of the German territory of 1937."

The final agreement with Warsaw, consequently, stressed both the recognition of the Oder-Neisse line and the renunciation of

force. There was an additional Polish note concerning the repatri-
ation of ethnic Germans and persons with close relatives in the
Germanies. Bilateral or multilateral obligations of either contracting party were specifically exempted from the effect of the treaty
and the borders were to be finally determined at a peace conference. As Walter Scheel wrote about the accusation that the federal
government was giving away the German eastern territories:

> We cannot dispose over something that has long been at the
> disposal of history; we cannot give up something we no
> longer possess. To lose one's homeland is bitter, to look on
> Breslau, Danzig, or Deutsch-Krone as Polish cities is bitter.
> But if at least after 25 years we take note of existing reality, it
> is not we who have created the reality. The Federal Republic
> of Germany has to shoulder the burden of the National
> Socialist legacy.[25]

The treaty with Poland was signed by Brandt and Scheel on
December 7, 1970, after nearly a year of negotiations, pending
ratification by the West German *Bundestag*. The treaty was put
in the proper perspective by the unofficial opinion coming from
Polish leaders that "now there really is no need anymore for a
peace treaty with Germany."

The ink was not yet dry on the Warsaw treaty when Prague
likewise pressed for negotiations to set to rest the ghost of the
Munich Agreements of 1938 which had partitioned Czechoslovakia. Czechoslovakia's bane of the interwar years had been its
multinational character: 51 percent Czechs, 23 percent Germans,
15 percent Slovaks, and the rest Hungarians and other nationalities. The bulk of the German-inhabited areas, the rimlands of
Bohemia and Moravia, were handed to Hitler by Great Britain in
the Munich Agreements on the assumption that the irredentism
of the Sudeten Germans was based on serious grievances against
the Czechoslovak government. Even the ensuing Nazi take-over
of the rest of the country still did not remove a certain sympathy
abroad for the German minority until the assassination of SS
leader Reinhard Heydrich and the Nazis' dreadful retribution
against the town of Lidice in 1942.[26] After that, the final expulsion
of the ethnic Germans of Czechoslovakia soon became a foregone
conclusion as the Czech exile leader Eduard Benes proclaimed over
Radio London (1944) that at the end of the war, Bohemia and

Moravia would see "a mighty revolution . . . a great people's revenge on the Germans and fascists whose end will be bloody and merciless." The revolution was bloody and merciless indeed, and hunger, epidemics, and massacres accompanied the expulsion of the ethnic Germans from Czechoslovakia.

The *Ostpolitik* toward Czechoslovakia began with Schröder's initiatives, which in 1967 produced a trade treaty and an exchange of trade missions, but nothing more. The Kiesinger-Brandt government, as will be remembered, had indicated its willingness to regard the Munich Agreements as null and void. Chancellor Brandt likewise has shown his interest in a reconciliation with Czechoslovakia and has finally moved toward concrete negotiations on renunciation of force, recognition of the pre-Munich borders, and humanitarian concerns. The negotiations, as this is being written, were still in progress.[27]

The Czechoslovak point of view is contained in a 1967 address of Foreign Minister Vaclav David to the United Nations in which he demanded that prior to a normalization, Bonn would have to acknowledge that the Munich Agreements were void *ab initio*. This also has been the Soviet position. David also insisted that Bonn would have to recognize the sovereignty of the DDR, a point the Polish negotiators had also brought up in the early stages of negotiating the Warsaw treaty. Significantly, the Poles quietly dropped this condition despite the urgings of East Berlin, which would have liked to make its recognition the *conditio sine qua non* of all of Bonn's renunciation-of-force treaties. The Czechoslovaks, who deeply resented the East German role in their 1968 invasion, may well decide to act likewise. The Mutual Assistance Pact of 1967 among the DDR, Poland, and Czechoslovakia may have created an "iron triangle" of defense, but not necessarily an *entente cordiale*.[28]

Notes

1   The Federal Assembly consists of the Bundestag deputies and a like number of deputies of the Länder diets. It serves as an electoral college to elect the federal president.

2   The FDP later in the year also proposed dropping the Hallstein Doctrine altogether when Cambodia, Iraq, and the Sudan recognized the DDR.

3   On this subject, see especially George F. Duckwitz, "The Turning Point in the East," *Aussenpolitik* (English ed.) 21:4 (1970), pp. 363-79, where the details of the treaty are discussed and related to earlier agreements of the

Federal Republic such as Adenauer's 1954 declaration at the London Conference "never to seek the reunification of Germany or the modification of the present frontiers of the Federal Republic of Germany by means of force."

4   Article 53 frees "enforcement action . . . against any enemy state [of World War II] . . . directed against any renewal of aggressive action by that state" from the need of authorization by the Security Council, where the Western Powers could veto it. Article 107 says: "Nothing in the present Charter shall invalidate or preclude action, in relation to any state which during the Second World War has been an enemy of any signatory to the present Charter, taken or authorized as a result of that war by the governments having responsibility for such action."

5   *Frankfurter Allgemeine Zeitung*, July 15, 1970.

6   For details, see Federal Republic of Germany, Press and Information Office, *The Treaty of August 12, 1970*. This collection of the relevant documents, notes, interviews, and press comments documents both the antecedents and the conclusions of the treaty.

7   Immediately preceding the Erfurt meeting, there was yet another campaign of harassment against West Germans going to West Berlin.

8   See the documentation in Federal Republic of Germany, Press and Information Office, *Erfurt, March 19, 1970*.

9   Chancellor Brandt had hinted, however, that diplomatic recognition might come in the long run provided East Berlin would relent and permit some humanitarian improvement of the personal relations between East and West Germans. East Berlin not only ignored the offer, but let it be known that it considered any West German concern for the people in East Germany an aggressive and discriminatory kind of interference in its domestic affairs. Regarding the public attitude toward recognition, the Social Science Institute of the University of Cologne conducted national surveys on the question of recognition of the DDR between January 1968 and February 1969. The positive responses in this period grew from one out of five to one out of three respondents, while the negative responses remained steady at slightly less than half of the sample. Respondents identifying with the FDP not only were most often in favor of recognition, but also became far more so than the SPD or CDU/CSU adherents during the year.

10   As Stefan Doernberg wrote in the SED monthly, *Einheit* (May 1970), p. 587, "no one, whether openly revanchist or hiding under phrases of peace, will succeed in turning back history and restoring an imperialistically dominated German nation."

11   Chancellor Brandt presented twenty points, including the mutual renunciation of force, an exchange of representatives of ministerial rank, mutual recognition of "autonomy," respect for the four-power agreements and for the de facto links between West Germany and West Berlin, admission to the UN, improved exchange of persons, goods, and information, and continuance of the favorable position of the DDR (despite the EEC barriers) in West German trade.

enabled him to establish a foothold among the rising young Communist elite of the DDR. A member of the Secretariat of the Central Committee and the Politbureau since 1958, he was an obvious successor to the septuagenarian Ulbricht for some time. Honecker is credited by some observers with the wrecking of the speakers' exchange of 1966 and has long enjoyed the reputation of an inflexible hard-liner opposed to any intra-German "bridge-building" or rapprochement.

12 See *Neues Deutschland*, August 15, 1970.

13 Erich Honecker was born in 1912 in the Saar, the son of a miner. He headed the East German Communist Youth (FDJ) from 1946-55, which

14 See, for example, Heinz Hoffmann, "Erfolgreiche Militärpolitik der SED," *Deutsche Aussenpolitik* 16:2 (1971), pp. 234-37. The difference between Ulbricht and Honecker was also evident from the changes in the program for the 8th SED Conference brought about by Honecker, who eliminated a planned discussion on the Federal Republic and its relations with East Germany and other Eastern states.

15 Foreign Minister Otto Winzer, for example, rather recently expressed acute alarm at a 1963 formula of Willy Brandt's according to which peaceful coexistence between the two Germanies denotes "a peaceful method of competition and *penetration*, an advancement of *transformation*" (italics by Winzer), which he interpreted as "undermining the socialist order of state and society" in the DDR, and as at the root of Brandt's 1970 refusal to grant diplomatic recognition (*Die Einheit* [May 1970], p. 592).

16 The Soviet Union first proposed such a conference in 1954 to forestall West German rearmament. Revived by Rapacky in 1964, the idea finally became capable of realization after 1968 when the Warsaw Pact agreed to full participation by the United States and Canada. See the communiqué in U.S. House of Representatives, Committee on Foreign Affairs, *Conference on European Security: Hearings before the Subcommittee on Europe*, 92nd Congress, 2d session, 1972, pp. 142-44.

17 See Otto Winzer's article on peaceful coexistence, *Die Einheit* (May 1970), pp. 594-96. See also Peter Florin in *German Foreign Policy* (June (1970), pp. 423-38.

18 Other participants are Albania, Austria, Cyprus, Lichtenstein, Malta, San Marino, Spain, Sweden, Switzerland, the Vatican, and Yugoslavia.

19 The Federal Republic expressed its hopes for achieving détente, security, and human communications through the conference in a preparatory statement in November 1972, and linked the conference to its well-known *Ostpolitik* goals. For an East German perspective, see Dieter Vogl, "Die Warschauer Vertragsstaaten und die europäische Sicherheitskonferenz," *Deutsche Aussenpolitik* 16:1 (1971), pp. 48-62, where great emphasis is placed on the participation of the Federal Republic and of the neutral states of Europe whether they are UN members or not. For nonmembers, such as the two Germanies, the renunciation-of-force agreement would take on a special meaning. For a chronology, see Boris Meissner, "The Soviet Union and Collective Security," *Aussenpolitik* (English ed.) 21:3

(1970), pp. 278-84. Meissner traces the notion of the European security conference from the Bucharest Declaration of 1966 and the Karlsbad Conference of the following year to the Finnish invitation to hold such a meeting in Helsinki. As he points out, the Soviet offer of dissolving the Warsaw Pact if NATO is likewise dissolved would still leave the Eastern Pact system completely intact because of the bilateral treaties among all the members, which provide for automatic assistance in case of attack and for the stationing of Soviet troops. See also Michael Palmer, *The Prospects for a European Security Conference* (London: Chatham House and PEP, 1971).

20   See Götz von Groll, "East-West Talks in Helsinki," *Aussenpolitik* 23:4 (1972), pp. 371ff., and Michael Palmer in *The World Today* (January 1972). The MBFR talks finally began in January 1973 in Vienna but involved only the Warsaw Pact and the NATO countries, after the big NATO powers became concerned about the influence of the small states on their defense policies.

21   See also *Deutsche Aussenpolitik* 17:5 (1972), pp. 844-51 and 872-99, and *Aussenpolitik* (English ed.) 22:3 (1971), pp. 283-86. The hearings before the U.S. House of Representatives, Committee on Foreign Affairs, Subcommittee on Europe, include a broad selection of documents and press comments. See *Conference on European Security*, appendix.

22   *Conference on European Security*, pp. 1-19, 37-50. As Assistant Secretary of State Martin Hillenbrand pointed out, the dismantling of NATO as a consequence of the conference is "not anticipated." The hearings also produced comments on the attitude of the State Department toward the *Ostpolitik*.

23   See also the West German interpretations in *Aussenpolitik* (English ed.) 23:1 (1972), pp. 14-35, and *Aussenpolitik* 23:4 (1972), pp. 371-82. The last-mentioned article, by a West German Foreign Office official, discusses procedures and likely agenda items in great detail.

24   In 1945, only 240,000 Jews were still in Poland, as compared to more than 3 million before the war. Since that time, anti-Semitic campaigns and emigration have reduced their number to perhaps 30,000.

25   See Federal Republic of Germany, Press and Information Office, *The Treaty between the Federal Republic of Germany and the People's Republic of Poland*, p. 43.

26   Up until that point, Sudeten German socialists in exile in London were still included in the exile leadership and a multinational federation was a distinct possibility for postwar Czechoslovakia, possibly including Poland. See Wenzel Jaksch, *Europe's Road to Potsdam* (New York: Praeger, 1963), chaps. 40-47.

27   In December 1973, the two governments finally came to an agreement.

28   See also James H. Wolfe, "West Germany and Czechoslovakia: The Struggle for Reconciliation," *Orbis* (Spring 1970), pp. 154-79.

Toward a New Balance of
Ostpolitik & *Westpolitik*

Why did Brandt and his Foreign Minister Scheel succeed in achieving their *Ostpolitik* goals where others had failed? The secret of their success lay in the timing and in their skillful linkage of the various measures and their ratification.

The Bonn-Moscow treaty as well as the one with Warsaw was not to come up for ratification until a "satisfactory" solution of the Berlin question was reached by the four powers: France, Great Britain, the United States, and the Soviet Union. Undoubtedly, the same applied to a treaty with Prague.[1] This made the Berlin settlement the crucial pivot of the relaxation of tensions in Europe, as indeed it should have been. Herein then lay Willy Brandt's grand design for the solution of the German problem in the East-West context. It consisted in tying all the loose ends of the *Ostpolitik* into a package dependent on four-power action in the most delicate point of friction, Berlin. The relations between the Federal Republic and the DDR were, of course, most vitally affected by any Allied guarantees or changes in the situation of Berlin, although neither of the two Germanies was a party to the four-power negotiations. The nature of the package placed the burden where it belonged, into the lap of the four powers, and made a settlement especially attractive to the least cooperative of them, the Soviet Union.

AT THE PIVOT: BERLIN

The Berlin problem began in the confusion of Allied planning for the postwar period. Since Germany was to be administered as one unit, the Allies decided to occupy the German capital jointly, with a sector for each occupying power. Since Berlin happened to be in the middle of the Soviet zone of occupation, this arrangement created a Western enclave as soon as cold war tensions began to mount. A Soviet land blockade of the Western sectors of Berlin occurred in 1948 in retaliation for the introduction there of the new West German currency. The blockade was broken by the famous airlift. The city council and administration split in two and the city was divided along the sector lines without, however, cutting off the movement of persons between the western and eastern parts.[2] East Berlin soon became the DDR capital and an integral part of the DDR, possibly in violation of the four-power status of Berlin. West Berlin was subjected to periodic harassment by the DDR since its isolation made it highly vulnerable to pressures.

The Federal Republic began to subsidize West Berlin[3] and to give it moral and political support while it continued to be an occupied city. More than fifty West German government agencies have been located there and public functions such as the election of the federal president or meetings of the West German political parties were frequently held in West Berlin. West German laws have often been made applicable to West Berlin by the local authorities and West German trade treaties frequently include West Berlin. Several of the treaties between Bonn and the Western occupiers oblige Bonn to support West Berlin.

The right of access to West Berlin from West German territory was embroiled in controversy from the beginning in 1945 when the American commander, General Lucius D. Clay, found that he could not maintain free access on just any routes available. He reluctantly agreed to a provisional allocation of certain specified land, rail, and air routes and even these have since been subject to curtailment whenever the Soviets or the DDR decided to exercise pressure on the city. Following the renewed Berlin crisis of 1958-59, the Soviet Union offered West Berlin the status of an unoccupied "free city" with guaranteed access, but Western suspicion of Communist infiltration techniques prevented agreement on this proposal. Instead, the United States was willing to reduce the size of the Western military presence in West Berlin and to agree to a mutual curbing of aggressive propaganda activities in both Berlins. President Kennedy, in his dramatic speech *"Ich bin ein Berliner"* (I am a Berliner), reasserted the American resolve to defend West Berlin and specified three essentials of the American position: (1) the Allied occupation rights, (2) free access, and (3) the viability of life in West Berlin. The right of self-determination of two million West Berliners was not to be sacrificed to the unrelenting pressures from the East.

But there was also good reason for the East German and Soviet concern about the island of freedom in the midst of their closed societies. The free movement of persons between East and West Berlin had attracted every year since 1949 between 300,000 and 500,000 East Germans via East and West Berlin to the Federal Republic, which by 1960 noted an influx of about 3.5 million East German refugees since the end of the war. They usually came without their belongings since unusual amounts of luggage would have alerted the East German police to their intention of *Republikflucht.* Many fled because of political oppression and persecution in the DDR. Those who were attracted by the higher living standards of the West were no less embarrassing to the East German "workers' paradise." They all brought their working skills and generally youthful energies, and in many cases the expensive professional training of doctors, teachers, and other professional persons. It was this heavy draining of skills and brains which on August 13, 1961, motivated Ulbricht with Soviet consent to build the Berlin Wall and elaborate mine fields and death strips all along the borders of the DDR with West Berlin and West Germany. Unlike West Germans, West Berliners were allowed to visit relatives and friends in East Berlin only on special occasions by means of passes granted (and often denied) by East Berlin.

The subject of Berlin was taken up again by the United States and the Soviets in mid-1969. When Willy Brandt made ratification of the Moscow treaty dependent on a "satisfactory" solution of the Berlin problem he indicated:

It is understood that the Four Power negotiations will result in assuring the close ties between the Federal Republic of Germany and West Berlin as well as unhampered access to West Berlin.[4]

The Berlin talks began in 1969 and, by mid-1971, had led to no less than twenty-five meetings and several near-breakdowns as well as premature announcements of agreement. More than once, the DDR attempted to aggravate the difficult situation by closing down or harassing the access routes. The CDU/CSU opposition, and to a lesser extent representatives of the government coalition, repeatedly went to West Berlin to "test" their right to meet there, generally touching off yet another wave of East German obstructions of their access to the city. Bonn made certain by means of monthly meetings that its demands on Berlin were in full agreement with those of the three Western ambassadors negotiating over Berlin. While one rarely heard any talk about Berlin as a *Land* of the Federal Republic anymore, there was a grim determination not to let the political links between the two lapse entirely.

The DDR was similarly determined, with Soviet support up to a point, to stop all West German official presence in West Berlin. As *Neues Deutschland* put it as recently as 1970, "There is only Berlin, the capital of the DDR, and the independent political unit West Berlin which is in the middle of and *on the territory of the DDR*" (italics added).[5] The original four-power agreements, of course, assign West Berlin neither to West Germany nor to East German territory. The Allied negotiators reminded the DDR during one protest against obstructions that East Berlin, too, was originally an integral part of the quadripartite Allied Komandatura of Berlin and that it was illegally integrated with the DDR. Bonn and West Berlin also insisted on the four-power status of all of Berlin, at least for tactical reasons. They argued that if the East Germans could grab East Berlin, West Germany should also have at least a special relationship with West Berlin. The Soviet Union eventually showed a willingness to concede this point although at the time it denied a West Berlin resident in a Russian jail the right to be represented by the West German embassy on the grounds that West Berlin was a completely separate unit. West Berlin Mayor Klaus Schütz called consular representation by Bonn one of the "musts" of a satisfactory settlement.

The question of the West German political presence in West Berlin was originally tied to the hopes for German reunification. In particular the West German Communists (KPD), who were still legal and represented in the *Bundestag* in 1949-53, were once ironically in the forefront of proposals to move the leading federal organs from Bonn to West Berlin. The SPD at the time advocated some minor transfers of federal agencies against the resistance of the Western Allies and Adenauer's CDU/CSU. Later it was the CDU/CSU which insisted in word and deed on a strong political presence in West Berlin, while the SPD strove to avoid outright confrontations on this issue with the DDR. The Soviets would have preferred severing all ties to Bonn, including the subsidies, and making West Berlin economically and, by implication, politically dependent on "its natural, East German hinterland."[6] The East Germans on their part objected to the West German "revanchist" activities in this "bridgehead against the DDR" and insisted on the "good conduct" of West Berliners, West Germans, and transients in West Berlin as a condition for their cooperation.

The thorniest problems were still the rights of access to the city. The DDR had long expressed the belief that all civilian travel between West Berlin and West Germany involved travel through the sovereign East German territory and should therefore be dependent on East German consent which could be suspended or revoked at will. The problem was indeed perplexing and there were proposals to solve it by means of an "Autobahn corridor" without off-ramps on the way, or a tunnel, or an elevated freeway for the same purpose of allowing unfettered transit.[7] Other proposals involved an international access authority composed of the four powers and the two Germanies. The DDR, and intermittently Moscow as well, had proposed leaving the regulation of access to direct negotiations between Bonn and East Germany or, with regard to the traffic of West Berliners to the East, West Berlin authorities and East Berlin. Some direct negotiations had indeed been held, such as involving the waterways. But in principle Bonn and West Berlin did not wish to let the four powers off the hook, and expected them at least to lay down the ground rules before any delegation of authority to the Germans took place. They did not relish the thought of being at the mercy of the changing East German moods which had led to countless obstructions in the past.[8] The DDR always pictured Bonn and West Berlin as the mischief-makers whose provocations were the sole reason for all the difficulties. When the DDR became sovereign in 1955, the Soviet Union delegated the control of civilian transit traffic to and from West Berlin to East German authorities, which became the basis of East German obstructions. Since 1968, the DDR has even required visas and increased transit fees for the civilian traffic through the DDR despite Western protests regarding the four-power rights over one undivided German territory.

It should be mentioned, however, that Bonn was not all that powerless against East German harassment. Bonn could have retaliated with its controls on intra-German trade, which has continued at a large volume throughout most Berlin crises, including the building of the wall. At this point in the negotiations, West Germans envisaged several alternatives. An unlikely outcome would have been to make West Berlin the eleventh *Land* of the Federal Republic in analogy to East Berlin, but still with four-power safeguards. The legal confirmation of the status quo would be the minimal solution, again with four-power safeguards, for which they might settle. A third solution was spelled out by Mayor Schütz: West Berliners were to be treated like West Germans visiting East Berlin. There had to be guaranteed access to West Berlin and an access authority to supervise access. The economic, financial and legal ties to Bonn were to be recognized and the transit traffic processed automatically. All this would have to be laid down in a four-power treaty rather than being based on the quicksand of East German assurances. By May 1971, the Soviets appeared ready to accept unhampered civilian access, consular representation,[9] and the freedom of West Berliners to visit relatives in East Berlin or in the DDR.

THE BERLIN SETTLEMENT

By mid-1971, the expectations raised by the bold gamble of the *Ostpolitik* had reached such a height that even the CDU was willing for the time being to withhold criticism of the kind of Berlin agreement that was evidently taking shape. CDU spokesmen noted, however, that the West German "presence" in Berlin had been curtailed. "For the first time since the end of World War II," declared Chancellor Brandt triumphantly on September 1, "agreements based on international law are creating clear conditions for access to West Berlin and for the relations between the city and the Federal Republic of Germany." Two days later, in the building of the long-defunct Allied Control Council for Germany, the foreign ministers of the four major Allied wartime powers initialed the Berlin Agreement, a first step toward a viable settlement.

The agreement reaffirmed the reserved rights of the four Allies and pledged they would respect each other's rights in Berlin and not attempt to change the status quo unilaterally or by threat of force. Four annexes to the agreement proposed details of (a) the civilian traffic between West Germany and West Berlin, (b) the relationship between the Federal Republic and West Berlin, (c) travel and communications between West Berlin and the surrounding East German territories, and (d) the representation of West Berlin interests abroad and the Soviet consular activities in West Berlin.

Regarding the first item, the Soviet Union assured the Western powers that the traffic of goods and persons across East German territory to and from West Berlin would be "facilitated and unimpeded." Some regulations of this traffic were specified and the details left to intra-German agreements. In the second annex, the Western powers reaffirmed the ties between Berlin and Bonn, provided that West Berlin not become a constituent part of the Federal Republic and the political organs of the latter not be convened in West Berlin. In the third annex, the Soviets gave equal visiting rights in East Germany to the West Berliners who had long been discriminated against as compared to West German or foreign visitors. This annex also promised to improve the ruptured communications between East Germany and West Berlin and to resolve the problem of enclaves such as Steinstücken by exchanges of territory, the details being left to intra-German negotiations. The fourth annex, finally, granted the residents of West Berlin West German consular representation abroad and in international organizations, and authorized the establishment of a Soviet consulate general in the Western sectors of the city. In a further exchange of letters with Bonn, the Western powers indicated which West German governmental agencies would be permitted to appear and operate in West Berlin for purposes of coordinating the relationships between the two entities.

The Brandt government immediately made it clear in a televised address that the Berlin Agreement was only the beginning of a settlement and that in many ways it accomplished little more than the sanctioning of the existing situation. Nevertheless, the former Berlin mayor said, "there are to be no more Berlin crises." And he stressed the sanctioning of access rights and the visiting privileges of West Berliners.[10]

The achievement of agreement among the four powers after seventeen months of seemingly hopeless wrangling met a very favorable public reaction at first. Even opposition spokesmen, who had occupied positions varying widely from the fundamental anti-*Ostpolitik* opposition of the old Gaullist wing to Schröder's mixture of procedural criticisms with substantive support, welcomed the great effort of the four powers at achieving a consensus. The announcement of President Nixon's visit to Peking, moreover, had focused the attention once more on the wide-ranging American strategy of relaxing international tensions in a way that could not but stress the fissures in the Communist bloc and reflect upon the wisdom of the *Ostpolitik.*

But soon a new chorus of opposition rose under the leadership of CDU Bundestag floor leader Rainer Barzel, who was himself running hard for the office of CDU national chairman and for his party's nomination as candidate for chancellor in the next parliamentary elections. Franz Josef Strauss and other CSU politicians quickly chimed in with critical statements about the Berlin Agreement. Barzel evidently hoped to rally the CDU behind his leadership by means of an all-out attack on the entire structure of the *Ostpolitik.* He criticized the government in particular for "having abetted Western concessions" to the Soviet Union during the Berlin talks and for promoting the permanent division of Germany. This was not a policy toward peace and security, he claimed, but "a confirmation of Soviet domination over a part of Europe . . . a cementing rather than an overcoming of borders, a policy oriented toward power instead of human rights, a policy loosening German ties to the West and not hospitable to the hopes of a United Europe."

Instead of lengthy rejoinders, the Brandt government turned to the next task at hand, the negotiation of details with the East German government. Once more, a momentum was developed in pursuit of the *Ostpolitik* which threatened to wrest the initiative from the hands of the critics. The negotiations began immediately, but were soon snagged by the refusal of the DDR negotiators to accept the West German interpretation of the exact wording of the Berlin Agreement among the four powers.[11] To make matters worse, there was another shooting incident at the Berlin Wall, injuring a young would-be refugee within a few days of the signing of the agreement. The DDR government had plenty of reasons to be displeased with the Berlin Agreement, which among other Soviet concessions to the West included the reassertion of Soviet residual rights in East Berlin and over the access routes to West

Berlin. Yet the Bonn negotiators could be rather certain that the Soviets would pressure East Berlin to stand by the details of the agreement. To increase this leverage, furthermore, Willy Brandt eagerly accepted an invitation to visit Leonid Brezhnev in Moscow to discuss the implementation of the treaty with Moscow and further steps toward a European Security Conference and the mutual reduction of forces.

East German stalling on implementation of the Berlin Agreement also evoked Western responses rather reminiscent of Brandt's and Scheel's procedural approach to *Ostpolitik*. Now the American envoy, Kenneth Rush, announced that the West would not sign the final protocol of the Berlin Agreement until "satisfactory results" had come from the intra-German negotiations. Secretary of State William Rogers and the NATO Council, furthermore, tied the European security conference to a Berlin settlement. Brandt added, in explaining the mention of UN membership for both German states in the final communiqué of his Moscow visit, that such membership application could not be made prior to achieving a modus vivendi between East and West Germany.

Finally, by the beginning of October 1971, the negotiations became more intensive and produced a first document, a protocol on postal relations between the two German states. State Secretaries Egon Bahr (Bonn) and Michael Kohl (East Berlin) settled down to the hard bargaining on further details of implementation just as the opposition CDU resolved its internal leadership crisis. Barzel was elected party chairman and soon CDU/CSU candidate for chancellor. He immediately began to assail the treaties with Moscow and Warsaw "as not a sound basis for an Eastern policy." He called for a new West German government which would conclude a treaty to "assure true rapprochement, détente, and peace."[12] Strauss, speaking at a convention of his Bavarian CSU, fulminated in a similar vein against Brandt's *Ostpolitik*. Willy Brandt, for his part, was awarded the Nobel Peace Prize and received a broad range of international support for his stand. But the lines of battle were clearly drawn.

By November, the intra-German negotiations were already going on at two levels, between Bonn and East Berlin, and between the West Berlin Senate and the East Germans. Brezhnev appeared in East Berlin to give further emphasis to the Soviet interest in having "all artificial barriers . . . dismantled which obstruct the peaceful coexistence of European states regardless of their social system." Honecker was unlikely to resist this kind of pressure for very long. The negotiations between Bonn and East Berlin indeed produced agreement after three months, but the official signatures were held up until the deadlock at the second level over intercity traffic[13] in Berlin could be broken. After mutual recriminations over who was to blame for the breakdown, East Berlin appointed a new negotiator, Peter Florin, while Bonn proceeded to dangle the initiation of the process of ratifying the Eastern treaties before Soviet eyes. Finally, on December 10, 1971, the two new agreements between Bonn and East Berlin and West and East Berlin were formally completed and initialed.[14] At the same time, the treaties with Moscow and Warsaw were formally submitted to the *Bundesrat* and *Bundestag.*

The Civilian Transit Traffic Agreement held no surprises over the Berlin Agreement. All former exclusions of categories of persons from the transit routes except for certain post-1961 refugees were eliminated, clearance of persons facilitated, and sealed shipments of goods freed from inspection. A joint commission was established to regulate and settle differences of opinion. East German security procedures were safeguarded against abuse by transit passengers. And the passengers and shippers, too, were to be freed from the harassments so common in the past. The second agreement between the DDR and the West Berlin Senate provided for visits of West Berliners of up to thirty days a year in East Berlin or other parts of East Germany. This arrangement contained certain restrictions such as barring post-1961 refugees from the DDR and limiting the use of private motor vehicles.[15]

Still, as Erich Honecker was quoted in *Neues Deutschland* (December 18, 1971), "these agreements were the first international obligations incurred between the Federal Republic and the DDR, and they involved once more a recognition of the borders of the DDR." He evidently found little else to cheer about. As he had stressed before the Central Committee early in December, the main thing to him about the Berlin settlement was that West Berlin was once more declared not to be part of West Germany.

What was the significance of the Berlin settlement for the relations between the two Germanies? Was it Soviet influence only that motivated the East Germans to come out of their cold war shell even though their demand for diplomatic recognition by the West still had not been met? The negotiators of the transit agreement already had a further draft of a general traffic agreement between East and West Germany lying before them which was tabled for the time being. The next major step had been named among Willy Brandt's twenty points at that ill-fated meeting in Kassel: a basic treaty defining the relationship between the two states, recognizing each other's territorial integrity, and pledging renunciation of force in their dealings with one another. Was there the hint of international recognition which the CDU/CSU professed to see?

The DDR at first recoiled from this proposal in the belief that Bonn's stress on German "national unity," the label of "inner-German relations," and the insistence on noninternational relations between the two German states were a trap. But the Soviet Union had accepted the particulars already at the time of the initialing of the Moscow Treaty, in mid-1970. The DDR leadership had not really changed its mind, even though it had cooperated up to a point in the Berlin settlement. As a SED Central Committee member pointed out in *Deutsche Aussenpolitik* in mid-1972, the contrast between the East German system and the "continuing revanchist goals" of Bonn called for a sharp demarcation in all matters and "international law relationships that could not be construed by the ruling circles of the Federal Republic to represent the allegedly continuing unity of the nation."[16] The conclusion of treaties and agreements between East and West Germany, thus, was seen by the DDR as part of the agenda of a new collective security system in Europe and not as steps toward German reunification.

THE RATIFICATION OF THE EASTERN TREATIES

The DDR leaders had come out of their cold war shell long enough to permit the closing of the arch of the *Ostpolitik*, a Berlin settlement. Could one expect the CDU/CSU opposition to do likewise, or would Barzel and Strauss attempt to defeat the entire *Ostpolitik* of the government when the Eastern treaties came up for ratification by the West German parliament? The motives of their opposition were obvious: the *Ostpolitik* was a radical challenge to the cold war shibboleths of twenty years of CDU/CSU government. Even though some of its aspects had been anticipated by CDU leaders such as Schröder, it was a plausible gambit to defeat the Brandt government by way of defeating the *Ostpolitik*.

Once the course had been decided, the arguments would follow easily enough. One could always claim that the progress of the *Ostpolitik* had been "too hectic," that the bargain struck was "not good enough," or that the Federal Republic had given too much and received too little. Barzel's formula was not a total rejection of the Eastern policy or of the relaxation of international tensions in Europe, but rather that the treaties were lacking in safeguards and that the Federal Republic had conceded far too much, namely, the rights of self-determination and free movement of the Germans in the DDR and of the refugees from behind the Oder-Neisse line. To demonstrate that the Soviet Union indeed interpreted the Moscow Treaty as giving international sanction to the borders in the East, he arranged to visit the Soviet leaders and to ask them.[17] Finally, he claimed that the *Ostpolitik* threatened to undo the Western ties of the Federal Republic and to turn it into another neutralist Finland.

The submission of the Eastern treaties to the West German parliament naturally focused everyone's attention on their chances there and on the rules of the parliamentary game. The government announced a time schedule for the three readings, proposing the first reading for February 23-25 and the second and third for May 3-4, 1972. Rumors also began to fly about certain SPD and FDP deputies of refugee origin whose defection might further diminish the slim, six-seat majority of the government parties in the *Bundestag*. Strauss darkly hinted that the government and the federal president had a secret understanding to dissolve the Bundestag and go to the people in case the treaties did not pass. Other CDU/ CSU spokesmen expressed their resentment of Soviet pressure for ratification and hinted that the treaties might also be held in violation of the preamble of the West German constitution. The government, on the other hand, trotted out official American statements of support for the *Ostpolitik* and Soviet statements assuring the Germans that German reunification and future border changes were not precluded by the treaties.

The first confrontation over the treaties occurred before the *Bundesrat*. The question of constitutionality came up before the Legal Committee of the *Bundesrat* in January. Five of the eleven West German *Länder* were governed by the CDU or CSU at the time. Their delegations met to decide on a strategy to defeat the treaties. The Legal Committee decided by a vote of seven to four that the treaties were constitutional[18] and eight to three that they were not subject to the absolute veto the *Bundesrat* enjoys on some subjects of legislation. The debate continued before the Foreign Policy Committee of the *Bundesrat,* in the *Länder* diets, and in various *Bundestag* committees. Strauss even came up with an alternative draft of the Moscow Treaty which stressed a formal renunciation by the Soviet Union of any rights of intervention under the UN Charter.

Early in February, the treaties came up before the plenary session of the *Bundesrat,* where the delegations of the five CDU/ CSU *Länder* had prepared a joint statement enumerating their "questions" and stating "conditions" for their approval of the accords. The statement reiterated previous CDU/CSU arguments that the Moscow Treaty might serve as an instrument of Soviet interference in the internal affairs of the Federal Republic, that the accord might jeopardize self-determination and reunification for Germany, that European integration might be handicapped, and that the Soviet Union did not formally renounce any rights of intervention on the basis of the UN Charter's "enemy state" clause. There was no guarantee that the Federal Republic would not have to recognize the DDR or a different citizenship for residents of the other part of Germany, the statement said. The Berlin settlement was termed unsatisfactory. The *Länder* governments were in full agreement with the goal of securing peace and détente, but the national and state unity of the German people must be a primary objective. "The recognition of a second German state under international law is out of the question . . . its membership in the United Nations is not to be furthered." The *Bundesrat* adopted the CDU/CSU statement twenty-one to twenty. The vote clearly heralded a negative decision, thereby making an absolute majority vote in the *Bundestag* mandatory. Willy Brandt had lost the first battle.

The debate became ever more heated as the government sought to refute the CDU/CSU charges and, among other things, newspaper allegations that the Eastern countries had been promised vast sums in reparations. Charges of "sell-out," "treason," and "demagoguery" were flying so that the party leaders had to call for a return to rational argument. Foreign statesmen everywhere expressed their support for the Eastern treaties. Soviet Ambassador Valentin Falin offered to obtain official answers to opposition queries and *Pravda* refuted the CDU/CSU claim that the treaties were interpreted differently by Bonn and by the Eastern partners. President Nixon called the Berlin Agreement "a milestone on the road to détente." His spectacular visit to Peking, furthermore, stole the headlines at just about the time of the first great *Bundestag* debate. Anyone but the CDU/CSU politicians could clearly see the international trend toward détente.

The first reading of the treaties was an occasion for spirited speechmaking and heated encounters,[19] but it hardly changed anyone's mind nor did it produce any arguments that had not been made before. Finally the treaties were referred to committee. Some independent newspapers commented on the unimpressive showing of the opposition, which had evidently done little to coordinate its line of argument. There was the mistaken impression among some observers that the CDU/CSU leadership had already resigned itself to the ratification as a soon-to-be-accomplished fact and was beginning to look ahead at the situation to follow.

More ominous at this time, perhaps, was the much-publicized defection of SPD deputy Herbert Hupka to the CDU. Hupka was the chairman of the Silesian Regional Association and a vice-president of the Union of Expellees. He and two nonvoting Social Democrats from Berlin were removed by the party from the Foreign Policy and Legal Committees of the Bundestag because of their outspoken negative views on the Eastern treaties. Hupka and one of the Berliners resigned, therefore, leaving the government coalition a margin of only four seats. Three FDP deputies, Wilhelm Helms, Gerhard Kienbaum, and Knut von Kühlmann-Stumm, also expressed some doubts about the wisdom of the *Ostpolitik*, thus again touching off speculations about the likelihood of new elections. Public opinion polls revealed broad public support for the *Ostpolitik*, a very encouraging circumstance for the government. However, there were also signs of acute friction between the two coalition parties, the SPD and FDP, which could spell disaster for the government and its *Ostpolitik*. One of the bones of contention was the debate over tax reform and, in this connection, the controversial figure of Karl Schiller (SPD), the "super-minister" of finance and economics. The other was the FDP's fear of falling below the 5 percent minimum of the votes in the impending state elections of Baden-Württemberg.

If the two coalition parties broke up, the Eastern treaties would never pass. And there were already threatening noises from the Soviet Union and other Eastern states about their wrath if the treaties failed to be ratified. But what could the CDU/CSU opposition expect to accomplish by overthrowing Brandt and defeating the ratification of the treaties? If the treaties fell through and Barzel became chancellor how could he hope to conciliate the East—perhaps by going along with Soviet desires for the European security conference? In that case, the East German delegation would sit with equal rights in the conference, having won the upgrading of its status without the quid pro quo of the Berlin Agreement. Or could the opposition really hope to renegotiate the treaties as desired with the cooperation of the disappointed Soviets and to get them ratified without losing face before the voters? Premier Kosygin made it very clear that the Soviet Union would not agree to renegotiating the treaty. The stakes were high and the opposition seemed to have given little thought to the morning after its assault might have succeeded.

At Easter time, the West Berliners were enjoying a foretaste of the benefits of the Berlin Agreement when an estimated half million people were allowed to visit in East Berlin. Berlin mayor Klaus Schütz, a Social Democrat, took this occasion for another appeal to the *Bundestag* and *Bundesrat* to ratify the treaties and put the Berlin Agreement in effect. In the meantime, also, the intra-German negotiations for a traffic treaty had proceeded apace and there were negotiations between Bonn and Moscow for a trade treaty, West German-Soviet trade having increased substantially during the preceding year. The trade pact was to include West Berlin as a special concession by the Soviet side. Even Erich Honecker during a visit to the Soviet Union and again in Sofia was quoted as expressing the most positive expectations of intra-German coexistence about the whole package of intra-German and Eastern treaties. This was all the more remarkable since on other occasions he had warned about the dangers of "Social Democratism" overwhelming the Communist purity of his regime.

The CDU/CSU spokesmen, however, demanded once more to see the negotiating protocols of the Moscow Treaty in order to authenticate various "leaked" statements they had released to the press on earlier occasions. They continued to demand renegotiation and, perhaps, a "German preamble" before the Eastern treaties as their price for ratification. Brandt would only agree to an all-party resolution of the *Bundestag* to accompany ratification. Such a resolution might include or stress the "Letter on German Unity" which Foreign Minister Scheel had addressed to Gromyko at the time. Brezhnev also confirmed that the treaties were not linked to an eventual peace treaty and agreed to publicize appropriately the contents of this letter which had expressed the German preoccupation with self-determination and reunification. Both of these points had been raised by the opposition.

Brezhnev hinted that the Soviet decision to sign the Moscow Treaty had also had to overcome considerable resistance among Soviet leaders mindful of the German invasion of the Soviet Union during World War II. As a goodwill gesture, the Soviet Union also released some 700 Germans detained since 1945. Public opinion polls among expellees from the Eastern territories disclosed that only a minority of these expellees still questioned the de facto recognition of the Oder-Neisse line. Three-fourths of them no longer expected the territories in question ever to be part of a German state again. Another poll in West Berlin revealed a majority of 60 percent of the residents to be in favor of the Eastern treaties. Only 14 percent opposed them and 26 percent expressed no opinion. Despite the obvious benefits to be expected for West Berlin, this could be considered a strong showing in the beleaguered city with its history of anti-Communism.

Just as the situation seemed to become clearer and the government reiterated the claim that the *Ostpolitik* was in the mainstream of international developments and that the three main demands of the opposition had been met, another coalition deputy, Helms (FDP), resigned over domestic issues and became an independent deputy.[20] The *Land* elections of Baden-Württemberg had brought a CDU majority victory, although the SPD and FPD could boast gains in their vote, too, and only small fringe parties like the NPD had lost ground. Opposition leader Barzel chose this moment, still before the final decision on the Eastern treaties, to move at the end of a budget debate for a constructive vote of no confidence against Brandt.[21] The authors of the motion cited the CDU/CSU's "desire for a constructive understanding with the East" and several domestic issues. They wished to save the Eastern treaties from failing by changing the government, renegotiating, and thus gaining broad majorities on the floor of the *Bundestag*. It was a bold gamble based probably on secret promises of wavering FDP deputies. Political excitement gripped the country. Protest strikes and demonstrations were held in favor of Willy Brandt. All three major parties reported a wave of spontaneous applications for membership, especially in big cities and including many prominent figures of public life. On April 27, the vote was taken. Rainer Barzel failed by two votes (247) to unseat Brandt.

Brandt immediately sought a new understanding with the opposition leadership regarding ratification of the treaties. There was no majority for anyone else, he stated, and the *Bundestag* might as well get on with the task at hand. At the same time, also, the new Traffic Treaty with East Berlin had been completed, which included some notable improvements for visits to East Germany and was accompanied by promises to broaden the opportunities for DDR citizens to visit the Federal Republic. But the crisis grew. The *Bundestag* took a vote on the budget and ended up stalemated 247 to 247. The other two wavering FDP deputies, Kienbaum and von Kühlmann-Stumm, then indicated their desire to resign their mandates, though von Kühlmann-Stumm still wanted to vote against the Eastern treaties first. There were also rumors of CDU deputies willing to vote for Brandt and his treaties but being restrained by party discipline from doing so. While the *Bundestag's* council of elders, i.e., the various party leaders, huddled over the best procedure for the ratification debate, the international situation again cast a long shadow over the drama in Bonn. Secretary of State Rogers announced his forthcoming visit to brief the government about President Nixon's impending trip to Moscow and to discuss East-West relations. It took little imagination to see in this a potent reminder for the CDU/CSU that the whole world outside was vigorously moving towards détente.

While the party leaders were negotiating over the details of an all-party resolution tying the treaties to West German foreign policy, having postponed the debate by a few days, a new poll of the Institut für Demoskopie dramatically revealed the popular support for the treaties in the Federal Republic. As it turned out, 52 percent of a representative national sample called for a speedy enactment of the accords while only 26 percent opposed them (22 percent having no opinion). If new elections were held at this time, the SPD would have received 49 percent, the FDP 5 percent, and the CDU/CSU only 45 percent. The CDU/CSU leaders could hardly have misunderstood the message contained in this poll. An election at this time would have spelled disaster for them and their fight against the *Ostpolitik.*

Nevertheless, there were substantial numbers of deputies in both camps who were irreconcilably opposed to any compromise even as the party leaders worked on the specifics of an understanding. They agreed on a date for the final vote and on a prior debate about the expansion of the Common Market as a gesture signifying the West German ties to the West. However, a "recognition of the EEC" by the Soviet Union demanded by the CDU/CSU was still considered unnecessary and meaningless by the government.

Joint commissions prepared a joint foreign policy resolution on European integration, intra-German freedom of movement, and the right to self-determination and reunification, but the resolution still was not adopted by the CDU/CSU leaders, who insisted that this resolution first be accepted as binding by the Soviet Union. The government considered such a procedure an attempt at amending the Moscow Treaty and would not hear of it, even though it had no quarrel with the contents of the resolution. Eventually agreement was reached on a joint resolution among the party leaders and in the presence of Soviet Ambassador Falin, though the latter could make no promises about how the Soviet Union would acknowledge receipt of it. A passage in the resolution stating that "the accords do not create a legal basis for the frontiers as they exist today" was reported to account for Soviet hesitation. The Brandt government addressed a special message of reassurance to Poland on the Oder-Neisse border. Eventually, Moscow accepted the resolution unchanged and promised to present it to the Supreme Soviet.

By mid-May, finally, the CDU Executive Committee voted twenty-four to one to ratify the Eastern treaties. This was not to say that such hard-liners as Strauss (CSU) or even Schröder (CDU) had given in, but it indicated the final breakdown of the domestic resistance to the *Ostpolitik*. The Executive Committee even issued a statement waiving party discipline, thus allowing each CDU deputy to vote according to his conscience. Several prominent CDU politicians immediately offered to support the treaties in the *Bundestag* and *Bundesrat*. Only Strauss' CSU held off pending a CDU/CSU parliamentary caucus meeting the next day at which the proper course of action would be decided. Even the White House expressed its pleasure at the signs of intraparty cooperation. The negotiators of the Traffic Agreement with East Berlin presented the fruits of their labors, which still required legislative ratification. State Secretary Egon Bahr began to speak of the next steps in the intra-German rapprochement, further facilitation of civilian traffic and a basic treaty defining the relationships between the two countries.

On May 17, 1972, the *Bundestag* approved the Moscow Treaty with 248 ayes, 10 nays, and 238 abstentions. The Warsaw Treaty was accepted by 248, rejected by 17, and there were 231 abstentions. The massive abstentions were due to the decision of the CDU/CSU caucus, which had found itself hopelessly split in three ways. The joint resolution passed with 491 votes and 5 abstentions. The *Bundesrat* voted 20 to 0 for acceptance of both treaties, with the 21 CDU/CSU delegates abstaining. Their abstention spared the government the embarrassment of having to try to override a negative *Bundesrat* vote with an absolute majority of 249 in the *Bundestag.*

A REVOLUTION IN THE
INTERNATIONAL RELATIONS OF EUROPE

The die had finally been cast in the direction of revolutionizing the status quo in Europe. The thicket of *junctims* making the ratification of one batch of agreements conditional on the ratification of another batch, and building yet further expectations of agreements on the resolution of the conflicts raised by the earlier conditions, had finally parted to reveal the shape of the things to come. The *Ostpolitik* had managed to bridge the chasm between the Eastern and Western states and a new, resurgent Europe was about to emerge from the welter of new agreements and in the crucible of the impending Conference on European Security and Cooperation. But there was still a final struggle of the rear guards of the old order against the completion of the work of the *Ostpolitik.*

The CDU/CSU, after years of adamant obstruction, had finally come around to the realization that it too could not afford to let the treaties fail. In voting to abstain, moreover, it had gingerly sidestepped the major issue that could have been its undoing in an election at this time. Instead, it could pursue its role as an opposition along the lines of several domestic issues that appeared to be far more promising for its eventual return to power.

The erosion of the slim majority of the government parties as a consequence of the struggle over the Eastern treaties induced CDU leader Barzel to call for the immediate resignation of the government two days after the ratification. Brandt demanded assurances of cooperation from the opposition, since under West German constitutional law the chancellor's resignation is followed by the dissolution of the *Bundestag,* and in the meantime the opposition can form a government if it can muster a majority. It was true enough that the governing SPD/FDP could no longer muster a majority to pass the 1972 budget or any other controversial legislation. The CDU and the CSU also had once more come to blows over various issues, but the solidarity of the government coalition was similarly rocked by the dramatic resignation of its super-Minister Karl Schiller, whose charges and recriminations followed the Brandt government from mid-1972 until the elections of November 1972.

In September, after months of hesitation, Brandt suddenly announced that he would indeed pose the question of confidence. His own cabinet had to topple him by withholding its votes and then the federal president dissolved the *Bundestag* for new elections. The FDP had already announced that it would remain in coalition with the SPD. Brandt made it clear that he would run on his record of the *Ostpolitik* and the Berlin and intra-German accords. The CDU/CSU named "the recovery of economic and political stability" their first priority and, in foreign policy, announced their preference for European integration and "intra-German agreements which truly improve the life of the people in divided Germany." Television debates among the party leaders focused especially on the *Ostpolitik,* inflation, social security, and intra-German relations—the Basic Treaty became a hot issue during the last weeks of the campaign.

The voters had their say on November 19, 1972, and their answer was a ringing endorsement of the *Ostpolitik,* including the Basic Treaty with East Berlin. They turned out in record numbers (91.2 percent as compared to 86.7 percent in 1969), and gave the SPD an edge over the CDU/CSU for the first time since the beginnings of the Federal Republic. The SPD won 45.8 percent (42.7 percent in 1969), the CDU/CSU 44.9 percent (46.1 percent in 1969), and the FDP an unexpectedly strong 8.4 percent (5.4 percent in 1969). Actually, the CDU/CSU lost only 17 of its 242 *Bundestag* seats (of a total of 496). The SPD picked up a mere 6 seats for a total of 230, while the number of FDP seats went from 30 to 41. Thus the SPD/FDP coalition had received a comfortable majority to carry on its *Ostpolitik* and a long list of domestic reforms. Pollsters attributed the success of the government parties to (1) a high turnout of young, new voters and people mobilized by the campaign, and (2) the popular response to the new initiatives, especially the Basic Treaty, by which the Brandt government overcame its slump in the polls of August 1972.

The ratification of the Eastern treaties after two years of uncertainty brought expressions of relief from many quarters and especially from the East. Czech Communist leader Gustav Husak, in particular, called for further negotiations to "restore normal neighborly relations." Observers noted that he neglected to repeat his earlier demand that Bonn would have to recognize the invalidity of the Munich Agreements of 1938 from the very beginning (*ex tunc*), which had been a bone of contention. Perhaps this denoted a new willingness to settle for less.

The ratification in Bonn and Warsaw completed the process of preconditions which Foreign Minister Scheel (FDP) had so carefully devised. As he pointed out now, the next sequel was the final enactment of the Berlin Agreement and entering into effect of the intra-German agreements related to it. The Traffic Treaty and further intra-German agreements were next, including such consequences as East and West German admission to the United Nations. The establishment of diplomatic relations with Poland, Hungary, and Bulgaria was another point on the agenda. With the completion of the Berlin-Eastern treaties package, furthermore, the time had come to prepare the Conference on European Security and Cooperation. And with this all-European conference, inclusive of the United States and Soviet Union, *Ostpolitik* and *Westpolitik* could once more be profitably joined for the benefit of all Europeans and their allies.

By mid-September 1972, indeed, Bonn had established full diplomatic relations with Warsaw and the Traffic Treaty with East Berlin was ratified by the *Bundestag*. It had even gotten around to preparing the establishment of diplomatic relations with Peking, which followed shortly after. The ambassadors of the four big powers were meeting once more to establish a consensus on their residual rights in Germany with respect to the status of both Germanies and their impending admission to the UN. A joint statement on this subject was expected after due deliberation with the respective governments.

Most significant of all, the Basic Treaty between the two Germanies was unveiled and initialed two weeks before the parliamentary elections, a treaty in which the Federal Republic "formally takes note of the DDR as a sovereign and equal state," though not as a foreign country, as Brandt pointed out in a newspaper interview. Welcomed by the U.S. State Department and associated with the new four-power accord, the Basic Treaty was immediately questioned by the CDU/CSU, which reserved to itself the right to renegotiate it after the elections because "it had not yet had an opportunity to examine all the relevant documents." In later pronouncements, chancellor candidate Barzel modified his first statements by an appreciable margin but Strauss fulminated against it all the more.

The Basic Treaty proceeded from the fact of the German division under Allied suzerainty without exactly recognizing such a division as permanent. It did pay tribute to détente, nonuse of force, and inviolability of borders, and pledged the two German states to (1) normal, good-neighborly relations; (2) sovereign equality, self-determination, and, among other things, the protection of human rights; (3) the discontinuance of *Alleinvertretung* by Bonn; (4) promoting European security and a reduction of armaments, especially the control of nuclear weapons; (5) steps toward economic, scientific, and cultural cooperation; and (6) an exchange of permanent missions between the two Germanies. As Willy Brandt put it in a press conference, this treaty was "the instrument for organizing cooperation under the prevailing circumstances," that is, "by way of settled coexistence" and without abandoning the notion of a common nationhood. It opened the way to "the normalization that is now possible" and made life easier in many ways in the two Germanies and in West Berlin, again without changing the legal status quo in such matters as citizenship or property. A number of practical cooperation and exchange agreements between the two states and including Berlin were to follow.

The importance attributed to this treaty by the Western powers and other governments can be seen from the hurried appeals of Bonn to NATO governments and others to hold back diplomatic recognition from the DDR until the Basic Treaty was ratified. India jumped the gun, however, and Finland was one of the first to offer recognition to both Germanies. But the NATO Council of Ministers at its December 1972 meeting promised to follow the West German plea. They pledged solidarity to extend support not only for Bonn's intra-German negotiations but also throughout the pending European security conference and any negotiations on troop reductions. French Foreign Minister Maurice Schuman proposed to the big Western powers that once the treaty was signed they were to open only preliminary contacts with the DDR, rather than establishing formal diplomatic relations, until the question of admission to the UN came up. Other NATO countries promised to postpone recognition at least until after the signing of the treaty on December 21. There was a feeling it might be somewhat unseemly for the Western powers to race each other to East Berlin even though the desire was evidently strong.

By this time, the long-expected wave of diplomatic recognitions of the DDR by many states other than the Federal Republic (which had insisted on "noninternational recognition") was obviously well under way. FDP leader and Foreign Minister Walter Scheel felt compelled to deny that this was "a bitter consequence" of the *Ostpolitik* and, in particular, of the Basic Treaty. On the contrary, he argued, it is "a natural outcome of these treaty negotiations and of the conclusions of the accord that the NATO members now establish contacts." This trend was already strong regardless of Bonn's policies, thus making it necessary for the Federal Republic to take the initiative and obtain concessions from Moscow and East Berlin while they still had something to offer the East. But the Basic Treaty and the Four-Power Declaration relating to the treaty and UN membership expressly reserved the final disposition of the German question to a peace settlement. "There was no reason in the meantime to discriminate against the DDR" as long as it showed some willingness to cooperate. The underlying formula, in other words, was that human improvements in the DDR and in West Berlin were well worth conceding international recognition, since German reunification was in any case unattainable in view of the irreconcilable differences between the two systems.

Needless to add, the CDU and especially the CSU[22] rejected this trade-off as well as the whole Basic Treaty with the DDR. There was some expression of dissent among the CDU deputies, however, which produced several points illuminating the predicament in which the party had found itself since 1970. The CDU/CSU must catch up to the international developments, the dissenters argued, and be realistic about the emergence of the DDR and the present Eastern borders which were now being recognized by practically everyone in West and East.

Indeed, it seems to be the normal course of major innovations in foreign policy that they can only begin with a realistic acceptance of world conditions as they are rather than as they never were or might have been years ago. The SPD learned this lesson the hard way during the long years of Adenauer's bold new departures in foreign policy. It was a painful process for the SPD leaders to give up their hardened rearguard action against his policies of European integration and of bringing West Germany into the Western alliance. Only after they had come to accept the new conditions could they set out for major departures of their own. It may well be a similarly painful process of accepting the achievements of their antagonists before the proud leaders of the CDU and CSU can stage a comeback.

THE CONTINUING PREDOMINANCE OF *WESTPOLITIK*

During their determined struggle against Brandt's *Ostpolitik,* the CDU/CSU leaders' weightiest, if not their most influential, argument pointed to an inherent conflict between further European integration and the Eastern policies. Granted that the West German policies toward the East presupposed a secure West German position within NATO and a sound economic one within the Common Market (EEC), this objection was far from absurd. One aspect in the preparatory talks for the Conference on European Security and Cooperation, for example, concerned the West German desire—shared by other EEC members and opposed by the East—to allow the European Community (EEC, ECSC, and Euratom) a mode of formal participation. Behind this request lay the concern that the Eastern Europeans should recognize the right of the EEC members to continue to develop without Eastern interference the process of economic and political integration they have begun and to which they accord priority over any all-European patterns of cooperation.

The European Community indeed commissioned its Political Committee (of political directors of each foreign ministry) and an ad hoc group to prepare a common strategy toward the conference, an absolutely necessary maneuver, since community members after January 1, 1973, were no longer free individually to conclude new trade treaties with nonmember states. These deliberations have furthermore been linked with those in the NATO Council, at least among the delegations from community countries. The Eastern Europeans for their part have felt a hearty dislike for the Common Market, its "economically discriminatory" policy, and even more for its ambitions to become a politically unified "superpower" and a vehicle for "Western European imperialism."[23] Within the EEC Commission, the views about the European security conference have ranged from positive views hoping for better relations with the Soviet Union or Eastern Europe (with the ulterior motive of making the satellites less dependent on Moscow) to the suspicion that the conference was a plot to substitute a weak all-European pattern of cooperation for the further political integration of the community.

The standard response of the Brandt government to these Christian Democratic criticisms has always been that Bonn's *Westpolitik* has been proceeding apace and that the *Ostpolitik* measures enjoyed substantial support among all of the Western allies.[24] Appearances have indeed fostered the impression of a very active and successful *Westpolitik,* especially with the dramatic expansion of the Common Market from the original six to nine members. To be sure, the demise of Charles de Gaulle and the persistence of pro-European leadership in Great Britain in the face of determined resistance at home account far better for the final coming about of that long-awaited event than anything the Brandt government did in its few years in office. Still, as Great Britain, Ireland, and Denmark[25] took on their official roles in the European Community on January 1, 1973, it was difficult for the critics to claim that no progress was being made toward European integration.

The impact of the event was further magnified by the surprising eagerness of the British to enter into the round of contacts and activities toward greater cooperation in political and defense matters which accompanied the expansion of the community. For many years, a potent argument against British membership in the Common Market had been that Great Britain was "not really interested in European integration" beyond the advantages of economic cooperation, and hence her membership would water down the heady spirit of European union. Now that she was actually joining, her government turned out to be nearly as keen on playing a strong political role in the community as any of the "good

Europeans" of long standing who had agreed at the Hague Conference of 1969 to turn their attention to political integration.

The European Community, in any case, has not been dormant since the middle sixties when the organs of the Common Market (EEC), the European Coal and Steel Community, and Euratom were merged. The EEC, in particular, achieved a complete customs union in 1968, when it also began to make greater strides toward a common agricultural policy. The summit conference at the Hague in December 1969 started off periodic consultations among the various foreign ministers on foreign policy, a concern hitherto completely left out of the essentially economic concerns of EEC. In mid-1970, serious negotiations began on the entry of Great Britain, Denmark, Norway, and Ireland. Later the same year, the members of the European Free Trade Area were consulted on the possibilities of association short of membership. Eighteen African countries have already become associate members who can draw on the European Development Fund. Mediterranean countries from the Middle East to Spain have varying arrangements with EEC.[26] By the end of 1970, an exciting year for *Ostpolitik,* the *Westpolitik* had already witnessed the first foreign ministers' meeting on world foreign policy and a survey of cooperation in science and technology had been started. Early in 1971, the community was given its own revenues and agreement was reached on the establishment of an economic and monetary union.

The formation of a huge trading bloc of 250 million people, with political ambitions, will not be without its drawbacks. As Willy Brandt pointed out in a recent article, the economic partnership between the United States and the Common Market appears to be headed for more competition and occasional conflict after many years of profitable cooperation. Yet there is nothing inevitable about the development of rivalry and he suggested, in fact, that "it would be desirable to give organic form to the economic dialogue between the U.S. and the Common Market."[27] The recurrent crises of the British pound and the American dollar by necessity have already produced consultations across the Atlantic. The enlarged EEC can afford to interact with the United States with less fear that greatly increased volume of American trade and capital will "take over Europe."

The Brandt government suggested a summit conference of the heads of government of the ten prospective members of EEC

(Norway had not yet opted out), following a conference on price stability and monetary union in September 1972.[28] President Pompidou, who had surprised Europe with proposals for a European confederation a year earlier, issued the invitations for the summit meeting. For this occasion, Bonn prepared an agenda which put *Ostpolitik* and *Westpolitik* in context. The first points on it were economic and financial monetary measures along with social security, including regional structural policy and the environment. Second were institutional reforms such as the strengthening of the Council of Ministers, the European Parliament, and the Economic and Social Committee. The third point called for "an organized dialogue" with the United States, better relations with industrialized countries, and trade cooperation with Eastern Europe and the developing nations. European political and intergovernmental cooperation also figured prominently on the West German agenda for the summit, leaving hardly anything for the opposition CDU to advocate.[29] In this context, *Ostpolitik* played a very modest role.

Joint environmental policies, an industrial policy to make the best use of the available resources, and the avoidance of the "institutional Balkanization" of many separate European organizations (Euratom and CERN, Eldo and Esro, the European Space Conference, OECD and the technical reports of the community) are the next items on the European agenda. They clearly point the way to a great leap into confederation. The time seems ripe and Bonn will certainly not hesitate to take the plunge. Perhaps, by 1980, the European Union will be a fact.

The European *Westpolitik* can be related more emphatically to the larger Western alliance. At the same time that Western Europe feels its burgeoning economic strength and there may be more intense economic competition ahead between Europe and America, at the same time that Europeans truculently stand up for their economic independence from America, the military gap between Europe and the U.S. has actually been widening. Europe is less able and perhaps less willing to be independent in its defense today than it was in the days of Charles de Gaulle. The European EEC members of NATO, to be sure, have formed a Euro-Group, launched a program to reinforce European defense, and pledged additional funds for their common defense. But they are not prepared to replace American troops and their nuclear and strategic deterrent power. They, including the West Germans, want to have their cake and eat it too, under the protection of the American nuclear umbrella.[30]

A concise summation of the relationship between *Westpolitik* and *Ostpolitik* is found in a statement by Foreign Minister Walter Scheel, who in a January 1973 radio address about future West German foreign policies said:

> The unification of Western Europe will share the foreground of political activity in 1973 with endeavors to facilitate a greater measure of cooperation between Western Europe and Eastern Europe.

However, the relatively equal salience of these two spheres does not correspond to the consequences to be expected from initiatives in both. The *Ostpolitik* is sensational because it breaks with twenty-year-old taboos of West German foreign policy. Its measures, however, bring about only relatively small if psychologically momentous changes. If a European Union inclusive of Great Britain results by end of the 1970s from the current endeavors, it may not be headline-making news and yet it would revolutionize the European scene more deeply than the small steps of *Ostpolitik* will.

Notes

1   There was even a proposal to tie the mutual balanced force reductions (MBFR) to a Berlin settlement, although the United States rejected any such link, just as the Eastern states refused to make the European security conference dependent on a normalization of intra-German relations.

2   See W. P. Davison, *The Berlin Blockade: A Study in Cold War Politics* (Princeton: Princeton University Press, 1958), and Hans Speier, *Divided Berlin* (New York: Praeger, 1962).

3   The subsidy took the form of about half of the Berlin city budget, occupation costs, tax write-offs for West German businesses located there, and other reimbursements.

4   Quoted in Federal Republic of Germany, Press and Information Office, *The State of the Nation, 1971*, p. 15.

5   November 13, 1970. To give West Berlin the status of a West German *Land* would violate the specific injunctions of the Western Allies against parts of the West German and West Berlin constitutions regarding this matter.

6   See Gerhard Wettig, "The Berlin Policy of the USSR and the GDR," *Aussenpolitik* (English ed.) 21:2 (1970), pp. 136-49.

7   Bonn came up with a proposal of sealing railroad cars in transit as was once done between the wars in the Polish corridor on the way to and from East Prussia.

8   Before the Erfurt meeting, also, there was always the fear of implied recognition of the DDR, or at least of the usual attempts of the DDR to inject the issue of recognition as a precondition into all negotiations.

9   The Soviet Union also expressed the desire to open a consulate in West Berlin, but for predictable reasons refused to subordinate this consulate to the Soviet embassy in Bonn.

10   For the text of the speech, see Federal Republic of Germany, Press and Information Office, The Berlin Settlement: *The Quadripartite Agreement on Berlin and the Supplementary Arrangements*, pp. 35-37.

11   The dispute originally concerned a passage about the relations between the Federal Republic and West Berlin, i.e., not even any of the subjects for immediate negotiations between Bonn and East Berlin. Nevertheless, East German resistance continued for quite some time in the form of statements in *Neues Deutschland* and on the air to the effect that no specific German translation of the agreement had been authorized by the four powers and that East German sovereignty over the access routes to West Berlin continued de facto.

12   The CDU nevertheless quickly came to the support of the government when the Soviet foreign minister hinted that the ratification of the Eastern treaties should be initiated even though the intra-German negotiations had not yet produced agreement. CDU spokesmen moved to strengthen the hand of the government in turning down this suggestion. On the other hand, the Soviets succeeded in making the entry into force of the Berlin Agreement dependent upon ratification of the Moscow Treaty.

13   The issue was over providing for immediate and nondiscriminatory entry from West Berlin to the surrounding East German areas. East Berlin probably saw in this matter a threat to the integrity of its borders with West Berlin, although no opportunities for East Germans to visit the West were involved, as yet.

14   A public opinion poll conducted by INFAS in West Berlin disclosed 55 percent of the respondents welcomed the settlement, while 30 percent were still dissatisfied with it.

15   For details, see *The Berlin Settlement*, pp. 61-94. For a rather colorful East German view of the Berlin situation, see Viktor Boldyrew in *Deutsche Aussenpolitik* 17:5 (1972), pp. 873-99. Boldyrew emphasizes that the DDR had already demonstrated its willingness to negotiate most of the details before September 1971.

16   See Harry Ott, "Zum Klassencharakter der Aussenpolitik der DDR," *Deutsche Aussenpolitik* 17:3 (1972), p. 429. Ott argues that the concept

of the nation in the DDR is, in its class character, "a socialist nation-hood," while that of the Federal Republic is bourgeois and based on the irreconcilable class conflict of bourgeoisie and proletariat.

17   The Brandt government had insisted that article 3 of the treaty only "recognized the geographical status quo," leaving international law sanctions to a future peace conference. The CDU/CSU strategy also hoped to delay ratification until after the state elections in Baden-Württemberg, in which it counted on winning a majority, thus changing the majorities in the Bundesrat in its favor.

18   The charges to be refuted were that they violated a constitutional man-date for reunification and a mandate to allow the "Eastern territories" eventually to accede to the West German Basic Law. Furthermore, the treaties were alleged to involve a cession of territory and to deprive Ger-man residents or former residents of citizenship without constitutional amendments to that effect.

19   See Federal Republic of Germany, Press and Information Office, *Erste Beratung der Ostvertraege im Deutschen Bundestag,* am 23., 24. und 25. Februar 1972.

20   Bundestag Deputy Helms is a Lower Saxonian farmer, not a refugee.

21   The constructive no-confidence vote requires that a majority of the house elect a new chancellor, presumably Rainer Barzel in this case, in place of the incumbent. Under the West German Basic Law it is not possible simply to vote a chancellor out of office without replacing him.

22   Immediately following the elections, CSU chairman Strauss even threat-ened to break up the common parliamentary caucus agreement of the CDU and CSU, stressing particularly the differences of degree on the *Ostpolitik* and German foreign policy in general. In February 1973, the Bundesrat majority of Christian Democrats rejected the Basic Treaty twenty-one to twenty, thus compelling the Bundestag to override their veto.

23   This gives some plausibility to the Christian Democratic demand that Eastern Europeans should first "recognize EEC" before the Federal Repub-lic would drop its objections to the international recognition of borders and of the DDR. Actually Brezhnev in a speech of March 1972 did "rec-ognize the reality of the Common Market" and asked for a similar "recognition of COMECON by European Community members. See also Michael Palmer, "The European Community and a European Security Conference," *The World Today* (July 1972).

24   In December 1972, the NATO Council once again reaffirmed its support for the intra-German policy of Bonn as well as for its policy of "peaceful reunification."

25   Norway, following a plebiscite, declined to join what was widely expected to be a "Europe of Ten."

26   See Commission of the European Communities, *The Enlarged Community* (Brussels, 1972), pp. 41-42.

27   "Germany's Westpolitik," *Foreign Affairs* (April 1972), p. 421. This idea
      was echoed in a press interview by U.S. Undersecretary of State Walter
      Stoessel in November 1972 and in Bonn's programmatic statements for
      the EEC summit conference of October 1972.

28   At this conference in Rome, the economic and finance ministers decided
      to establish a European Fund for Monetary Policy Cooperation and other
      measures to cope with currency crises. The conference looked toward the
      establishment of the Economic and Monetary Union, beginning with a
      European "currency calculating unit."

29   Barzel still called on the European Community to strengthen its author-
      ity for social policy, environmental protection, development aid, and
      anticyclical economic policy.

30   The emphasis in European defense is still mostly on conventional arms
      and there is a consensus that there would be no point in reducing troop
      strength before an MBFR is agreed upon. If they occur, such troop cuts
      would presumably weigh the continental European powers, save France,
      against the Warsaw Pact exclusive of the Soviet Union, which would
      be weighed against the American strength in Europe.

CHAPTER 7

The Making of
German Foreign Policies

The making of foreign policy in the context of the political environment in any contemporary sovereign state has at least four salient aspects. One, the minds of the policy makers and their publics, has already been explored in the first three chapters of this book. The underlying attitudes toward the international system and the specific foreign policy images of large groups of people and their leaders are the broader dimensions of the foreign policy-making mind. How particular leaders actually pursued these images in given situations over the years constitutes the narrative of the last four chapters. But this account would not be complete without a further look at the other three aspects of German foreign policy making: the capabilities of the two contemporary German systems and the anatomy and physiology of their policy-making apparatus.

THE ECONOMIC MIGHT OF WEST & EAST GERMANY

Nation-states cannot get their way in the world without a certain amount of power as defined in an instrumental and relational way. There are many aspects to the measurement of the power of a state. The economic and military capabilities of the two Germanies in their political environment will be stressed here. Economic power by itself is a potent means of influence in foreign relations, especially through foreign trade. In Willy Brandt's pursuit of *Ostpolitik,* for example, it is doubtful that he could have induced the Soviet Union and the other East European states to negotiate those agreements with Bonn, had it not been for the large trade deals and offers of credit extended to them. Relations with Bonn would be far less attractive to the East if Bonn did not have something to offer, economically and technologically, to the closed and in many respects backward economies of the Iron Curtain countries.

Economic resources are also the single most compelling precondition to military power, the power to deter or compel other countries in foreign relations. Only countries of a certain size and economic modernity can afford the luxury of well-equipped modern armed forces, as the debate over nuclear armaments of medium-sized powers has illustrated all too well. The fateful impact of Adolf Hitler on the world was based on the simple fact that a man of maniacal obsessions was permitted to become the absolute ruler of a country with sufficient resources to make war on and enslave a quarter of the globe. At the same time, the example of Hitler's war machine should also alert the student of international relations to another crucial aspect of the role of economic and military capabilities in foreign affairs. It would be rather simple-minded to picture world politics merely as a mechanistic system of states of varying capabilities. The actual use of one's capabilities to compel other states depends on the prevailing attitudes and images of foreign policies. The German capabilities once misused by Hitler are again quite considerable today, even though today's superpowers dwarf the Germanies. But, as emphasized earlier, the will to use this power for war and aggrandizement no longer appears to be present.

A good point of departure for examining the economic capabilities of both Germanies is a comparison of their prewar status with current developments. Before World War II, the German borders of 1937 enclosed about 182,000 square miles. The Oder-Neisse areas, including East Prussia, make up about 24 percent of this area, the DDR another 23 percent and the Federal Republic and West Berlin a little more than half. Of the 69.3 million inhabitants of prewar Germany, 43 million lived in the West, where today there are 57 million, an increase which accounts in part for the rapid economic recovery. In the DDR area, there were 16.7

million before the war and there are somewhat more than 17 million today. The postwar migration of most of the 9.6 million living beyond the Oder-Neisse line in 1939 evidently benefited mostly the Federal Republic.

As for the degree of industrialization, both West and East Germany were remarkably similar before the war and even showed about the same population density. Prewar West Germany, however, was an agricultural import area, while East Germany was reasonably well balanced. The Oder-Neisse areas were agricultural surplus areas with only a few industrial concentrations in the industrial Silesian coal basin and the light industries near Königsberg and Stettin. The loss of their heavy industry and bituminous coal left a considerable gap for the DDR, while West Germany still has the Ruhr, the powerhouse of the German economy. The prewar industrial heritage of the DDR included machine industries and locomotives, synthetic rubber and gasoline, and plenty of electric power.[1] Trade between the two halves of Germany was intensive, and West Germany was particularly involved with exporting and importing goods from abroad. Today, both West and East Germany's economic power rests largely on their prodigious capacity for exports.

The postwar development of West Germany has often been called an "economic miracle" because of the utterly desolate condition of the German economy in the first three years after the war. The "miracle" can be explained with (1) the availability of skilled labor due to the population increase, (2) the funding and modernization of German industry under the Marshall Plan, and (3) an uncommonly good market situation with high domestic demand and favorable circumstances abroad. Most of the rapid growth took place in the 1950s even though the early 1950s were still marked by substantial unemployment (9 percent in 1951). In 1958, the index of industrial production already stood at 232 percent of the level of 1936. The growth rate was highest in chemicals and synthetic fibers, electric power, electronics, vehicles, shipbuilding, construction, and consumer goods. West German trade naturally lost most of its intra-German and Eastern partners and shifted instead to the United States and Western Europe, especially the Common Market in the 1960s. The gross national product of West Germany passed the 1936 level in 1950 and doubled it in the 1950s with an average annual growth rate of 9.6 percent. In the 1960s, the growth rate slowed down to an annual average of 4.8

percent, but still kept abreast of the growth rate of the DDR (4.5 percent) during its most prodigious development. The unemployment rate in West Germany practically disappeared by the late 1950s except for certain economically disadvantaged areas, such as areas close to the dividing line with the DDR. Instead, the West German economy began to attract masses of foreign workers from Italy, Spain, Greece, Turkey, and Yugoslavia in numbers fluctuating between 0.5 and 3 million.

East German development never had a Marshall Plan and, as will be remembered, suffered a great deal from selfish Soviet economic policies. In 1950, its gross national product was still 20 percent below the 1936 level and even in 1957, it had surpassed this level by only 20 percent. Nevertheless, the annual growth rates in the mid-fifties began to exceed those in the Federal Republic, although not for long, as seen above. Unemployment in East Germany was considerable in the late 1940s and early 1950s, in spite of the socialist economy, but disappeared later on, in part due to the migration to the West. Today, the DDR also faces critical labor shortages, which are remedied in small ways by exchanges such as the current trainee program which brings young Hungarians to the DDR.

The East German economy of the 1950s showed the imbalances typical of Communist planning. Mining, basic investment, and production goods were favored by economic expansion, while consumer goods were slighted. The living standards in East Germany were at a depressed level in the 1950s and despite some improvement have still not caught up with those in the Federal Republic and West Berlin. Car ownership in the DDR is still a rarity, as compared to the Federal Republic where one in five persons owns a car. Television set ownership has just about caught up. Rents, health care, basic foods, and simple consumer goods are cheaper in the DDR, while the more sophisticated consumer goods are priced far out of the common range. Proportionately, more East Germans than West Germans (51 percent versus 44 percent) are gainfully employed, especially married women. In the 1960s, DDR wages rose by only 30 percent, while in the Federal Republic they rose 86 percent with the result that the gap in real family income has grown from 32 percent to 45 percent. Even in social security benefits, the Federal Republic exceeds the per capita proportion expended by the DDR by 50 percent. Agricultural production, in particular, limped woefully behind at about two-thirds of the prewar level until after the collectivization drive of the late fifties and early sixties. Once collectivized and rationalized, East German agriculture gradually overcame its handicaps and began to outproduce other socialist countries by the late sixties.[2]

Economic power also should be measured in terms of the ability of a country to survive the vicissitudes of shifting alliances among powers. At the time of the renunciation-of-force negotiations with various Eastern states, for example, a common line of criticism was that Bonn's trade deals with the East, especially its purchase of Russian oil, would make it dependent on the Soviet bloc. Figuratively speaking, the Soviet Union could just turn off the oil faucet to exert pressure whenever it wanted to. Oil is one of the necessities West Germany has to import. The size and diversification of the West German economy, and of its energy sources in particular, however, give it enough autonomy to withstand such manipulations, however annoying, and to make them in fact rather unattractive to the Soviets. This is not a relationship comparable to that of prewar Germany and the various Balkan countries, whose dependence on German trade was quasi-colonial. Due to the shifts of West German trade from prewar times, Bonn's trade with the East today is rather modest and generally below the levels of American trade with the Eastern bloc.

Bonn is far more vulnerable to American trade restrictions, although even there the expanding Common Market[3] has by now created an ample margin of safety against sudden crises, such as that which struck the Weimar Republic with the New York crash of 1929. Within the Common Market, West Germany is today economically and especially industrially the most powerful country, though easily balanced by the admission of Great Britain with its remaining Commonwealth ties. With the admission of Great Britain, the new Common Market, with a population on a par with the Soviet Union and economic power on a par with the United States, will constitute a third great bloc capable of true economic autonomy in the last quarter of the twentieth century, once monetary cooperation and political consultation overcome the remaining incongruities.

East Germany, after a brief fling with the world market in the early sixties, is still very dependent on the Soviet Union, with which it does about 40 percent (45-50 percent before 1962) of its trade volume, and from which it derives 13 percent of its energy needs, all in the form of oil.[4] Until the increases of the last three years, about three-fourths of East German trade has been with the Soviet bloc. The renewal of the trade treaty between Moscow and the DDR in December 1965 was widely interpreted as the resumption of an exploitative relationship in which the Soviet Union was getting advantages which no trade ministry in its right mind would concede of its own free will. To heighten the impression, one of the chief economic planners, Dr. Erich Apel, committed suicide at the time as if in reaction to the sellout of East German economic interests.[5] However, the nature of the exchange of sophisticated East German industrial goods for Soviet raw materials almost automatically required special privileges for the Soviets in order to spare them the usual economic consequences of such a relationship. The total foreign trade volume of the DDR, measured in dollars, amounted to about one-seventh of the West German trade volume in 1969. In the meantime, this ratio may have improved somewhat, but it is still very far from the ratio between their respective populations and areas. The DDR chiefly exports lignite, machinery, electric appliances, and photographic materials, while it has to import iron, steel, coal, and crude oil from the Soviet Union and its COMECON partners.

GERMAN MILITARY CAPABILITIES, EAST & WEST

Under the Kaiser and even more under Hitler's program of "total mobilization" for war, an enormous war machine was launched and maintained on the foundation of the existing economic base of the *Reich*. A reunified Germany even today would be an industrial giant ranking third in the world behind the United States and the Soviet Union and could probably put forth a commensurate military posture. What about the two German successor states in this respect? West Germans are often fond of pointing out how the DDR is armed to the teeth in contrast to themselves. Defense expenditures in 1970, indeed, accounted for 5.9 percent of the gross national product of the DDR, as compared to only 3.8 percent in West Germany. Of every 1,000 inhabitants, the Federal Republic has 8 in the *Bundeswehr* and 0.3 in the border police, while the DDR has 11 in the National People's Army (NVA) and 18 in the workers' militia.[6]

The difference in military emphasis is also obvious to the casual visitor to East Germany. The goose step is still very much in fashion there in public parades and in the changing of the guards, while the "inner guidance" agency of the West German *Bundeswehr* from the very beginning undertook to banish all reminders of the days of Prussian militarism. West German army life is so relaxed and unmilitaristic that at times there has occurred a serious morale problem among officers of all ranks. Gone with rare exceptions are the days when recruits were brutalized by drill sergeants and when it was generally assumed that a man had to be "broken in" in denial of his individuality until he would become a mere automaton in uniform. There are well-established complaint procedures throughout the army, culminating in an ombudsman who reports directly to Parliament. Owing to the interpretation of what role a "democratic army" should play in a democratic society, furthermore, there is a conspicuous lack of militaristic popular propaganda building up soldiering as a popular, heroic ideal, as was common before 1945. Instead, West German recruits receive an education in civics and officers are trained to project a democratic posture with hardly any of the old officers privileges and perquisites of the old German army.[7] And there are large numbers of conscientious objectors, to show the other side of the coin.

The DDR, of course, also supplies political education in Marxism-Leninism to officers and men in order to make them into stalwart fighters for communism. The spirit of the East German army can be gauged from the overtones of official conferences and addresses, such as the recent conference of NVA delegates in Dresden, where the martial militancy of the Communist movement mingled easily with the customary bombast of the German military. As the chief of the Political Main Administration (PHV) of the NVA, Admiral Verner, reported in a warlike style to this conference in the presence of Erich Honecker:

> Under the leadership of the party, the members of the army accomplished a great deal in the fight (*Kampf*) to realize the resolutions of the VIIth SED party convention. Side by side with the Soviet army and the other brother armies, they reliably secured the state borders, the air space, and the coastal areas. Thereby, the armed forces of the DDR rose to the challenge of the military-political situation and made their contribution to the successful enforcement of the foreign, security, and military policies of the party. Firmly inte-

grated with the socialist defense alliance, the NVA has always been ready to guarantee the military superiority of socialism and to rein in the imperialistic enemy in Europe.[8]

The speaker also emphasized that "the NVA is the first official German army whose mission and deeds fully agree with the interests of the working class." This statement, related to the concept that the class struggle still goes on and the class enemy rules in Bonn and Washington or perpetrates liberal reforms in Prague or Budapest, gives proletarian internationalism a new direction. Instead of the accustomed, pacifistic overtones, it calls upon the East German soldier in alliance with the Red Army to do battle against Bonn, the Western alliance, or the interlopers of liberalism in the socialist camp.

The admiral also developed the educational ideal of the "socialist soldier personality" from these premises of the international class struggle:

> The socialist soldier is a better soldier because he understands the purpose behind his soldiering and identifies to the last consequence with the class mission of our military. Solid, basic knowledge and convictions are required to make his understanding of what he is "for" and what he is "against" the indispensable foundation of his civic consciousness and a never-ending source of his revolutionary fighting spirit.

The "socialist" relationship among officers, noncommissioned officers, and men, the speaker further said, is the special responsibility of the party agencies within the armed forces. It is this socialist relationship which is "a decisive factor in producing military superiority against aggressors." The "imperialistic class enemy" is not to be underestimated, for

> in the 1970s we must expect an enemy who will not only modernize his arms and equipment with immense material, scientific-technological, and financial means, but will steadily increase his moral aggressiveness.

The East German army began to take shape, according to Defense Minister Heinz Hoffmann,[9] when the SED Politbureau decided in March 1949 to give full and unconditional support to the Soviet armed forces in case of war against the Western imperialists who had just split Germany in two in violation of the Potsdam Agreements. Central Committee resolutions of 1951 and 1952 anticipated the likelihood of imperialistic aggression with the formation of People's Police shock troops and, in 1952, the establishment of the Garrisoned People's Police for purposes of combating invading counterrevolutionaries and policing the border. The Paris Treaties of 1954 and the subsequent inclusion of West Germany in NATO finally gave the signal for the DDR to join the newly formed Warsaw Pact. Early in 1956, the People's Chamber, the East Berlin parliament, established a Ministry of National Defense and founded the National People's Army (NVA) along the guidelines worked out earlier by the Central Committee.

It is not without interest to compare the timing and the personnel and organizational problems of West German rearmament with this account. To begin with, it is difficult to find an equivalent in a Communist society to the pluralistic concert of critical voices from the churches, youth organizations, trade unions, and various veterans' organizations which greeted the idea of rearmament in the Federal Republic. Not only was it intensely unpopular among the "reeducated," demilitarized German people, especially the young, but even the die-hard veterans and officers of the Nazi army were far too upset about the public dishonor heaped upon "the German soldier" to welcome German rearmament within NATO.

The idea of German rearmament appears to have been adopted in Bonn in the fall of 1950 in response to fears of a Korea-like invasion by the DDR People's Police troops. In November 1950, the first defense commissioner, Theodor Blank, was appointed. The actual development of a West German army did not come until 1955, when a Personnel Advisory Board made up, among other members, of resistance fighters and survivors of Nazi concentration camps was established for the purpose of screening the applicants for officers' positions of the rank of colonel or higher. The board acquitted itself admirably of the task of separating the old German army chaff from the democratic wheat, even though there was occasional criticism of some of its decisions.

In the meantime, political wrangling broke out again over the removal, by constitutional amendment, of the conscientious objection clause in the constitution and its replacement with legislation. The introduction of conscription was another object of intense political discussion in parliament as well as in the streets. Amid the controversies and occasional cases of misfits from the old officer corps, however, the new spirit of the *Bundeswehr* took shape under the guidance, in particular, of Count Wolf von Baudissin, whose reforms aimed at the concept of a "citizen in uniform." To the consternation of other European army officers, Baudissin wanted his soldiers to enjoy the freedom of speech and written expression, to be able to read anything without censorship, and to be under legal obligation to raise formal complaints against superiors' orders that seemingly were contrary to law or morality. Many of his ideas found acceptance in the 1956 Soldiers Act and the 1957 Guidelines for Military Education of the Defense Ministry.

At about the same time, also, the *Handbook of Inner Guidance*[10] and the Federal Military School of Inner Guidance at Koblenz began their assignment of inculcating the attitudes of a democratic and constitutional system into the officer corps. As the Defense White Paper of 1970 put it:

> Based on this concept (the citizen in uniform), leadership and civic education, or *innere Fuehrung*, implies the development and application of methods of modern leadership in the military field. It comprises the principles to be applied in education and training, welfare and personnel management . . . Thus, the principles of leadership and civic education are not a sort of wash to be worn and discarded at will . . . No one who rejects them is qualified to command our soldiers . . . [in enumerated soldiers' duties]. For the first time in German history, however, the soldier has been given more than just a set of duties to perform; he also has constitutional rights. The soldier is at all times entitled to unqualified respect for his human dignity . . . Furthermore, every soldier is entitled to develop his personality freely . . . he has the right to wear civilian clothes when off duty, to wear his hair as he pleases, and to shave or grow a beard as he chooses . . . Similarly, a soldier is entitled to express his opinion freely . . . The Basic Law accords him the freedom of information and opinion as well as the freedom of assembly and coalition (but not of partisan activity while on duty).[11]

Under the *Kaiser,* German generals and drill sergeants were fond of calling their brutal military training a "school of the nation." Today, the *Bundeswehr* has become something of a democratic education for the masses, frequently making up for the authoritarian residues of German homes and schools.

In the East German army, as DDR Minister Hoffmann relates proudly, the officer corps of the new DDR army had to be created almost from scratch. Ninety percent of the officers of the Garrisoned People's Police in 1956, while loyally proletarian, had only a grade school education, which did not give them the ideological and military science training expected of them. Today, over 90 percent of the NVA officers have *mittlere Reife* (10th grade education) and 40 percent have graduated from secondary schools. About 20 percent have attended a university, including "hundreds of officers and generals" with diplomas from Soviet military academies or even from the Soviet General Staff Academy. Their armaments include some of the most modern Soviet equipment ever handed to a satellite country—and the DDR often received them before other satellites did. Well-trained officers and recruits —more than 75 percent with a tenth- or twelfth-grade education and almost 95 percent with completed vocational training— facilitate the handling of this sophisticated equipment.

The DDR army recruits, moreover, come from an environment that is highly supportive of the People's Army and army careers. Almost 80 percent of today's recruits, according to Hoffmann, had the benefit of premilitary training in the public schools. This training includes strategic field games and the use of small weapons, and begins by the time students are about twelve or thirteen years old. Prior to premilitary training, there are elaborate fraternization rituals which bring school children to the military bases where they can sample the chow and climb into tanks. The object of these rituals is, of course, the early development of affection for the NVA, military hardware, and a soldier's way of life. They are unlikely to give much encouragement to the traditional pacifist sentiments of the socialist movement, although the DDR has been more permissive toward conscientious objectors than other satellite countries or the Soviet Union itself.

There has been no West German equivalent for this premilitary training and promilitary indoctrination since the Hitler Youth (HJ) ceased functioning in 1945. There are, of course, also the Communist youth organizations, the Pioneers and the Free German Youth (FDJ), who are very active in the school and peer group environment of the DDR and help to suppress antimilitary sentiments in East German youth. Finally, there is the stream of official propaganda in praise of the People's Army and the military parades such as the one which took place early in 1971 in East Berlin in violation of the four-power status of all of Berlin. Even if the population at large is skeptical of the "international class struggle" posture of the NVA, it will hardly ever hear a critical word about the military establishment of the DDR.[12]

The military overemphasis in the DDR, however, also has to be seen against a background of uncertain loyalties. At the time of the workers' uprising in East Berlin, in June 1953, the People's Police units called in generally refused to attack the insurgents and were soon kept away from the scene for fear they would join the rebels. Since 1952, some 30,000 members of the NVA are said to have deserted to the West. Since the building of the wall in 1961, hundreds of NVA soldiers and border policemen have taken advantage of their role and fled to the West. At the same time, however, other East German border policemen have shot down and maimed or killed refugees as if they were rabbits. The question remains, in any case, whether the NVA units could really be expected to fight with West German troops in an armed clash unless they were "sandwiched between or in front of Soviet forces."[13] It is not even certain today they would actually fight against the socialist brother armies of a reformist satellite regime, for example, unless they were cornered.

An intra-German armed clash might well conjure the chaotic vision of thousands of West German and East German soldiers defecting in droves back and forth while heaps of abandoned military equipment pile up unused: they called a war and everybody ran. And it is not just a question of Germans fighting Germans. The problem of fighting morale goes far beyond the question of national loyalties into the psychology of the nuclear standoff. Unlike earlier peacetime eras, the long interlude of peace under the shadow of the mushroom-shaped cloud has not led to a regression to the usual projective mechanism of hating a foreign nation and identifying with one's own nation, right or wrong. Neither has it created a generation of Eichmanns, of banal bureaucrats or technocrats who unfeelingly press the buttons of the deadly machinery of modern war.[14] Instead, the new generation on both sides of the Berlin Wall appears to have sensitive stomachs and an astounding readiness to opt out of any organized attempt to involve it in actions that outrage its sensibilities. The myth of the German soldier's obedience to the death of officers' orders (*Kadavergehorsam*) is dead in spite of the East German eagerness to maintain under the red flag what worked so well under the black-white-red and swastika banners. Perhaps the German soldier's bellicosity under orders from 1870 to 1945 was never anything but a sublimation of the aggressiveness and frictions of a society in the throes of rapid modernization which has more or less run its course by now.

Western strategists have suggested that from the point of view of the Soviets, the military "unreliability" of the East German National People's Army (NVA) would indicate a "forward strategy" of pushing on into West Germany in case of war rather than allowing the hostilities to take place on DDR territory. The equipment of the six NVA divisions, however, is hardly designed for offensive war and not even a match for other Warsaw Pact armies. Eighteen hundred T55, T54, and T34 tanks and twenty-four air force and support squadrons of MIG 17s, 19s, and 21s hardly amount to an offensive striking force. The NVA is evidently meant to be merely a defensive army, unless it is combined with the twenty Soviet divisions in the DDR and with other Warsaw Pact armies nearby. Behind this evident weakness of the East German defensive posture probably lies the distrust of the Soviet Union in the loyalty and reliability of the common East German recruit. The memory of the revolt and military defections of June 1953 have not disappeared. In the first half-dozen years alone after the Berlin Wall was built, moreover, some 500 NVA soldiers defected to the West.[15] The Soviet Union and the Warsaw Pact would be reckless not to draw these uncertainties into account in their defense planning. The DDR, on the other hand, is thus made all the more dependent on Soviet protection against any threat to its security and may look upon any MBFR negotiations or other disarmament talks between the Soviets and the West with suspicion.

Does the DDR really fear military aggression from the "revanchists" in Bonn? Or is all the propaganda of apprehension a deliberate, self-serving ploy to maintain a tight rein over the country? There may well have been some contingency planning in East Berlin to anticipate a *blitzkrieg*-like lunge of West German forces into East Germany. Western voices at the time of the 1953 uprising, Dulles' "roll-back" doctrine, and the Western refusal to recognize East Germany as a legitimate regime all may have contributed to apprehensive feelings in East Berlin. Even the strategic considerations regarding "localized" or "limited" wars in Western military planning have aroused Communist fears, an equivalent of de Gaulle's rhetorical question about American reliability: would the Russians really risk their cities and industry over East Berlin at the moment of truth? The Soviets, of course, keep twenty Russian divisions stationed in East Germany as a token of their loyalty and, perhaps, also in case of an uprising or invasion there or elsewhere in their satellite empire. Yet in spite of this, the *Ostpolitik* of Willy Brandt has raised new fears of a Soviet-West German détente at East Germany's expense. Defense Minister Hoffmann characterizes the *Ostpolitik* as follows:

> The current *Ostpolitik* of the Bonn government is designed for the seventies and constitutes the attempt to adjust to the new balance of forces in Europe and to pursue the unchanged goals of West German imperialism with different means, finesse and, if necessary, by subterfuge and over the long haul . . . By a systematic and well-aimed preparation for all forms of the military use of force, military blackmail, open or covert aggressions, Bonn military policies seek to realize the strategic goals of the West German monopoly bourgeoisie. It corresponds both to the tactical ideas of circles who prefer to eschew the use of military force or plan to use it only as the conclusive phase of their flexible *Ostpolitik,* and to those on the extreme right, who absolutely prefer the immediate use of military force to change the status quo in Europe.[16]

In any event, the DDR has 137,000 men under arms backed up by an estimated 350,000 border police and workers' militia-men.[17] The Russian divisions, discreetly stationed in forested areas and segregated from the civilian population, amount to about 180,000, considerably more than the NVA commands. And they have superior armaments, presumably including strategic nuclear weapons. In neighboring Poland, by comparison, a mere 30,000 Russians form a token force next to 275,000 Polish soldiers. Even in subdued Czechoslovakia, the Russian troops number only 80,000, as compared to 230,000 native regulars. The size of the Soviet force in the DDR must be an indication of the height of the stakes there from the point of view of the Soviet Union.

On the other side of the wall, there are 486,000 West Germans in the *Bundeswehr* (frequently stationed abroad), air force, navy, and the border and other operational police forces.[18] The twelve *Bundeswehr* divisions account for about 278,000 men, to which is added the American presence of about 225,000 and the reduced British and Canadian representation, which until a few years ago amounted to about 50,000 Englishmen and 6,000 Canadians. Again, the sheer size of the foreign military presence in relation to the native NATO troops in West Germany is startling. And these figures do not account for the larger nuclear weapons under the control of the American army. The *Bundeswehr* operates with some of the most sophisticated American equipment, including some items, such as the *Starfighter,* which reportedly may have exceeded the capabilities of many German air force pilots, resulting in a continuing, macabre scandal of fatal crashes.

The military capabilities of both East and West Germany, then, are not to be regarded as autonomous forces of considerable potential. Rather, they should be viewed in the context of their respective alliances, which have concentrated such heavy reinforcements in the strategic locations of the two Germanies. The two military blocs of NATO and the Warsaw Pact have nearly 3 million soldiers at the ready, half of them on German soil. Twenty-eight Soviet and twenty-nine non-Soviet divisions with a total of 855,000 men and 13,650 battle tanks stand in the northern tier of Eastern Europe, the DDR, Poland, and Czechoslovakia. Another twenty-nine Soviet divisions and 6,500 tanks are deployed in Western Russia within easy striking distance. The Warsaw Pact can get strategic support from 3,400 fighter and 4,480 tactical aircraft, not counting surface-to-air missiles.

The corresponding NATO area (Allied Forces Central Europe), plus Schleswig-Holstein and Denmark, is ready to field the challenge with twenty-six divisions of 703,000 men, including two French divisions, 6,600 tanks, 510 fighter and 2,800 tactical aircraft, as well as surface-to-air missiles. Further manpower would have to be raised from beyond the Atlantic Ocean. The 700 medium-range ballistic missiles on the Soviet side have to be countered with the 80 Polaris missiles on five American and British submarines, naval aircraft from the U.S. Sixth Fleet in the Mediterranean, or the British and Turkish bomber forces. On the seas, the Warsaw Pact nations command a heavy preponderance, although they are still more or less bottled up in the Baltic except for the recent Soviet move into the Mediterranean.[19]

In the face of such concentrations of military forces and weapons in and around the Germanies and their ties to them, the armies of both the DDR and the Federal Republic appear to have relatively little weight of their own. In fact, it would seem more appropriate under the circumstances for the Germans on both sides of the wall to pray that there will never be any open hostilities between the two sides in Central Europe. For open warfare would inevitably escalate to the level of the huge forces present on both sides and very likely turn both Germanies into a wasteland. Such a clash would very likely also trigger a nuclear holocaust. As the West German Defense White Paper of 1970 put it succinctly:

> Today we have before us a new type of soldier. His mission is responsive to a completely new challenge; though he is trained to use weapons of great destructive power, this is done for the sole purpose of preventing their ever being used.[20]

THE ANATOMY OF
GERMAN FOREIGN POLICY MAKING

Foreign policy making in both Germanies and everywhere else, for that matter, is a highly oligarchic and centralized process. Except for certain key issues and the long-range trends of public opinion, policies are made and changed by relatively small groups and few people. In the Federal Republic foreign policy making tends to be more constrained by the formal structures and procedures determined by the Basic Law. In the DDR, on the other hand, there is a greater degree of integration of actual policy making with the Communist Party (USSR).

The West German Basic Law established a federal republic of ten *Länder*, but foreign policy is almost exclusively a federal prerogative. The *Länder* participate in federal policy making through the appointive upper house, the *Bundesrat*, which has to approve most legislation and finance bills relating to foreign commitments. Constitutional amendments such as the ones implementing the Paris Treaties of 1954 generally require *Bundesrat* approval, though during the heyday of Adenauer's foreign policies in the 1950s the *Bundesrat* was often ignored. The *Länder* can conclude agreements with foreign countries or with the Vatican, provided the subjects fall within their legislative competence. Even then, federal approval is necessary and the federal government can also require the *Länder* to implement its foreign commitments. There was a time once in pre-1933 German federalism when the states had important military prerogatives and the right to participate in the selection of regional army commanders. Of this, nothing remains but the nominally regional character of the "readiness" police troops (*Bereitschaftspolizei*). In the conclusion of treaties affecting one or more *Länder*, the state governments have a right to be informed and consulted but they cannot veto the resulting action.

Within the federal government, the Basic Law gave the right to determine foreign policies chiefly to the federal chancellor and his cabinet. The *Bundestag*, too, has an important role through its Foreign Affairs Committee and its general legislative and financial powers, but in practice its role is not one of proposing policies, but rather of deliberating policies initiated by the executive. The same applies to defense policy except that here the budgetary aspects are more prominent, which at least in theory gives the *Bundestag* more of a veto.[21] The sorry precedent of military autonomy under the Weimar Republic led West German policy makers to take care that the military be subjected to civilian control. The minister of defense is the commander in chief of the armed forces and the Defense Committee of the Bundestag has special privileges of continuing to meet between legislative sessions and special investigatory powers.

The role of the *Bundestag* in foreign policy making has tended to fall under the shadow of a succession of rather charismatic chancellors. Konrad Adenauer used to play fast and loose with his supporters in parliament and was frequently accused of failing to keep them informed of his foreign policy maneuvers. Erhard was perhaps the weakest of the four chancellors to date and content to leave the initiative in foreign affairs to Foreign Minister Schröder or, alternatively, to the German Gaullists in his party. Kiesinger's career from the chairmanship of the *Bundestag* Committee on Foreign Affairs under Adenauer into political obscurity and regional politics is perhaps typical of the situation. In spite of his many brilliant speeches on foreign policy in his

earlier career, most Germans had hardly heard of him when he reemerged as a dark horse candidate for chancellor in 1966. While he was chancellor he was perhaps the most adroit in his handling of the docile *Bundestag*. Willy Brandt, by contrast, has the dynamism and charisma of a popular chancellor, but has fared less well with the suspicious *Bundestag* in spite of the transparent character of his foreign policies. In addition to the Defense and Foreign Affairs Committees, the committees on All-German Affairs, Borderland Questions, Expellees, and the Budget Committee are frequently involved in foreign policy.

The dominant role of the chancellor in foreign policy making was fully intended by the makers of the West German Basic Law of 1949. They went out of their way to create a strong parliamentary executive by such means as giving the chancellor a legally preeminent position within the cabinet and making it difficult for the *Bundestag* to overthrow him. The *Bundestag* has to elect a successor in order to vote the chancellor out of office. The other ministers are responsible to him and can be dismissed by him. The Basic Law also clearly states the chancellor's prerogative to "lay down the guidelines of policy." Adenauer was his own foreign minister in the early days of his tenure and, after Brentano became foreign minister, continued to dominate foreign policy in a way comparable to the domination of French foreign policy by President de Gaulle. The framers of the Basic Law took away much of the strength the presidency once had had under the Weimar Constitution, leaving a mere figurehead without an emergency or military command role. Nevertheless, the federal president still receives ambassadors, pays official visits abroad, and has to put his signature on bills and treaties before they can become law.

There are also other formal structures which play an important role in the making of foreign policy. One such agency is the Chancellery, which under Chancellery Minister Horst Ehmke (SPD) became particularly effective as a liaison and coordinator of all the ministries. Individual political appointees as state secretary, such as Hans Globke under Adenauer or Egon Bahr, the chief negotiator of the *Ostpolitik*, under Brandt, also can become important and influential policy makers in their own right. The ministers of foreign affairs, defense, finance, economic cooperation (development), economics, refugees and expellees, and all-German affairs are all influential and fairly autonomous agencies of foreign

policy making within their respective bailiwicks who can prepare and plan their policies with the held of an expert staff. The cabinet as a body is an important advisory body to the chancellor. There have also been a few occasions when important disputes over foreign policy were brought before the Federal Constitutional Court over legal technicalities such as whether the German *Reich* was still in existence and its obligations applied to the Federal Republic. Finally, there are intracabinet councils such as the Federal Defense Council and information-processing agencies such as the Federal Press and Information Office.

As Karl W. Deutsch and Lewis J. Edinger have pointed out, a chancellor with a strong majority in the Bundestag, such as Adenauer enjoyed between 1953 and 1961, will have largely a free hand in charting his own course in foreign policy. If he has only a plurality in the Bundestag and is in coalition with another party, he is far more in need of the cooperation of the legislature and the president.[22] Adenauer succeeded in attracting a coterie of backbenchers and devoted supporters, his "Chancellor Party." Without this special appeal, a chancellor can be successful only if he enjoys the strong support of his own party. Willy Brandt evidently has assembled a strong party team with such SPD leaders as Herbert Wehner, Horst Ehmke, Helmut Schmidt, Georg Leber, and many others, whose solidarity and cohesion amid the hue and cry of the opposition have allowed him to pursue his risky course in foreign policy.[23] He has been fortunate in winning the full agreement and cooperation of the FDP in his foreign policy, a feat which had eluded the CDU/CSU time and again.

A discussion of the formal policy-making structures of the Federal Republic should not ignore the organized links of Bonn to regional organizations such as the European Community (Common Market, ECSC [Schuman Plan], Euratom), European Monetary Union, WEU, and NATO. The regular channels and frequent consultations through these organizations are an important source of European and other foreign policies as long as Bonn strives earnestly to advance European integration and to coordinate its policies with those of its allies and neighbors, as through the foreign ministers' meetings started in 1970. Under the Franco-German Friendship Treaty, there are also regular consultations at several levels between the two governments. German-American consultations and, more recently, the frequent contacts of Bonn with the Soviet Union, Poland, and the DDR have established further

structures through which Bonn foreign policies are often influenced. In the last analysis, the network of West German diplomatic and trade representations around the world is another transmission belt of policy-modifying information.

How does the DDR make foreign policy? In spite of an increasing volume of studies of the East German system, there is still a dearth of detailed studies of the policy-making apparatus of the DDR. DDR foreign policy appears to be made mostly at the very highest levels of the East German Communist party, the SED. The SED enjoys a virtual monopoly of political control, in spite of the presence of other puppet parties such as the East German CDU, LDP (Liberals), DBD (peasants), and NDP.[24] These small "petty bourgeois" parties have been encouraged to remain, of course under reliable pro-Communist leadership, although their social bases, such as small business or the independent peasantry, have disappeared with collectivization. These parties and the SED-dominated mass organizations, the trade unions, youth and women's organizations form the National Front which presents candidates without opposition at "election" time in the DDR. Within the SED, the principle of "democratic centralism" effectively centralizes control at the top while leaving the grass roots a modicum of free discussion and elective mechanisms to keep them happy.

A West German political scientist, Peter C. Ludz, has suggested that the rise of a new generation of managers and experts in the 1960s constituted a counterelite which is subtly pushing aside the men of the old party apparatus of the SED to make room for long-overdue reforms. Such young counterelites appear to have been behind liberalization in the other satellites, too.[25] However, the party apparatus in the DDR still appears to be solidly in control today, while it was the New Economic System and other attempted reforms that had to yield ground. It was Erich Apel, the young economic planner, who committed suicide, and old party man Ulbricht who railroaded the 1965 trade treaty with the Soviet Union through the ratification process against all opposition.

The formal institutions in the DDR are the Council of Ministers and the Council of State, the ten-member nominal head of the East German state similar to the Soviet Presidium. The Council of State dates from 1960, when President Wilhelm Pieck died and his office was abolished. Ulbricht, who was already SED secretary and vice-chairman of the Council of Ministers, had himself elected chairman of the Council of State, which thereupon increasingly took over the functions of political leadership and co-ordination, leaving the Council of Ministers to supervise the economy. The members of both bodies generally occupy positions in the top party councils, the Politbureau or the Central Committee, although there have been passing trends away from the old party dominance. The young counterelites of the 1960s tended to start out with state administrative careers rather than with the party. While such a trend might indeed denote an increasing autonomy of the state from the state party, there is no evidence that the young counterelites ever became directly influential in foreign policy making. To be sure, the temporary attempt of DDR trade in the early sixties to seek a position in the world markets rather than continuing to rely on the Eastern bloc was a major step in the direction of an autonomist foreign policy. But the gallant promoters of this and other reforms appear to have lost their battle for East German autonomy from the Soviet Union.

General foreign policy making in the DDR, as in most Communist countries today, involves both the top party organs and the top organs of the state, such as the Council of State and Winzer's Foreign Ministry in the Council of Ministers. New policy changes are initiated and discussed by the Foreign Policy Commission (APK) of the Politbureau. The interlocking personnel of the top party and state organs makes it difficult to say in any particular case where action originates and how it is transmitted from the one to the other.[26] Formally, the APK sends its proposals to the Central Committee (ZK) of the SED and to the Foreign Policy Committee of the *Volkskammer*, the East German Parliament.

The Central Committee, a body of about 150 members and candidate members, is the major coordinating and consultative body, although it still has not shaken off the reputation of being merely a sounding board for the decisions of the Politbureau. The Central Committee and the Politbureau also include the leaders of the mass organizations which will promote the policies adopted at the top as the "mass line." The biggest sounding board of the DDR, however, is the People's Chamber (*Volkskammer*), a legislative body composed of about 500 delegates of the parties and mass organizations. The People's Chamber never seems to originate any bills of its own but only takes unanimous action on bills submitted from outside the parliament. Although the 1968 constitution assigns formal sovereignty to this body, there is no evidence that the People's Chamber would ever rise to this challenge.

As with the Federal Republic, there are also the regular channels which tie the DDR leadership to the Warsaw Pact, COMECON, and, most significantly, to the Communist Party (USSR). Unfortunately, again, there are only surmises and guesses of how and to what degree the Soviet Communist leadership keeps the SED leaders in line. With the exception of the 1965 trade treaty, disagreements have tended to be so discreetly hidden from view that it is difficult to draw a line between coercion and free will. The defense minister of the DDR has since 1956 been a first deputy supreme commander of the Warsaw Pact forces, the supreme commander always being a Soviet marshal. The stature of the NVA within the pact has grown conspicuously over the years, although all of its forces, unlike those of the other members, are under the Supreme Command. Thus, the DDR, just like West Germany, has no autonomous national army either. The commanders of the Soviet troops stationed in the DDR, moreover, can declare a state of martial law there at any time without having to give any official explanation. The SED party has the NVA well penetrated: 75 percent of the officers and nearly as high a proportion of the noncommissioned officers and enlisted men now are party members. The political reliability of the NVA has undoubtedly improved under these conditions.[27]

As for COMECON, the DDR is fully represented on all the representative bodies, the Assembly, the Conference of National Delegates, the Executive Committee, the International Bank for Trade and Cooperation, and the twenty-two permanent commissions, of which three (chemical industry, construction machinery, and industrial equipment standards) are headquartered in East Berlin. Unlike the other COMECON nations, the DDR has always been anxious for very close economic relations with the Soviet Union. Indeed, with 18 percent of Soviet trade, it is the Soviet Union's most frequent partner. The Soviet Union in turn, as will be recalled, occupies the same position in DDR trade with over 40 percent of that trade.

There are also further formal structures which would be examined more closely if their influence on DDR foreign policy were known. One such structure is the propaganda apparatus, the newspapers and other periodicals of the SED, radio and television, and the other communications media under party control. While the communications elites cannot be expected to play a checking or pluralistic role as in free societies, they do constitute a potent segment of the party leadership and are in a favorable position to have an accurate overview and to express opinions on matters of foreign policy. The same is true of the diplomatic service and of the military leadership as such. It is also not unlikely that the academic establishment, including the more recently created social science institutes and academies, plays an increasing role behind the scenes in analyzing situations and interpreting relevant literature. What Communist would argue with a pertinent Lenin quotation? The internal security and intelligence apparatus, finally, may also have its weight since it has some control over the sources of information for the making of foreign policy.

THE PLURALISTIC FORCES
OF WEST GERMAN FOREIGN POLICY

The rules and structures of policy making aside, West German foreign policy tends to follow the resultants of many complex parallelograms of group pressures and opinions of various publics. The seeming prominence of Chancellors Adenauer or Brandt and of official policy-making oligarchies should not completely overshadow the role of the broader group setting. The officials' actions are embedded in the lively give-and-take of public opinion and in the play of the pluralistic forces of political competition. Indeed, the official government policy often seems to be buffeted about by storms of criticism and at best to follow the path of the least resistance.

The strongest group forces in West Germany, at least in the making of foreign policy, are the political parties. The Christian Democratic Union/Christian Social Union (CDU/CSU) has had a plurality almost from its dramatic beginnings in the immediate postwar era and, for the years from 1953 to 1961, even a majority of the vote. Except for a labor wing, the CDU/CSU tends to be a rather conservative party which represents mostly business and professional people, farmers, the lower middle classes, and the churches. Its foreign policy has always been rather pro-European and, except for the German Gaullists, Atlanticist. The line between Gaullists and Atlanticists was never an easy one to draw since some Gaullists, such as Strauss, are really quite pro-American as well. Since the decline of de Gaulle's influence in Germany, the division between the hard-liners and the doves, especially on the *Ostpolitik* issues, is more characteristic of where the CDU/ CSU stands in foreign policy today. Due to the competitive system, also, the great desire of the CDU/CSU to get back into power makes the party far more inclined to follow a hard line against Brandt's *Ostpolitik* than it might do otherwise.

From the CDU/CSU leadership, there are important links to prominent parts of the press. The large Springer newspapers *Die Welt* and *Bildzeitung* often are the handmaidens of the CDU/ CSU hard-line opposition, and so are many smaller, local papers. The party also has newspapers which usually speak for it, such as the *Rheinischer Merkur*.

The party, furthermore, is well connected with prominent circles and associations of West German business and industry, such as the Employers Associations (BDA), the Federation of Industry (BDI), the chambers of commerce, and the chambers and other organizations of handicraft, not to mention the farmers' association (DBV) and related groups. Some groups are expressly interested in foreign trade or shipping. Unlike the news media, these interest groups rarely have an elaborate foreign policy line. They do have vested interests, however, in the issues of economic cooperation with the West as well as the East. On the questions of *Ostpolitik*, for example, they may well decide that it makes good sense to trade with the Iron Curtain countries, just as they favored Adenauer's westward-looking policies. On the other hand, the refugee and expellee organizations[28] have a particularly strong position in the CDU/CSU and their current opposition to Brandt's *Ostpolitik* is hardly economically motivated.

The second major party, whose popular vote over the years has been inching closer to the 50 percent mark, is the Social Democratic Party (SPD), which can look back on more than a century of tradition. The SPD represents the broad stream of the German labor movement chastened by the three traumas of the First World War, the resultant schisms (which led to the secession of Independent Socialists and Communists), and Nazi totalitarianism. The great war taught them the perils of patriotism, the Communist exodus set them off from the revolutionary left, and Nazi persecution made them appreciate constitutional safeguards and liberties. Their postwar leader, Kurt Schumacher, the great antagonist of Konrad Adenauer in the early years, also learned another lesson while languishing in Nazi concentration camps:

not to scorn the nationalistic feelings of his fellow Germans lest a demagogue like Hitler take advantage of them again.

From 1945 on, an underlying regard for the German nation has colored SPD foreign policy. At first in sharp and unrewarding opposition to the European policies of the Adenauer administration, the SPD continued to feel a deep obligation to the Germans in the East and to restore the traditional German relations with Eastern Europe. Thus, even though the SPD in the 1960s came around to a full acceptance of the European and defense policies of Adenauer, the intra-German initiatives and the *Ostpolitik* of Willy Brandt's team grew in principle from the earlier propensities of the SPD. The logic of the *Ostpolitik*, which brought the SPD around to an acceptance of the Oder-Neisse line, may in time lead it on toward the complete recognition of the DDR, provided the voters continue to lend it their support.

The SPD is closely linked to the giant trade union federation, the 6.5 million members of the DGB, and to other labor organizations. The DGB has often exhibited strong preferences in foreign and defense policy. Its leaders have generally shared the SPD's anti-Communism and initial reserve against a united Europe and NATO entanglements. In the 1950s the DGB played a prominent role in the massive demonstrations against German rearmament and, in particular, against nuclear weapons. The SPD also has in recent years acquired a larger following among professional people, some writers such as Guenter Grass, and among the young, although the student New Left has treated it with all the fury revolutionaries reserve for mere reformists. A number of daily newspapers also support the SPD, as well as its own weekly, *Vorwärts*. The public radio and television networks are governed by boards on which the SPD is represented along with other parties and major organizations in order to avoid any blatant bias.

It should be mentioned also that the SPD is a party which has always prided itself on its high degree of unity and solidarity. While there may be occasional factions and groups engaged in heated debates on certain policies, it is considered good form for the opposing individual or minority to accept the will of the majority in the end. There are, of course, individual and group differences of opinion among hard-liners and progressives or between the right and the left wing. But there is no comparison between this and the factionalism in the CDU/CSU, where the Bavarian affiliate, the CSU, even insists on a completely autonomous organization. There has never been anything in the SPD, therefore, like the bitter rivalry for leadership between Adenauer and Erhard, Schröder and Strauss, or Barzel and his rivals for the leadership of the party in opposition.

The third major party, the Free Democrats (FDP), also looks back upon a long and proud tradition, although its antecedents, for a hundred years prior to 1948, were always split into a right- and a left-wing liberal movement. Liberalism in foreign affairs has long meant a commitment to the German nation-state founded by Bismarck and put to the test on the battlefields of World War I. Right-wing liberalism, such as that of the German People's Party (DVP) of Weimar, generally meant a strident nationalism and commitment to the old order. Left-wing liberalism, such as that of the Weimar Democrats (DDP), often mixed pacifism and inter-nationalism with nationalism. The DVP produced a Stresemann, the DDP a Max Weber, but in the end the voters of both deserted them in favor of the Nazis. The two souls of German liberalism are still very much alive in the FDP today, although they express themselves more as a conservative, business-oriented strain and a kind of cultural, personal freedom-minded liberalism. Both have in common, however, an underlying nationalism which led them on toward intra-German contacts and *Ostpolitik* plans long before and always a step or more ahead of the SPD.

The FDP enjoys good relations with the business and profes-sional world and also with the German farmers. The latter have rarely expressed strong feelings about foreign policy except for their opposition to the politics of European agricultural integra-tion, but tend to be nationalistic and traditional in orientation rather than the contrary. There are also several important news-papers and periodicals that are considered to be close to the FDP point of view in foreign policy, such as *Der Spiegel* and *Die Zeit,* and also the conservative *Frankfurter Allgemeine Zeitung.*

The FDP has been very important in West German politics because the two larger parties have long been so evenly matched as to make coalition with the FDP a likely precondition for their getting into power. Adenauer's coalitions and that of Erhard gen-erally included the FDP, although the latter party was often unhappy in them and, at times, walked out in a huff. Only Kiesinger's coalition (1966-69) was a "grand coalition" with the SPD, excluding the FDP. Brandt's coalition again is with the FDP and has had a margin, after the walkout of three right-wing liberals, of only six seats. Unfortunately, the electoral base of the FDP has been slipping gradually since the immediate postwar days, when it enjoyed 12-15 percent of the popular vote. Since 1966, the FDP representation at the state level has been lapsing so badly in several state elections that there was considerable doubt in 1973 whether the FDP would receive the minimum of 5 percent of the popular vote[29] necessary to reenter the Bundestag. It came as a surprise to many people when the FDP received 8.9 percent of the vote, probably helped by Social Democratic ticket-splitters on the second ballot.

In addition to the three major parties and associated groups and communications media, there have always been small parties, especially of the extreme right or left, in postwar Germany. Most of the time they fail to poll enough votes to surmount the minimums placed in their path by the electoral laws, or they succeed, only to lose out again at the next election. A typical example of this rapid rise and decline was the Expellee Party (BHE) of the early fifties, which at first evoked great fears of its becoming a revanchist force of over 10 million. It turned out to be not only quite tame but astoundingly short-lived. The BHE was not an extremist force and could hardly be assigned to the left or the right. It was interested mostly in bread-and-butter benefits for its poor refugee constituents. There have been a few other small parties competing here and there.

The West German Communists (KPD) polled up to 10-14 percent in some areas during the first postwar years, but then suffered greatly from the impact of Soviet policy in East Germany, the forcible merger of the KPD and SPD into the SED of East Germany, rising prosperity, and the outbreak of the cold war. In the second Bundestag elections of 1953, they no longer received enough votes to be represented and subsequent state and local elections had the same effect at the lower levels. The foreign policy of the KPD in those days used to be a carbon copy of Soviet and SED foreign policies, anti-American, antiimperialistic, and, at times, stridently nationalistic. Like the SED, they criticized all the other West German parties for condoning "the division of Germany by the imperialists in violation of the Potsdam Agreements."

In 1954, the KPD was outlawed along with the neofascist Socialist *Reich* Party (SRP) under provisions to curb subversive, anticonstitutional movements. But in the sixties, no such measure was undertaken against the German Peace Union (DFU) although it was known to have many an old Communist in its leadership.

The DFU campaigned a great deal against nuclear involvements but never made the grade at the federal or state level. Its campaign funds were rumored to have come from the DDR. Eventually the Communists themselves were readmitted under the name DKP. Their electoral strength has not shown much improvement but they were able to muster large numbers of demonstrators at Kassel whose chief concern appeared to be the diplomatic recognition of the DDR.

Right-wing movements were denied a license in the days of the occupation, with the exception of conservative states' rights parties such as the German Party (DP) of Lower Saxony and the Bavaria Party (BP). After 1949, however, a long succession of neofascist splinter groups with names such as German Right Party (DRP), Socialist Reich Party (SRP), or German Bloc competed with varying success at both levels. In 1951, the SRP polled a high mark of 11 percent in Lower Saxony, which prompted the federal government to initiate court proceedings to have it outlawed. Other splinter groups grew in its place, often with interchangeable leadership and with the support of certain newspapers and periodicals as well as neofascist youth groups.

The latest of these parties, the National Democratic Party (NPD), became the subject of a surprising amount of attention in the American press in 1966 when it polled between 5 and 9 percent in several state elections. Like other neofascist groups before it, the NPD scrupulously avoids anti-Semitic propaganda and advocacy of hatred against other nations, which are subject to legal penalties. Its leaders even deny that it is "a successor party" of the old Nazi party, although a large number of its leaders are ex-National Socialists of record. The foreign policy of the NPD is as muddled as the rest of its policies, composed of some Gaullist elements, some stridently anti-American and even pro-Soviet elements, and an obsession with the presence of large numbers of foreign workers in Germany. Among the extreme right, there are also some prominent expellee leaders and groups such as the uniformed Youth of the German East, as well as some veterans' organizations. After a few initial successes which gave it representation in several *Land* diets,[30] the NPD again began to decline, although there will undoubtedly be other neofascist parties in the years to come.

Not all the groups and periodicals are easy to classify along political lines. Many make a point of their nonpartisanship and independence, which is frequently necessary for their effectiveness and good reputation. Both the Protestant churches (EKD) and the Catholic church today do not wish to be identified with any one party. They believe in their special moral mission to speak out occasionally on questions of foreign policy. In the case of the Catholics this has often meant a strong anti-Communist, even antisocialist and antiliberal bias, but also a commitment to the European community and international understanding. The Protestant churches have been particularly open to Eastern contacts even though they have suffered a good deal of persecution and harassment in the DDR, which just recently cut the remaining ties between the Protestant churches in the DDR and the Federal Republic. Similarly uncommitted to any one political party is the academic community, which occasionally comes out with manifestoes on subjects such as the nuclear arms race. Professors and scientists in German society, it should be noted, command very high status and respect which give their political opinions more weight than they would have in the United States. Some of them also exercise considerable influence through radio, television, or journalistic careers which may stress foreign policy expertise. Finally, there are also groups such as the German Foreign Policy Association or the German Association for the United Nations, which cultivate serious discussion about their subjects.

In a country like Germany where foreign policy has always tended to be regarded as a *Wissenschaft* (science) rather than as an appropriate area for democratic pluralism, there will always be a bias in favor of the expert, whether he is a crafty Bismarck or an owlish-looking professor. The rather limited range of alternatives of West German, or for that matter East German, foreign policies has further increased the general suspicion toward pluralistic group pressures and the free play of opinions in the Federal Republic, not to mention in the DDR. Nevertheless, West Germans have by now become accustomed to the tugs and pulls of a free society on foreign policy making. The confrontations at Kassel were perhaps an extreme example of how opinions can clash in a democracy. But it is impossible not to sense the note of pride, however wistful, in *Der Spiegel's* description of the happenings at Kassel:

> This is a free country. Everybody can do or not do what he pleases, as long as he obeys the laws. Anybody here can also

go out and demonstrate for his own convictions or against the convictions of the next guy. . . . This we wanted to show to the people we always used to call the brothers and sisters from the 'occupation zone.' And God knows, we did it.[31]

Notes

1 See Wolfgang F. Stolper, *Germany Between East and West* (Washington: National Planning Association, 1960), pp. 4-5. See also Henry C. Wallich, *Mainsprings of German Revival* (New Haven: Yale University Press, 1955).

2 See Jean E. Smith, *Germany Beyond the Wall* (Boston: Little, Brown, 1969), pp. 135-36. The completion of the collectivization drive, the building of the wall, and the economic reforms of the New Economic System (1963) form the cornerstones of today's East German economy. On the last-mentioned subject, see also Arthur M. Hanhardt, Jr., *The German Democratic Republic* (Baltimore: Johns Hopkins University Press, 1968), pp. 90-100 and the sources cited there.

3 In 1968, of 100 billion marks of West German exports, 37 went to Common Market countries, another 23 to the European EFTA countries, 12 to North America, 13 to development countries, and only 4.5 billion to Eastern bloc countries. Federal Republic of Germany, Press and Information Office, *Jahresbericht der Bundesregierung 1968*, appendix, p. 29. In 1969, the Federal Republic held second place among exporting countries, with 10 percent of world exports as compared to a DDR share of 1.5 percent. See Federal Republic of Germany, Federal Minister for Intra-German Relations, *The State of the Nation 1971*, p. 51. This document also contains detailed comparisons of vital statistics between the two Germanies, pp. 101-16. Comparisons of broad areas of law can be found in Federal Republic of Germany, Federal Minister for Intra-German Relations, *Bericht der Bundesregierung und Materialien zur Lage der Nation*, 1971 and 1972.

4 In 1969, 68 percent of DDR exports went to COMECON countries. Forty-two percent went to the Soviet Union, including 60 percent of DDR machinery exports. Ten percent of the exports go to the Federal Republic as part of an intra-German trade volume well in excess of a billion dollars a year. West Germany is the second most frequent trading partner of the DDR, whereas the DDR is only in eleventh place on Bonn's list of trade.

5 See also Welles Hangen, *The Muted Revolution* (New York: Knopf, 1966), pp. 3-5.

6 *Bericht der Bundesregierung und Materialien zur Lage der Nation 1971*, p. 45. In percent of GNP, West Germany expenditures for defense are also considerably below those of Great Britain, Portugal, Greece, Turkey, and France, in Europe. In absolute figures, West German defense came to

22.7 billion West German marks and East German defense to 6.7 billion East German marks (exclusive of the cost of 300,000 persons employed in the civil militia) in 1970.

7   See Federal Republic of Germany, Press and Information Office, *White Paper 1971-1972: The Security of the Federal Republic and the Development of the Federal Armed Forces*, pp. 79-80.

8   *Neues Deutschland*, May 23, 1971.

9   See Heinz Hoffmann, "Erfolgreiche Militärpolitik der SED," *Deutsche Aussenpolitik* 15:2 (1970), pp. 226-37. Hoffmann is currently defense minister and a member of the SED Central Committee. He was with the Communist legionnaires of the Spanish Civil War and, in 1963, was given command of the Warsaw Pact forces in a multinational maneuver as a gesture of recognition of the role of the DDR in the Warsaw Pact.

10   See the brief excerpts in Walter Stahl, ed., *Education for Democracy in West Germany* (New York: Praeger, 1961), pp. 210-17.

11   Federal Republic of Germany, Press and Information Office, *White Paper 1970 on the Security of the Federal Republic of Germany and on the State of the German Federal Armed Forces*, pp. 121-22.

12   These militaristic practices stem less from the Prussian than from the Soviet example. See, for example, Robert G. Wesson, "The Military in Soviet Society," *The Russian Review* 30:2 (April 1971), pp. 139-45.

13   R. L. Garthoff, quoted in Hanhardt, *The German Democratic Republic*, p. 104. See also the other sources cited there.

14   L. J. M. van den Berk is beside the point when he contends that "the original scorn of the soldiers for any military organization and their suspicion that the armed forces might be employed against the Federal Republic of Germany are increasingly thrust into the background by a certain pride in mastery of the military craft and in not being inferior to the soldiers of other countries," as quoted in Hanhardt, *The German Democratic Republic*, p. 104. This playful attitude only holds so far as the weapons are not used against people. The real test may prove their fighting morale a hollow promise.

15   See also Eberhard Schulz and Hans Dieter Schulz, *Braucht der Osten die DDR?* (Opladen: C. W. Leske, 1968), pp. 86-89 and 102-7.

16   See Hoffmann, "Erfolgreiche Militärpolitik der SED," p. 235. The quotation is followed by a lengthy list of the purported West German steps to prepare military aggression.

17   There is some confusion of figures. U.S. Arms Control and Disarmament Agency, *World Military Expenditures 1970*, p. 11, lists 196,000 members of the armed forces and "paramilitary forces" maintained at $7,398 per man. In 1964, according to official sources, there were 80,000 in the army, 11,000 in the navy, 15,000 in the air force, and another 400,000 in the border police, shock troops, and workers' militia of the DDR. The *Frankfurter Allgemeine Zeitung*, June 18, 1971, stated East German troop strength as 90,000 army, 16,000 navy, 25,000 air force, 47,000 border guards (evidently included in the *World Military Expenditures* figure),

880,000 trained reserves, 90,000 police, 350,000 workers' militia, and 600,000 other paramilitary mass organizations.

18 *World Military Expenditures 1970*, p. 10. In 1965, a total of 450,000 included 278,000 in the army.

19 See *White Paper 1970*, pp. 17-20.

20 Ibid., p. 115.

21 On this point see especially Elmer Plischke, "West German Foreign and Defense Policy," *Orbis* 12 (Winter 1969), pp. 1111-12.

22 Karl W. Deutsch and Lewis J. Edinger, "Foreign Policy of the German Federal Republic" in Roy C. Macridis, ed., *Foreign Policy in World Politics*, 3rd ed. (Englewood Cliffs, N.J.: Prentice-Hall, 1967), p. 125.

23 See also Arnold J. Heidenheimer, *The Governments of Germany*, 3rd ed. (New York: Crowell, 1971), p. 162, who calls Brandt the "party Chancellor" in a pun on the "Chancellor Party" of Adenauer.

24 See also James H. Wolfe, "Minor Parties in the German Democratic Republic," *East European Quarterly* 4:1 (1970), pp. 457-78, and R. Barry Farrell's "Foreign Policy Formation in the Communist Countries of Eastern Europe," *East European Quarterly* 1:1 (March 1967), pp. 31-74.

25 See Peter C. Ludz, *Parteielite in Wandel* (Cologne: Westdeutscher Verlag, 1968), and the same author's *The German Democratic Republic from the Sixties to the Seventies*, Harvard Center for International Affairs, Occasional Paper no. 26 (Cambridge, Mass.: November 1970).

26 See especially the description of how the decision to invite Willy Brandt to Erfurt came from the Politbureau before the Council of Ministers proclaimed it as its own. There had to be connections between the section for West Germany in the Foreign Ministry and the Central Committee secretary for international contacts, which reports to the Politbureau. The SED secretary most likely remained in constant contact with the planning and execution of the undertaking. Premier Stoph, the principal East German figure of the encounter, was at the time also a member of the Politbureau and presided over the Council of Ministers. Foreign Minister Winzer was a member of the Central Committee and thus likewise a logical transmitter of party decisions to the state organs. Even the minor executives in the ministries are party members and therefore likely to make certain that the will of the party is done. See Anita M. Dasbach-Mallinckrodt, *Wer macht die Aussenpolitik der DDR?* (Düsseldorf: Droste, 1972).

27 See Ludz, *The German Democratic Republic from the Sixties to the Seventies*, pp. 65-66. It is also remarkable how many of the highest army leaders, such as Heinz Hoffmann and Admiral Verner, are men of a Communist revolutionary background dating back to the Spanish Civil War or to Weimar.

28 The most prominent are the League of Expelled Germans (ZDV), the regional associations (*Landsmannschaften*), and the Silesians and the Sudeten Germans among the latter. As was pointed out earlier, the

expellees have prominent representatives in all the parties, but particularly in the CDU/CSU and in extreme right-wing groups.

29   West German electoral law provides a hurdle of 5 percent on the second ballot in order to discourage splinter parties. Most of the *Länder* have similar restrictions. There are two ballots per voter in every election, one for a candidate to represent the local district and one for a party. It is the percentages on the second ballot that are reported in the newspapers.

30   In several cases, such as in Hesse and Bavaria, the crisis of the FDP coincided with the triumph of the NPD, as the FDP would lose just enough votes to fall below the 5 to 10 percent hurdle while the NPD would attract just enough votes to inherit most of the lost FDP seats. In the meantime, the declining popularity of the NPD, which had attracted a motley collection of protest voters of all kinds, has cost it nearly all representation on any level of government again.

31   May 25, 1970, p. 32.

The Two Germanies on the Threshold of a New European Era

The two Germanies have not only come a long way since the defeat and division of 1945-48; they have also been most intimately connected with the very core of the developing and unfolding European scene. They were at this core because of their central location in Europe and at the cutting edge of the Iron Curtain and of cold war friction. As this exploration of the West German foreign policy culture showed, they are literally living the uncertainties and transitions of the vital European center. Their lack of trust in the international system in the 1950s and early 1960s reflected their precarious position on the edge of the two opposing power blocs. Their straining for a new identity above the flawed identity of the German nation helps to explain their receptiveness to Adenauer's European solution to the German problem. Their sense of impotence amid the threats and crises of a divided world is mirrored in their mute hopes of manipulating the only instruments available, their government, its allies, and the international organizations to which the Federal Republic was admitted. Their perception of their friends and enemies rounds out the image of the West German foreign policy culture and can, with opposite signs and few other changes, be applied to the East German minds as well, as long as the rather different relationship between the elites and the masses in the two countries is taken into account.

219

It is against this background, then, that the foreign policies proposed and carried out by different sets of East and West German foreign policy elites should be visualized. Foreign policy makers by definition labor at the interface between the internal dynamics of a political system and the external challenges of its environment. Older traditions of German foreign policy, specific policy postures of the past, and the dynamics of social and generational change tie together the past and the present. The problems of securing the German nation-state faced by Bismarck or Stresemann are not all that different from the search of postwar East and West Germany for security. Adenauer, too, drew on an older German and European tradition in his spectacular feat of leading the Federal Republic into European integration and into the Western alliance. His accomplishments appear without equal because of the seemingly hopeless state of Germany, both West and East, at the outset of his undertaking. Yet he was favored by circumstances and an international environment that allowed Western Germany no other choice but the one between resurgence as a prosperous, well-armed ally of the West and continued misery and stagnation as a fought-over neutral. Walter Ulbricht had even less choice in "the other Germany."

The *Ostpolitik* of Willy Brandt and Walter Scheel, and perhaps of some of their predecessors in thought, if not in action, has been based on the solid foundations built by Konrad Adenauer. It is not a radical departure from these foundations, as the current resurgence of *Westpolitik* clearly shows. Who would have thought in the days of Charles de Gaulle that within a year of his demise the movement for European integration would gather such momentum and take aim at a United States of Europe by 1980? The *Ostpolitik* chiefly concentrated on the blind side of the earlier *Westpolitik*, a blindness that originally grew from necessity. In the changed international atmosphere of the 1970s, the *Ostpolitik* is perfectly attuned to the global trend toward winding down the cold war, defusing the Berlin time bomb, and reconciling the West Germans to their neighbors in the East. In time even the resistance among the leadership of the SED and the CDU/CSU will give way to the understanding that Europe is entering a new era of cooperation and understanding which presents no threat to either one of the two Germanies.

REFERENCE MATTER

Selected Bibliography

DOCUMENTS

Commission of the European Communities. *The Enlarged Community.* 1972.

Democratic Republic of Germany (East Germany), Deutsches Institut für Zeitgeschichte. *Dokumente zur Aussenpolitik der Regierung der DDR.* 14 vols.

———, ———. *Statistisches Jahrbuch.* Annual. 1971.

Federal Republic of Germany (West Germany), Auswärtiges Amt. *Die Bemühungen der deutschen Regierung und ihrer Verbündeten um die Einheit Deutschlands 1955-1966.* 1966.

———, Bundesministerium für innerdeutsche Beziehungen. *Bericht der Bundesregierung und Materialien zur Lage der Nation 1971,* also *1972.* 1971, 1972.

———, ———. *Literatur zur deutschen Frage.* 1966.

———, ———. *SBZ von A bis Z.* 10th ed. 1966.

———, ———. *The State of the Nation 1971.* 1971.

———, ———. *Texte zur Deutschlandpolitik.* 11 vols. 1966-73.

———, Press and Information Office. *The Berlin Settlement: The Quadripartite Agreement on Berlin and the Supplementary Arrangements.* 1972.

———, ———. *Bundeskanzler Brandt: Reden und Interviews, 1969-1971.* Hamburg, 1971.

———, ———. *Deutsche Politik.* Annual, 1960-67.

———, ———. *Deutschland im Wiederaufbau.* Annual, 1950-59.

———, ———. *Erfurt, March 19, 1970, a documentation.*

———, ———. *Erste Beratung der Ostverträge im Deutschen Bundestag.* February 23-25, 1972.

———, ———. *Facts About Germany.* 6th ed. 1966.

———, ———. *Jahresbericht der Bundesregierung.* Annual, since 1968.

———, ———. *Kassel, May 21, 1970, a documentation.*

———, ———. *Kurt Georg Kiesinger—Reden und Interviews.* 1968.

———, ———. *Regierung Adenauer, 1949-1963.* 1963.

———, ———. *The State of the Nation, 1970.* 1970.

———, ———. *The State of the Nation, 1971.* 1971.

——, ——. *The Treaty between the Federal Republic of Germany and the People's Republic of Poland.*

——, ——. *The Treaty of August 12, 1970, between the Federal Republic of Germany and the Union of Soviet Socialist Republics.* 1970.

——, ——. *Treaty on the Non-Proliferation of Nuclear Weapons.* 1969.

——, ——. *White Paper 1969 on the Defense Policy of the Federal Republic of Germany.* 1969.

——, ——. *White Paper 1970 on the Security of the Federal Republic of Germany and on the State of the German Federal Armed Forces.* 1970.

——, ——. *White Paper 1971-1972: The Security of the Federal Republic of Germany and the Development of the Federal Armed Forces.* 1972.

——, ——. *Willy Brandt—Reden und Interviews, 1968-1969.* 1969.

Siegler, Heinrich von, ed. *Wiedervereinigung und Sicherheit Deutschlands.* 2 vols. Bonn and Vienna: Verlag für Zeitarchive, 1967.

——, ——, *Vertrag über die Grundlagen der Beziehungen zwischen der BDR und DDR.* 1973.

Tudyka, Kurt P. *Das geteilte Deutschland.* Stuttgart. 1965.

U. S. House of Representatives, Committee on Foreign Affairs. *Conference on European Security: Hearings before the Subcommittee on Europe.* 92nd Congress, 2nd session, 1972.

PERIODICALS

Aussenpolitik. Quarterly, since 1949 (English edition since 1970).

Deutsche Aussenpolitik. Bimonthly, since 1950. (*German Foreign Policy* since 1970). East Berlin.

Deutsche Fragen. Monthly, since 1954.

Die Einheit. Monthly, since 1945. East Berlin.

Europa-Archiv. Weekly, since 1947.

Jahrbuch der Deutschen Gesellschaft für Auswärtige Politik. 1955, 1956-57, 1961, 1962, 1963.

Neues Deutschland. Daily.

Orbis. Quarterly, since 1957.

Der Spiegel. Weekly, since 1947.

United Asia. Special issue "20 Years of GDR" 21:5 (October 1969).

Die Zeit. Weekly, since 1945.

BOOKS & ARTICLES

Adenauer, Konrad. *Erinnerungen.* 4 vols. Stuttgart: Deutsche Verlagsanstalt, 1965-68.

Altmann, Ruediger. *Das deutsche Risiko.* Stuttgart: Seewald, 1962.

——. *Das Erbe Adenauers.* Stuttgart: Seewald, 1960.

Amme, Carl H., Jr. *NATO Without France. A Strategic Appraisal.* The Hoover Institution on War, Revolution and Peace. Stanford: Stanford University Press, 1967.

Apel, Hans. *DDR, 1962, 1964, 1966.* Berlin: Voltaire Verlag, 1967.

———. *Wehen und Wunder der Zonenwirtschaft.* Cologne: Wissenschaft und Politik, 1966.

Bell, Coral. *The Debatable Alliance.* New York: Oxford University Press, 1964.

Benoit, Emile. *Europe at Sixes and Sevens.* New York: Columbia University Press, 1961.

Besson, Waldemar. *Die Aussenpolitik der Bundesrepublik.* Munich: Piper, 1970.

Birnbaum, Immanuel. *Entzweite Nachbarn.* Frankfurt: Athenäum, 1968.

Bluhm, Georg R. *Detente and Military Relaxation in Europe.* London: ISS, 1967.

Bracher, Karl Dietrich. "The Foreign Policy of the Federal Republic of Germany," in Joseph E. Black and Kenneth W. Thompson, eds., *Foreign Policies in a World of Change.* New York: Harper and Row, 1963.

Brandt, Willy. *Aussenpolitik, Deutschlandpolitik, Europapolitik.* Berlin: Berlin-Verlag, 1968.

———. "Germany's Westpolitik." *Foreign Affairs* (April 1972), pp. 416-26.

———. *A Peace Policy for Europe.* New York: Holt, Rinehart and Winston, 1969.

Calleo, David P. *Europe's Future: The Grand Alternatives.* New York: Norton, 1967.

Camps, Miriam. *European Unification in the Sixties.* New York: McGraw-Hill, 1966.

Clay, Lucius D. *Decision in Germany.* Garden City, N.Y.: Doubleday and Co., 1950.

Cornides, Wilhelm. *Die Weltmächte und Deutschland.* Tübingen: Wunderlich, 1961.

Craig, Gordon A. *From Bismarck to Adenauer.* Baltimore: The Johns Hopkins Press, 1958.

Croan, Melvin. "East Germany," in Adam Bromke, ed., *The Communist States at the Crossroads.* New York: Praeger, 1965. Pp. 126-39.

Dasbach-Mallinckrodt, Anita M. *Wer macht die Aussenpolitik der DDR?* Düsseldorf: Droste, 1972.

Deutsch, Karl W., and Edinger, Lewis J. "Foreign Policy of the German Federal Republic," in Roy C. Macridis, ed., *Foreign Policy in World Politics.* 3rd ed. Englewood Cliffs, N.J.: Prentice-Hall, 1967. Pp. 102-52.

———, and ———. *Germany Rejoins the Powers.* Stanford: Stanford University Press, 1959.

———, et al. *France, Germany and the Western Alliance. A study of elite attitudes on European integration and world politics.* New York: Scribner's, 1967.

Dulles, Eleanor L. *One Germany or Two.* Stanford: Hoover Institution, 1970.

Edinger, Lewis J. *Politics in Germany. Attitudes and Processes.* Boston: Little, Brown, 1968.

Fjalkowski, Juergen. *Berlin Hauptstadtanspruch und Westintegration.* Opladen: Westdeutscher Verlag, 1967.

Florin, Peter. *Zur Aussenpolitik der souveränen sozialistischen DDR.* East Berlin: Dietz Verlag, 1967.

Freund, Gerald. *Germany Between Two Worlds.* New York: Harcourt, Brace, 1961.

Freymond, Jacques. *The Saar Conflict, 1945-1955*. New York: Praeger, 1960.

Gasteyger, Curt. *Europe in the Seventies*. London: ISS, 1966.

Hanhardt, Arthur M., Jr. *The German Democratic Republic*. Baltimore: The Johns Hopkins Press, 1968.

Hanrieder, Wolfram F. "German Reunification, 1949-1963," in Roy C. Macridis, ed., *Modern European Governments: Cases in Comparative Policy-Making*. Englewood Cliffs, N.J.: Prentice-Hall, 1968.

———. *The Stable Crisis*. New York: Harper, 1970.

———. *West German Foreign Policy, 1949-1963. International Pressure and Domestic Response*. Stanford: Stanford University Press, 1967.

Heidenheimer, Arnold J. *The Governments of Germany*. 3rd ed. New York: Crowell, 1971.

Herz, John H. *The Government of Germany*. New York: Harcourt, Brace, Jovanovich, 1972.

Hiscocks, Richard. *The Adenauer Era*. New York: Lippincott, 1966.

Hornby, Lex, ed. *Profile of East Germany*. New York and South Brunswick: A. S. Barnes and Co., 1966.

Jacobsen, Hans-Adolf. *Nationalsozialistische Aussenpolitik 1933-1938*. Frankfurt: Metzner, 1968.

———, and Stenzl, Otto, eds. *Deutschland und die Welt*. Munich: Desch, 1964.

Jaksch, Wenzel. *Europe's Road to Potsdam*. New York: Praeger, 1963.

Institut für Demoskopie. *Jahrbuch der öffentlichen Meinung*. Allensbach, 1947-55, 1957, 1964, 1969.

Kaiser, Karl. *German Foreign Policy in Transition; Bonn Between East and West*. London: Oxford University Press, 1968.

Kaltefleiter, Werner. "Europe and the Nixon Doctrine: A German Point of View." *Orbis* 17:1 (Spring 1973), pp. 75-94.

Keller, John W. *Germany, The Wall and Berlin*. New York: Vantage Press, 1964.

Kissinger, Henry A. *The Necessity for Choice*. Garden City, N.Y.: Doubleday Anchor, 1962.

———. *The Troubled Partnership*. Garden City, N.Y.: Doubleday Anchor, 1966.

Kitzinger, Uwe W. *The Politics and Economics of European Integration*. New York: Praeger, 1963.

Klein, P.; Kroeger, H., et al., eds. *Geschichte der Aussenpolitik der DDR-Abriss*. East Berlin: Dietz Verlag, 1968.

Kopp, Fritz. *Kurs auf ganz Deutschland?* Stuttgart: Seewald, 1965.

Ludz, Peter C. *The German Democratic Republic from the Sixties to the Seventies*. Cambridge, Mass.: Harvard Center for International Affairs, 1970.

———. *Parteielite im Wandel*. Cologne: Westdeutscher Verlag, 1968.

Lust, Peter. *Two Germanies*. Montreal: Harvest House, 1966.

Lyon, Peyton V. "The German Problem," in Adam Bromke, ed., *The Communist States and the West*. New York: Praeger, 1967.

Majonica, Ernst. *Deutsche Aussenpolitik*. 2d ed. Stuttgart: Kohlhammer, 1965.

———. *Möglichkeiten und Grenzen der deutschen Aussenpolitik*. Stuttgart: Kohlhammer, 1969.

Mampel, Siegfried. *Dis Stellung der DDR im Sowjetischen Paktsystem*. Berlin: A. W. Hayn's Erben, 1966 (Sonderdruck aus "Recht in Ost und West").

Mehnert, Klaus. *Der deutsche Standort*. Stuttgart: Deutsche Verlagsanstalt, 1967.

Meissner, Boris. *Die Breshnew-Doktrin.* Cologne: Wissenschaft und Politik, 1969.

Merkl, Peter H. *Germany: Yesterday and Tomorrow.* New York: Oxford University Press, 1965.

————. *The Origin of the West German Republic.* New York: Oxford University Press, 1963.

Mittag, Günter. "Die Stellung der DDR in der Welt." *BZG—Beiträge zur Geschichte der Deutschen Arbeiterbewegung.* East Berlin, 1964, no. 5.

Nesselrode, Franz von. *Germany's Other Half; A Journalist's Appraisal of East Germany.* London: Abelard-Schuman, 1963.

Osgood, Robert E. *Nato: The Entangling Alliance.* Chicago: University of Chicago Press, 1962.

Osten, Walter. *Die Aussenpolitik der DDR.* Opladen: Leske Verlag, 1969.

Plischke, Elmer. "West German Foreign and Defense Policy." *Orbis 12* (Winter 1969), pp. 1111-12.

Richardson, James L. *Germany and the Atlantic Alliance.* Cambridge, Mass.: Harvard University Press, 1960.

Richert, Ernst. *Das Zweite Deutschland. Ein Staat der nicht sein darf.* DDR. Frankfurt: Fischer Bücherei, 1964.

Robson, Charles A., ed. *Berlin: Pivot of German Destiny.* Chapel Hill, N.C.: University of North Carolina Press, 1960.

Scheel, Walter. "Europe on the Move." *Foreign Affairs* (Fall 1971), pp. 62-76.

————. "German Foreign Policy and the Developing Countries." *Central Europe Journal* 14:1 (January 1966).

Schmidt, Helmut. *Strategie des Gleichgewichts.* Stuttgart: Seewald, 1969.

Schröder, Gerhard. "Germany Looks at Eastern Europe." *Foreign Affairs* (October 1965), pp. 15-25.

Schulz, Eberhard, and Schulz, Hans Dieter. *Braucht der Osten die DDR.* Opladen: C. W. Leske, 1968.

Schütz, Wilhelm Wolfgang. *Rethinking German Policy.* New York: Praeger, 1967.

Schwarz, Hans-Peter. *Vom Reich zur Bundesrepublik.* Neuwied: Luchterhand, 1966.

Sethe, Paul. *Oeffnung nach Osten.* Frankfurt: Europäische Verlagsanstalt, 1966.

Shell, Kurt L. *Bedrohung and Bewährung.* Cologne: Westdeutscher Verlag, 1965.

Smith, Jean Edward. *Germany Beyond the Wall.* Boston: Little, Brown, 1969.

Speier, Hans. *Divided Berlin.* New York: Praeger, 1961.

————, and Davison, W. Phillips, eds. *West German Leadership and Foreign Policy.* Evanston, Ill.: Row, Peterson and Co., 1957.

Stehle, Hansjakob. *Nachbar Polen.* Frankfurt: S. Fischer, 1963.

Strauss, Franz Josef. *Herausforderung und Antwort.* Stuttgart: Seewald, 1968.

Szaz, Zoltan M. *Germany's Eastern Frontiers.* Chicago: Regnery, 1960.

Ulbricht, Walter. *Whither Germany?* Dresden: Zeit im Bild, 1966.

Vali, Ferenc A. *The Quest for a United Germany.* Baltimore: Johns Hopkins Press, 1967.

Vogelsang, Thilo. *Das geteilte Deutschland.* Munich: DTV, 1966.

Von Guttenberg, Karl Theodor. *Wenn der Westen will.* 2d ed. Stuttgart: Seewald, 1965.

Wallich, Henry C. *Mainsprings of the German Revival.* New Haven: Yale University Press, 1955.

Weinberg, Gerhard L. *The Foreign Policy of Hitler's Germany*. Chicago: University of Chicago Press, 1970.

Wettig, Gerhard. *Entmilitarisierung und Wiederbewaffnung Deutschlands*. Munich: Oldenbourg, 1967.

Wildenmann, Rudolf. *Macht und Konsens als Problem der Innen- und Aussenpolitik*. Frankfurt: Athenäum, 1963.

Willis, F. Roy. *France, Germany, and the New Europe, 1945-1967*. New York: Oxford University Press, 1967.

Winzer, Otto. *Deutsche Aussenpolitik des Friedens und des Sozialismus*. Berlin: VEB, 1969.

Woitzik, Karl-Heinz. *Die Auslandsaktivität der Sowjetischen Besatzungszone*. Mainz: von Hase & Köhler, 1967.

Index